Yale Historical Publications, Miscellany, 121

Women and Men
on the Overland Trail

John Mack Faragher

New Haven and London   Yale University Press

Printed in the United States of America by
The Vail-Ballou Press, Inc., Binghamton, N.Y.

Library of Congress Cataloging in Publication
Data

Faragher, John Mack, 1945–
    Women and men on the overland trail.

    (Yale historical publications: Miscellany; 121)
    Bibliography: p.
    Includes index.
    1. Family—The West—History—19th century.
2. Women—The West—History—19th century.
3. Frontier and pioneer life—The West—
History—19th century. 4. Overland journeys to
the Pacific. I. Title. II. Series.
HQ553.F37   301.42′0978   78-10290
ISBN 0-300-02267-0
        0-300-02605-6 pbk.

11   10   9   8   7   6   5   4

For the men and women of my family;
to my mother, father, and grandmother

Contents

Tables

Preface

As a historian I have come to greatly respect the midwestern people of this study, respect them too much to use them casually as foils for polemics. I have tried to base my analysis and judgment on standards that these people would have understood. But as a historian writing over a hundred years later, I bring ideas and values with me that belong uniquely to my own time. These perspectives are very much a part of my years of struggle with the contemporary women's movement and consequently are ones that these men, and most of these women, would neither have understood nor accepted. But acknowledging, with the Chinese, that women hold up half the sky, that in other words only women and men together can make and reproduce society, it seems clear that only the radical perspective of feminism can provide the concepts necessary to reconstruct our past, to liberate it from the shackles of its own ideologies. It is my belief that an important step in creating a society of free and equal women and men is the creation of a history of women and men in their real connectedness.

This study first began to germinate several years ago when I was working as a research assistant for Professor Robert V. Hine in the history department of the University of California at Riverside. Bob's probing curiosity and persistent questions kept me burrowing for answers. To him I owe the query that motivated my original look into the materials of this study: Was the western experience a plus or a minus for women? Although not a formal question of this study, this question has informed many aspects of my work, and I have tried to sum up my answer in the final chapter.

Professor Howard Lamar of Yale University introduced me to the emigrant diaries and recollections of the overland trail, and despite his own ongoing research with them, helped to foster my work. In a seminar with Howard I came to understand the importance of a cross-sexual perspective on the history of marriage and the family; this was the second motivating idea of the research. Howard generously shared his own insights and ideas about the overland experience with me both in seminars and in informal office chats and has taken the time to listen to my findings. Throughout what seemed to me a long and frustrating period of research, writing, and production, he was patient, encouraging, and enthusiastic.

An earlier draft of some of these ideas appeared in a 1973 article coauthored with Christine Stansell.[1] Although many of the ideas of that piece have been recast, entirely revised, and, in a few cases, rejected here, the time spent preparing, writing, and evaluating that article have been crucial to the development of my thinking.

Michele Hoffnung read the chapters in draft, then as a dissertation, and again for this version. Her criticisms have resulted in considerable rethinking and rewriting on my part; her insight more than once saved me from substantial errors. I offer my lasting thanks, especially, for her willingness to put aside her own work and listen to problems having to do with mine. She has patiently helped see me through my obsessions with the study as only a dear friend and comrade can.

I would also like to thank the National Endowment for the Humanities for a Youth Grant for travel and research; my students at Yale University and the University of Hartford for the past three years, who have listened to my ideas about men and women in the West and sometimes offered ideas of their own that clarified things considerably; the reference librarians of Sterling Memorial Library at Yale, who answered my questions, guided me skillfully to sources I could not otherwise have found, and helped to make my many hours writing in the Linonia and Brothers Room a most pleasant working experience; the helpful staffs of the Beinecke Library, Yale University, the Newberry Library, Chicago, the Kansas State Historical Society, Topeka, Kansas, the Bancroft Library, University of California, Berkeley, and the Huntington Library, San Marino, California; Paul Henderson, for providing transcripts of privately owned manuscript diaries; David Musto and Edmund Morgan, as well as the entire History Department at Yale University, for their support and encouragement; Edward Tripp and Alexander Metro of Yale University Press, who introduced me to the details of publication; and Joan Rosenstock, who taught me a good deal about writing by her skillful editing of the manuscript.

The criticism and encouragement of friends and colleagues have measurably improved the manuscript. I remain responsible for its imperfections as well as its contributions.

Introduction: Perspectives, Setting, Sources

A curious conceptual problem pervades the history of the
nineteenth-century American family. Historians of women and
the family are convinced that the nineteenth century was a
period of increasing differentiation in the social roles of women
and men, so much so that one can speak of distinct male and
female subcultures within the larger context of American society.[1] Yet men and women continued to live and work together
within families. Indeed, so the argument runs, marital and
conjugal relationships took on even more significance in a society where the web of family and community interaction was
rapidly disintegrating under the pressures of modernization.[2]

Herein lies the historical problem. It is precisely the separation of the sexes in the mid-nineteenth century that makes it
difficult to reconstruct the dynamic of married life. There are
severe problems in writing the history of the inarticulate;
people rarely leave documents of their daily, not to mention
their family, lives. But these problems are compounded for a
study of families as dynamic groupings in the nineteenth century. To the extent that women and men functioned within the
boundaries of their most significant role definitions, domestic
worker and mother on the one hand, producer and breadwin-
ner on the other, the sexes performed different work and
shared different experiences, so that men, when they wrote,
mainly left indications of their relationship to the productive
aspects of their lives, while women contributed sources for an
understanding of their relationship to domestic life. Women's
and men's artifacts give us some indication of the sexual boundaries that informed their understanding of their place in the
social and family order, but in their isolation from each other
these artifacts are mute about the complex dynamic that transformed these differential roles into a structure for marital relationships. We have been left with a fragmented picture of
nineteenth-century social life which emphasizes the separation

of the sexes but is unable to show how the family operated as a
meeting ground of divergent roles.

This study is structured by an interlocking set of hypotheses
designed to confront this conceptual and methodological
problem. Although in mid-nineteenth-century mid-America
the work, the family and public roles, and the thoughts and the
feelings of men and women differed fundamentally, marriage
and family making were social norms highly valued by both
sexes. The cultural expectation was that husbands and wives,
despite their difference, would reach some ordered harmony
within the bonds of marriage. This harmony was achieved
through a conflictual process integral to each marriage relationship that defined the terms, set the goals, and determined
the acceptable conflicts and accommodations, given the divergent interests of the sexes. The different social power of men
and women was put to a test of strength in the marriage-
defining conflict. This process, which husbands and wives were
both committed to by dint of their commitment to marriage,
was a struggle between the sexes. The key then, to an understanding of nineteenth-century marriage is an appreciation and
evaluation of the place of sexual struggle in the social order.

In marriage, some succeed while others fail, some are happy,
some not, some are able to agree upon a definition for their
relationship, others seemingly are able to agree on very little.
Apart from biography there is little one can say about these
variations. In its broad outlines, however, the marital struggle
takes place in socially determined ways. In nineteenth-century
rural North America, men enjoyed a monopoly on public life;
the vast majority of women had to accept the position in the
social order occupied by their husbands, fathers, or brothers.
Women enjoyed a private social and cultural life which they
created themselves, but it was of little consequence in the allo-
cation of social responsibility and power. Because of their
greater resources and higher overall social importance, most
men entering marriage already had the upper hand. In large
measure any study of marriage under circumstances of male
social dominance will be a study of a struggle between men and
women that includes the continuing subordination of wives,
women's social and emotional battle against that subordination,

and the alternatives of accommodation or resistance to patriarchy.[3]

In order to undertake such a historical examination of marriage in its dynamic aspects, it is essential not to misconstrue the evidentiary sources. One must be aware first of what might be called the behavioral transformation problem. It would not do to conclude that women were actually gentle, home-loving creatures, men assertive and worldly-wise competitors, after nothing more than a critical glance at *Godey's Lady's Book* and *Hunt's Merchant Magazine,* since it is one of the functions of social role prescriptions to create such deceptions in order to convince historical subjects that the roles laid down for them are nothing but cultural reflections of their natural selves. Historians must understand these pressures on people to conform but they cannot allow themselves such gullibility. The object of historical scholarship is to show how prescribed norms and values reflected, conflicted with, or were translated into behavior. What is required, then, are sources that provide systematic information about the behavioral regularities of daily life, as well as insight into popular values and beliefs.[4]

Secondly, it would not do to reach solid conclusions about the way a set of reciprocal roles fit together and contradict each other on the basis of evidence drawn exclusively from the ranks of only one of the role players. The role set of husband-wife, like the more discussed set of master-slave, must be treated as a unit; without masters there can be no slaves, and without husbands no wives. This is, as Eugene Genovese writes, an organic antagonism. The lives and destinies of men and women have always been intertwined, and the true history of one must always be, in part, a history of the other.[5] The antagonism cuts both ways; women's history can no more be written solely out of the private communications of woman to woman than can men's history be written from business evidence.[6]

This study takes as its central problem a reconstruction of the relationship between men and women in marriage in the mid-nineteenth-century Midwest. To do this it utilizes personal records of both men's and women's daily lives to examine family behavior in its cultural context. Demographic reconstitution has been the device most widely used to look into the lives of families, and it will be put to use here. But family reconstitution alone can tell us little of the relationships of work, affection, and power within the family. In order to understand marriage it is necessary to analyze work and the division of labor, attitudes and beliefs about the proper roles for men and women, and those social groupings, including the family, that mediated the participation of women and men in the social order. Finally it will be necessary to examine the relationship of women and men, the sexual struggle itself.

The experience of midwestern families in the overland emigration to the Pacific coast provides a remarkable opportunity for this kind of behavioral and cultural study of nineteenth-century married life. Men and women together participated in most of the annual spring and summer family emigrations that inched across the 2,000 miles of continent between the Missouri River and the Pacific coast from 1843 until the 1870s, when transport by transcontinental railroad became available. Despite the overwhelming masculine prejudice of our backward glances at the American West, in the day-to-day experience of wagon travel the emigration was not a he-man but a family experience. As Mary Elizabeth Warner, an emigrant of 1853, wrote, "They talk about the times that tried men's souls but this was the time [that tried] both men and women's souls."[7] In itself the trail experience was no more remarkable than ordinary family life and struggle; indeed, men as well as women responded to their overland emigration in typical family ways. But the fact of emigrating such a great distance across such monumental terrain was so unusual that many husbands and wives took to writing about it. They wrote about the trail but also about the family lives they lived while traveling. The emigrants bequeathed us an abundance of diaries, letters, and written recollections providing a cross-sexual description of a common family event. The quality of the extant men's and women's accounts varies widely, but overall they contain a wealth of information about individual and family behavior, attitudes, and beliefs. In the nineteenth century, at any rate, a better opportunity for historical study of family life would be difficult to come by.

I approached this study of the Overland Trail through the back door, interested more in the kind of historical materials the emigrants left than in the experience itself. Perhaps this in part justifies the appearance of yet another study of this classic and intrinsically fascinating moment in the history of the nineteenth-century United States. Still, despite the thousands of pages in print, interesting scholarly interpretations of the Overland Trail experience are a relatively rare commodity, and there is ample room for new scholarship.[8] Moreover, examined through the lenses of masculine and feminine experience, the Overland Trail acquires a new historical shape.

The overland route across the North American continent traced its way through great river valleys leading to and from the natural highway over the Rockies at South Pass. From its mouth on the Missouri near Omaha, Nebraska, the Platte River cuts a broad valley corridor west across the Nebraska plains and well into the high country of Wyoming. Feeder streams lead right into the opening of South Pass. Western slope rivers provide routes from the continental divide to the northern or southern range of the Pacific mountains.

In 1812 a few lonely traders returning east to the States from Astor's isolated fur-trade outpost on the northwest coast stumbled into South Pass and the route by way of the Platte. The meaning of the discovery of the pass was not lost on Westerners, already eyeing Louisiana Purchase lands west of the Missouri. "It appears," wrote an editor for the *Missouri Gazette* in 1813, "that a journey across the continent of North America might be performed with a waggon, there being no obstruction on the whole route that any person would dare to call a mountain."[9] But a general consensus that western lands were largely barren, combined with the general availability of land in the Midwest, placed a quarter-century damper on enthusiasm for overland emigration by way of the newly discovered route.

Gradually, however, the conditions were created for a popular family emigration of massive proportions. Beginning in 1823 and continuing through the twenties and thirties the route was used for the traffic of the American fur trade. In 1830, the American Fur Company for the first time took provi-

sion wagons across the pass to the fur trader's rendezvous on
the Pacific side of the divide, fulfilling the hopes for wagon
travel expressed seventeen years before. Fur traders could
move their goods with pack animals, but families needed wagons. Now it had been demonstrated that the means for family
emigration across the Rockies was available, and during the
1830s West Coast propagandists accordingly began official and
popular agitation for Oregon and California emigration.

As the best midwestern lands were taken, and settled conditions began to restrict opportunity, many people turned their
eyes westward, across the deserts and plains to the Pacific
coastal valleys, but one question remained: could women and
children make the trip? When in 1836 and again in 1838 the
American Board of Commissioners for Foreign Missions sent
men *and* women missionaries to Oregon mission stations it
seemed that here, at last, was proof of the feasibility of family
emigration. The editor of *The Oregonian and Indian's Advocate*,
published by the Oregon Provisional Emigration Society, took a
lesson from the journey of the six missionary couples:

> Six white women . . . have already crossed the prairies to
> Oregon. . . . And we are assured by their own testimony
> that they were in better health and spirits at the end than at
> the beginning of their journey, having found it extremely
> pleasant. . . . This shows, we think, the feasibility of this
> route for ladies, and even children. Now if these ladies,
> making the tour in this manner, retained and improved
> their health, to what conclusions must we come? Must we
> not say that a larger company of families, who would move
> more slowly, be better provisioned, and take advantage of
> circumstances which these could not control, could, with
> the most perfect safety to health, pass from Missouri to
> Oregon?[10]

The first emigrant company to the Pacific, composed of one
hundred persons, mostly men, embarked two years later and
another male company the next year, in 1841. Finally a large
train of over a hundred people, mostly families, left in the
spring of 1842. It was this emigration and the one of the

following year, both publicized by John Charles Frémont's widely read reports of his exploring expeditions along the route and over South Pass, that convinced many thousands of midwesterners that the trip was, in the words of the *Daily Missouri Republican*, "little else than a pleasure excursion, requiring scarcely as much preparation as a journey from St. Louis to Philadelphia thirty-five years ago."[11] The overland emigration to the Pacific coast was finally under way in earnest.

The emigrants followed more than one overland trail, since cutoffs and new routes were born during each of the nearly thirty years of travel, and in open country emigrants spread their wagons out for miles to avoid eating each other's dust. Nonetheless, the general route they followed was the same one that had been known since 1812 (see accompanying map).[12] They thought of this route as a series of distances between strategic landmarks; this helped them, as it may assist us, in comprehending the enormous overall distance they had to travel. Each day's tally of miles was pitifully small–twenty miles a day was a goal, fifteen was more typical–and the emigrants needed interim goals to break up the two-thousand-mile journey. The first leg took them from the Missouri River to the army's Fort Kearny on the Platte River in central Nebraska Territory, a distance of as much as 320 miles from embarkation points south in Missouri but less than 200 miles from the western border of Iowa. They traversed this distance in generally mild and pleasant early May weather, moving over rolling plains amid plentiful supplies of grass, wood, and water. It was a lovely and deceptively easy way to start a perilous trip. Relatively simple river crossings presented the only early obstacles. By making good time, they could reach Fort Kearny on the Platte by late May.

Most did not stop to rest but pushed on to the second leg, up the Platte to Fort Laramie. Here the land turned drier and the grass brown in the increasing heat of June. There was no wood, but the buffalo dung which littered the valley was a good substitute fuel. Along the south bank of the North Platte, buttes and rock formations (Courthouse Rock, Chimney Rock, Scott's Bluff) the likes of which emigrants had never seen gave warn-

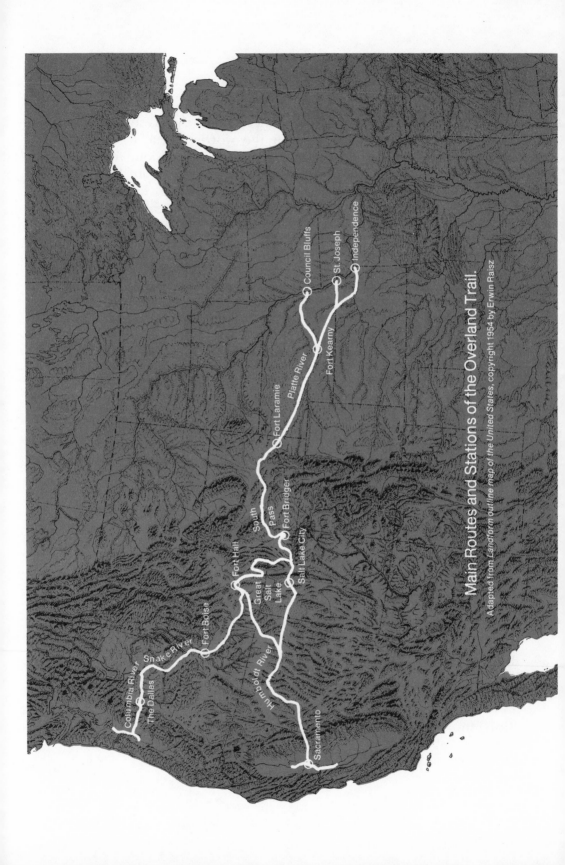

Main Routes and Stations of the Overland Trail.

Adapted from *Landform outline map of the United States*, copyright 1954 by Erwin Raisz.

Independence

St. Joseph

Council Bluffs

Fort Kearny

Platte River

Fort Laramie

South Pass

Fort Bridger

Salt Lake City

Great Salt Lake

Fort Hall

Fort Boise

Snake River

Humboldt River

Columbia River

The Dalles

Sacramento

ing of strange sights to come. As they approached the western reaches of the Platte the summer nights turned quite cool, a sign that they were making the gradual ascent to the summit of the continental divide, which by then lay another 300 miles to the west.[13]

After some 300 miles along the Platte, the emigrants arrived at Fort Laramie. A lingering landmark of the American fur trade, taken over by the army in the early 1850s to provide emigrant protection, the fort was an important supply post for the travelers.[14] But after only a day or two of rest the wagons were again on the road to South Pass, traveling through rough, dry, hilly country. The road left the protection of the river after Fort Laramie and headed across barren flatlands of alkali beds and sulfurous springs for the Sweetwater River. When the emigrants reached its banks they encountered more natural wonders: Independence Rock, "the register of the desert," where they left their names carved in the soft stone; Devil's Gate, where the Sweetwater cut spectacularly through a 400-foot-high rock wall; Ice Slough, where winter ice could be harvested from beneath the swamp grass, even during July when the emigrants passed. Finally they reached South Pass, 280 miles from Fort Laramie; an easy grade took emigrants up to the 8,000-foot summit so imperceptibly that they hardly realized it when they crossed the divide. South Pass was conquered in mid-July, but summer nights high in the Rocky plateau were so cold that ice formed on the tops of the water buckets.

Beyond South Pass the open country offered several possible ways to link up with the Western river routes. Some emigrants headed south to Salt Lake (especially after the 1850s, when the Mormons attracted them with their supplies and curious customs), some chose desert cutoffs due west, but most swung south, following water and timber 110 miles to mountain man Jim Bridger's supply station, then headed back north another 230 miles to the Hudson's Bay Company's Fort Hall on the Snake River.[15] The emigrants reached Fort Hall in mid-August, after nearly a month of regular and monotonous but relatively easy traveling since the divide. From the Missouri they had now traveled over 1,200 miles in some three-and-a-half months.

About two-thirds of the overall distance had been eaten up, but only a little over half the total time required for the trip; this was because the hardest and slowest traveling was yet to come.

A couple of days out of Fort Hall, California and Oregon emigrants parted company. Californians headed 150 miles south to connect with the headwaters of the Humboldt River (in northeastern Nevada), passing some spectacular rock formations along the way. The stretch was rather easy, but by this time patience and interest were wearing thin, and the trip seemed interminable, further travel almost unbearable. The 370 miles more along the banks of the Humboldt, through deadly dry, hot country, took another long, hard, and monotonous three weeks. When the Humboldt finally gave up, its waters dissolving into the Nevada sands without being deposited into any sea or lake, it was a signal for the beginning of the hardest and most demanding parts of the trip; these came at exactly the time when the emigrants were least prepared and most exhausted. By this time it was well into September, and they had no time to rest, for fear that an early winter would trap them in the snowy California mountains. At the Humboldt Sink they first faced a 55-mile waterless, grassless desert, for which they had to haul feed and water, and plan on losing oxen. Then it was 70 miles up the eastern slope of the Sierra Nevadas, following one mountain river or another to the summit, hoisting wagons over rock formations and easing them down slides with the use of ropes and chains. Finally, after the pass, the emigrants slowly drove down the last 80 to 100 tortuous, twisting miles of western slopes to the great Sacramento Valley, still green in the October light.

Oregon emigrants feared no better. Indeed, many chose the trail to California in order to avoid the hardships of the road to Oregon. Out of Fort Hall the emigrants clung to the cliff ledges along the south bank of the Snake River, passed the spectacular American Falls, and bore northward with the flowing waters. After 175 miles of difficult travel, they crossed and left the Snake, headed north to the Boise River, and followed its bottomlands for 100 miles to another Hudson's Bay facility, Fort Boise. Here they made three difficult crossings in succession, fording the Boise, again meeting and crossing the north-flowing Snake, and within days fording the Malheur. The road skirted the eastern edge of the dry scrub desert of southeastern Oregon for 150 miles, making at least six more substantial crossings, until it approached the dreaded Blue Mountains, looming up dark and solid ahead. Here the Oregon emigrants had the worst of it, making the grades only by the grace of ropes, pulleys, and quickly made winches, descending by using the same ropes and sheer human muscle power to restrain the wagons. The road, now barely a trace, moved the emigrants from the mountains through the wasteland below the Columbia River and after 200 miles of desolation landed them at The Dalles on the Columbia. Here forward wagon travel was stopped by the cliff walls along the river, and most emigrants ferried the final 100 miles down the Columbia—at a substantial cost in tolls, as well as risk to life and property. After 1845, some took the long Barlow detour around the southern slope of Mount Hood to avoid the ferry. Finally, one way or another, sometime in October, the emigrants reached their destination at the mouth of the Willamette.

Both Oregon and California emigrants traveled nearly 2,000 miles from their Missouri River starting points; counting travel time from home, some people were on the road a total of nearly eight months. The trip introduced them to natural wonders, thrills, discomforts, and fears they had never thought to experience. It was not a trip for the fainthearted; perhaps it was only for the foolhardy.

Historians estimate that from the 1840s to the 1870s as many as two hundred and fifty thousand to half a million individuals traveled this overland route to the Pacific Coast and other parts of the West.[16] For most of these emigrants the trip was a spectacular event in their lives, unlike anything they had done before or would ever do again. Impressed by its uniqueness, many recorded their once-in-a-lifetime experiences in letters or diaries; later even more reconstructed those parts of the journey that memory had preserved in recollections. Western bibliographers, archivists, and historians have located and catalogued nearly 800 of these documents of personal experience. This study is based on 169 narratives written by family members on the trail; of these I was able to reconstitute the genealogies and traveling parties of 122 emigrant families.[17]

Because they were contemporary records, the diaries are the most reliable and interesting material. Overland diaries were records of a particular and limited experience; most began and ended with the trip itself. As Arthur Ponsonby has noted in his study of English diaries, the immediacy of the material is both the strength and weakness of diary records. People write about the things that impress them at the moment, not about what prolonged consideration shows to have lasting importance.[18] Diaries, especially those with long, rambling entries, reveal what was on the minds of the writers. There were, of course, subjects of interest that were considered too indelicate or too dangerous to commit to paper, but the confidentiality of the diary still makes it a more open and honest reflection of contemporary thought and feeling than other sources.

Historians read and interpret, as diarists wrote, in the light of their own subjectivity. The use of a content-analysis method to test the underlying values of the diaries offered a way of assessing their thematic content by which I could hope to avoid simply reading in my own preconceptions.[19] The results of the content analysis indicate that the bulk of men's and women's concerns fell into three broad areas: the practical aspects of the trip, the health and safety of traveling kith and kin, and the natural beauty of the landscape.

Men and women diarists filled a substantial part of their entry pages with simple notations of the things they had done that day. Certainly the most impressive facts of life during the emigration were the practical matters at hand. For those involved, women as well as men, the six-month trek across the continent was experienced day to day as sixteen hours of hard, often grueling work. Rest and relaxation at one location were paid for in forced marches at another, as emigrants hurried to beat the winter snows over the Pacific mountains. Some emigrants lamented their work load: Helen Carpenter worrying that because of their work women had "no time for sociability," or George Belshaw complaining that there was no end to his responsibilities as captain.[20] But most merely noted without comment the work they had to do.

The emigration itself was undertaken for the eminently practical reasons of economic improvement. Men and women shared a strong concern for economic matters: purchases, miscellaneous costs along the trail (especially tolls at the river ferries, which galled the best-humored of emigrants despite the savings in time), and the economic potential and use of the land. This last was most important. The majority of emigrants were on their way to find and lay claim to new lands, and they kept practicing their skills at assessing farmlands throughout the trip. "These blackhills is not worth one cent for any human being," William Kahler complained in eastern Wyoming.[21] Just a day out of Topeka, Thomas Cramer began his own boning up by noting that "this is truly a lovely prairie country, finely watered, very fertile and possessing some timber."[22] Women were equally sensitive to this economic dimension. Traveling across Iowa, Amelia Hadley wrote that "notwithstanding all the fine land I would not live here if you would give it to me, the great trouble would be so far from market."[23]

In diaries the concerns of the everyday predominate, and it is consequently no surprise that emigrants' preoccupation with their own and their families' health, comfort, and safety was a second main theme. In any constantly kept-up diary, one might well expect a comment on the writer's state of health in nearly every entry; under the extraordinarily strenuous conditions of the trail, with regular changes in water quality, a poorly balanced diet, and closer contact than usual with potentially contagious social groups, along with high levels of individual exertion and lowered powers of resistance, writing on health took its place immediately after notes on work as a topic of concern. Henry Allyn's diary entry for May 2, 1853, was typical of the entries of many emigrants: "Could sleep but little on account of a vehement cough. Lay restless and wished for the day. . . . John Wesley is feeble though better; he drove team some today. I am very feeble and keep to my bed today. My cough continues with sickness of stomach, vertigo and headache."[24] Other related subjects included concerns about the safety of the party, the comfort, or lack of it, along the trail, and the need for rest.

These were travel diaries, and as Ponsonby notes, a preoccupation of travel journals is the shifting and changing natural or human scene.[25] So it was with the emigrants. The social scene, mainly their family lives, remained pretty much a constant, but the emigrants were startled and in some cases overawed by the imposing natural landscape and strange climate through which they passed. In terms of sheer preponderance, men and women emigrants mentioned the beauty of the setting more than any other single subject. On the thirteenth of July, 1851, P. V. Crawford's party halted at midday after finding the hot springs and geysers near Bear River, west of South Pass. "Here we lay the balance of the day, contemplating the grandeur," he wrote.[26] Such brief notations occur on nearly every page of every diary text. On the other hand, notes on natural wonders could run on for pages as men and women described their first encounters with the plains or mountains or their attempts to scale the heights of Chimney Rock or Devil's Gate. To the emigrants the West through which they passed included both the most beautiful and most desolate sights they had ever seen. Every person seemed to adhere to a naturalistic aesthetic standard which appreciated the landscape as God's artistic masterpiece.

These three broad themes—practical matters, health and safety, and natural beauty—account for over two thirds of the measured content of both men's and women's diaries. It is in the remaining content, as well as in the style of the writing, that the diaries of men and women as whole documents differ sharply. Women were concerned with family and relational values—the happiness and health of the children, family affection, home and hearth, getting along with the traveling group, and friendship, especially with other women. Men were concerned with violence and aggression—fights, conflicts, and competition, and most of all hunting. These divergences between men's and women's diaries are important for an understanding of the values and priorities of husbands and wives, and later chapters will take up these differences in detail.

Most important to note at this juncture, however, is the essential similarity of men's and women's writing. Content analysis complements this evaluation by indicating that men and women appreciated the overland experience in similar

ways; in other words, that men and women shared the same
orientation to what was important: a naturalistic aesthetic, hard
work, good health, and practical economic considerations. The
diaries indicate, first and foremost, that these mid-nineteenth-
century men and women were part of a common culture, that
they were, indeed, more alike than different.

Men and women shared a basic common outlook that was in
part the cultural product of their common identity as partners
in marriage. Men as well as women were full of aesthetic appreciation; women as well as men were practical and
economy-minded. This agreement on essentials was what
allowed marriages to endure. The new social history has emphasized the subjectivity and self-direction of subordinate
classes and groups, a critical step in reconstructing the history
of class, race, and sexual struggle. Rather than focusing exclusively on their distinctive history, however, one should examine
them in the light of the cultural and social practices which
bound groups together, as men and women were bound together in marriage.

1

The Overland Emigrants

The written record of the overland emigration was left by all kinds of people: city and country folk, college graduates and the barely literate, old and young, rich and poor. Nonetheless, there was a social homogeneity among the writers that reflected the common background of the emigrants, most of whom were poor farmers from the Mississippi Valley. As Francis Parkman observed in 1846, the overland emigrants came from "the extreme Western states."[1] Three-quarters of the writers left homes in Indiana, Illinois, Iowa, and Missouri, and most of the rest came from closely bordering areas. In 1850 the Midwest was overwhelmingly agricultural. No northern states were more totally devoted to agriculture than these; almost 90 percent of the adult male workers of the Midwest were farmers, compared to only about two-thirds in the Atlantic and New England states.[2] Within this region the emigrants came from solidly agricultural, nonurban counties.

Emigrant occupations correspond with this profile. Six out of ten male heads of household were farmers. The other men worked at jobs common to a rural or small-town setting: carpenter, blacksmith, cooper, county teacher, doctor, editor, and especially itinerant or parish preacher. Judging from the way almost everyone took up the farmer's calling in Oregon and California, farming must have been a general skill known to most of these men.[3]

Most of the emigrants took up the move with a farmer's motives; they wanted to claim new and better farmlands. Over a quarter of the writers of the diaries and recollections stated unequivocally that new agricultural land was *the* motive in their decision to emigrate. Clarence Danhof has put it well: "The impulse toward removal to the West did not arise from a desire to recreate the pattern of the eastern farm left behind, but came from a vision of a rich soil producing an abundant surplus of products, readily salable for cash upon markets which, if not immediately available, would certainly develop and could somehow be reached."[4] Many were leaving a bad economic situation: unable to find cheap but productive lands, unhappy with the out-of-the-way location of the lands they owned, burdened with debt.

John and Cornelia Sharp are examples of these land-hungry emigrants, willing to undergo extreme hardship for new opportunities. A couple in their late thirties with a growing family of children, they had struggled unsuccessfully for years to make their poor farm in Washington County, Ohio, pay. In 1848 John decided that they could do better in Oregon. After a strenuous ride of over 900 miles on their homemade Ohio River flatboat, the couple and their seven children disembarked in Independence, Missouri. The Sharps rented two one-room cabins and scratched out a mostly corn diet from the poor soil, all the while working for wages to accumulate the necessary cash for the trip. It took four years, and even then John had to borrow $500 from a nearby brother-in-law for the outfit. All these were acceptable sacrifices for new land to farm.[5]

Oregon and California offered cheap, abundant, and rich lands. Phoebe Judson, who traveled there in 1853, remembered their reason for emigrating quite distinctly: "The motive that induced us to part with the pleasant associations and the dear friends of our childhood days, was to obtain from the government of the United States a grant of land that 'Uncle Sam' had promised to give to the head of each family who settled in this new country."[6] A year earlier this motive had inspired the refrain of a popular camp song:

> Come along, come along—don't be alarmed,
> Uncle Sam is rich enough to give us all a farm.[7]

Certainly other reasons were important: milder winters, a healthier climate, an escape especially from malarial chills and fever. Reasons of health motivated nearly all the emigrants, as Parkman noted.[8] Indeed, a large number decided to emigrate specifically for a change in climate and, they hoped, an improvement in their health.[9] Others went to join family members

who had gone earlier. Most left for these and a combination of
other, more idiosyncratic reasons. But in general, the promise
of free land and changed economic circumstances was the primary attraction for the Judsons, the Sharps, and their midwestern peers. These farmers were motivated by a desire to trans-
form the material conditions around them; the emigration was
the most obvious consequence of their willingness to change.[10]

Historians have commonly judged the emigrants to have
been "perennial movers," and indeed, most emigrants had
moved before.[11] All but 10 percent of the male heads of household had been born in areas outside the Midwest. An examination of the mobility histories of families who made the trek
shows that only 22 percent of the male heads of household had
made no moves as adults.[12] The majority had moved at least
once, many twice, some three or more times. As one would
expect, the number of moves increased with age.

But more interesting, most men made their moves at the
same general points in their lives. Nearly all had moved westward from their parents' homes in their early twenties (46
percent) or had made a similar move westward within the first
two years of marriage (38 percent). Many men moved a second
time in their middle thirties; among the men who had been
married at least fifteen years by the time of their overland
emigration, 80 percent followed their initial move west with a
second move, again westward, some ten years later. The combination of these two moves typically took a man from his
birthplace on the east coast first to the Appalachian or Ohio
River region and finally to the western frontiers of Illinois,
Iowa, or Missouri.

The association of westward moves with particular points in
men's lives suggests that the life cycle of families was influential
in the nature and timing of emigration. Families, like institutions and individuals, have their own unique histories. These
histories, however, are punctuated by epochal events common
to all—marriage, the birth of children, their departure at
majority, death. Family sociologists conventionally divide
families into four types corresponding to all these stages: newly
married couples, still childless; families with all children under
fifteen years; families in which the oldest child has reached

fifteen; and couples whose children have grown and left to establish families of their own.[13]

Families of each stage are represented in the group of reconstituted emigrant families. Unfortunately the only comparable set of data I have found are drawn from rural North Carolina society in 1934,[14] but if one assumes a similarity between the two populations, it becomes apparent that young families were traveling in proportion to their numbers in the society, while mid-stage families were underrepresented and newlyweds more preponderant. In both populations there were very few independent mature families.[15]

A reexamination of the mobility histories by these structural family types shows a strong association between family stages and movement.[16] On the average, families moved once for each stage of the life cycle they passed through. Mobility, then, was correlated with the first three stages of the family life cycle.

Few newlywed men had previously moved as adults; for them the move to the coast would mean setting up their first homes and farms. Honeymoon emigrations were a tradition. Second-stage couples—those with young children—had also first moved at the time of their marriages, from Pennsylvania to Indiana or from Kentucky to Missouri. Now these young families were making their second major move. After eight or ten years of marriage, six to eight years farming the same ground, perhaps setting aside a few savings, these families felt secure enough to try improving their situation with a move to the coast.

The men of the third family type had come to the agricultural frontier in just such a move, as husbands in young families. The move to the coast was to be their third major move. We are on safe ground when we speculate that families in each stage undertook their moves to the coast with differing perspectives, perhaps even differing motives. For the couples of the third stage, with near-grown children soon to set out on their own, the move was perhaps a last chance to find the kind of home and farm suitable for their later years, perhaps in a region of abundant good land where their children would not be tempted so far afield in their own search for a place to settle.[17]

The emigration to the coast was, of course, made possible by a variety of objective social developments: large-scale economic and diplomatic trends, the discovery of gold in California, and changing technologies, to name a few. Social events and trends opened possibilities and framed the context for choices by individual men and women. The actual decision to emigrate, however, was made within the personal logic of each family, a subjective process controlled by the movement of the family life cycle. The willingness to pick up and leave the old farming life for a better one—the willingness to change—was so strong that it seemed almost institutionalized. The overland emigration was fundamentally bound up with family life. Because of the traditions that the mobility histories reveal, we can be reasonably certain that emigration at these points was culturally sanctioned; the only question was where they would go.

The emigrants were willing to move, certainly. But relocating was also a question of resources. Unfortunately there is no way to make an objective determination of the emigrants' economic condition from their written documents. We do know that they came from a region with the lowest per capita wealth in the nation.[18] According to their own testimony, they were an unprosperous lot. Almost two-thirds of the emigrant writers were silent about their economic status, but of those who did write about it, nearly half the emigrants thought of themselves as poor and another third as middling.[19] Considering their ages, of course, the newlywed and young families had not yet had the time to acquire much wealth.

At any rate, few emigrants had much financial flexibility. Peter Burnett, emigrant of 1843, knew his audience when he wrote that "the trip to Oregon is not a costly or expensive one. An individual can move here as cheap if not cheaper than he can from Tennessee or Kentucky to Missouri."[20] Agricultural historians, however, point out that the initial costs of farming were not insubstantial. The preparations for a trip across the continent and investment in new farmlands in the valleys of the Willamette or the Sacramento required some personal capital.[21] Emigrants had to have some means, but how much?

Contemporary estimates as well as historians' hindsight both suggest that farmers would have been safe to start with from

$500 to $1,000 in cash or property.[22] Few emigrants could come up with funds like those; each farmer would need carefully to assess his needs, hoping to meet them with ingenuity and sagacity in lieu of funds. He could count first of all on his own and his family's labor, and very possibly the help of neighbors, in clearing fields, fencing, constructing a first rude shelter and outbuilding, and digging his well. He could hope to meet subsistence costs of the first year by temporary employment with the Hudson's Bay Company or at Sutter's Fort in the 1840s, or in the stable Oregon or heady California economies of the 1850s. Farm animals and seed could also be purchased with this income. Draft animals and a wagon would come with the family over the trail.

The essential costs, then, were those of the trip itself. The trail's special conditions required a new set of goods, although some household and farm goods could be converted for trail use. The means of transportation—a wagon, oxen, and running gear—were the most expensive, coming close to $400. The wagon had to be constructed with care for the journey: strong enough to transport provisions for six months, but light enough for a reasonable team. Emigrants commonly employed a 2,000 to 2,500-pound farm wagon with a flat bed about ten feet long with two-foot sides. It had to be made of well-seasoned hardwood to stand the trip's great extremes of temperature and moisture; an ordinary farm wagon would not do. Emigrants were particularly careful in the purchase of a wagon. Other skilled farmers, to economize and be sure, took the time to make their own. Benjamin Bonney remembered that his father "put in his spare time for months making a strong sturdy wagon in which to cross the plains."[23] A wagon of this size loaded with some 2,500 pounds required a team of six mules or more commonly four yoke of oxen. Since emigrants were completely dependent upon these animals, keeping weight down to conserve the animals' strength was all-important. The provisions for the entire trip and all the baggage would have to conform to the weight limitations of the team.[24]

The limitation on weight showed most obviously in the emigrants' diet. People prepared to exist on the staples of bread, bacon, and coffee, but these were not sufficient. The list of supplemental foodstuffs mentioned by emigrants is long, but reducible to an essential ten or fifteen. Some of these could be brought from home, but most of the trail fare was special and had to be purchased in quantity. A family of four would be lucky to spend less than $120 for food stores. Cooking utensils too were purchased specially for the trip, and contemporary estimates suggest a minimum of $20 for a four-person mess.

Each family would already possess firearms, but the Indian presence was sufficient inducement for many to trade up in quality or add to their store. There was also a healthy supply of powder, lead, and shot to buy: $60 or $70 for arms.[25]

With these minimums, an emigrant family could count on spending an initial $125 to $150 per person before crossing the Missouri. If the oxen, rifle, and foodstuffs such as bacon, lard, and dried fruit could be brought from the family farm, the cost could be cut down to $70 per person. To this had to be added cash for toll ferries (established on the trail as early as 1847), emergency provisions along the way, and cash for the first few weeks on the coast while the men were looking for work.[26] For some, raising this kind of money was no problem. Wealthy farmers like James Frazier Reed of Sangamon County, Illinois, purchased his stores with savings. But for most, the investment required liquidating their property holdings, and many emigrants sold their household goods as well as their farms to finance the move. Here again is evidence of the willingness to change: most left with all their wordly goods loaded in the wagons.

Purchased goods, plus other necessary items brought from home—candles, towels, soap, articles of personal hygiene, sewing supplies, changes of clothing, and essential tools—must have weighed in at around 550 pounds per person. For one quarter of the families, weight presented no problems, since they took extra wagons over and above the minimum required and enjoyed considerable cargo space (2,500 to 3,500 pounds was the general range). Most emigrants, however, were pressed to economize and tried to carry their weight in the fewest possible number of wagons. Economic pressures pushed another quarter of the families beyond the weight limits and forced them to overload at the outset of the trip. In 1852 Eliza Brooks an-

swered her husband's call to join him in California and packed
her five children and goods into a single four-yoke wagon. She
brought along two laying hens and drove two cows, so the fresh
eggs and milk along the way may have allowed her to cut the
weight of her foodstuffs; nonetheless, the wagon must have
been loaded with well over 2,500 pounds of provisions alone.[27]

Most families, however, conformed to the minimum requirements set by their size and took the necessary number of
wagons. A family of four could make the trip in a single wagon,
although in such a move there was very little capacity for cargo,
perhaps space enough for an additional 300 pounds. Ezra and
Eliza Meeker, their son, and Ezra's brother Oliver traveled to
Oregon in a single wagon in 1852, James and Lavinia Porter,
their infant son, and her brother in 1860.[28] But because of their
size, the majority of families were compelled to take more than
one wagon. A single vehicle simply could not be crammed with
enough provisions for all. Since each wagon could be loaded
with 2,500 pounds, emigrants generally had a little extra space;
on the average families should have been able to pack in cargo
weighing 1,000 to 1,200 pounds.

Within these limits, without overloading, what could a family
take? With an eye to a farmer's priorities, we can surmise that
the means of production were at the top of the list. The farm
tools were the first items packed after the essentials. The writer
of an advice circular for the 1843 emigration suggested that
"each man should have the necessary implements of husbandry
to go right to work and each mechanic should take his tools with
him." This counsel was nearly universal. Joel Palmer warned
against taking "useless trumpery" but urged farmers and
craftsmen to take a long list of tools "as it is difficult getting such
articles" on the coast.[29] Any room left over was probably allocated according to the priorities of individual families. Some
took books, others household articles, extra clothing, perhaps a
camp oven, or some items of furniture. To be sure, these last
were the first items to go overboard when the going got rough.

This emigrant outfit—wagon and team, provisions, arms, and
other essentials—was designed as a mobile household for one
family. Most emigrants outfitted mainly at home, in family
groups, buying their goods at local establishments. Planning for

the trip as a family set the pattern and the material basis for the entire journey. Except for the collective planning of some single men during the Gold Rush there was little experimentation with larger-than-family economies. Each family expected to be mainly self-supporting and most work would be performed in the context of the family economy.

Outfitted and packed up, emigrant families headed out sometime in the late winter or early spring for the Missouri River towns known as the jumping-off places. Nearly three-quarters of the families traveled to the Missouri in their family wagons.[30] For many this first section of the trip was a lark; roads were generally good, accommodations readily available at inns or friendly farmhouses. Often the route was set so the travelers could visit friends or relatives on the way. For others the early parts of the trip were more of a shakedown cruise. Late winter storms and the thaw frequently flooded roads, making them temporarily impassable and the going slow. Perhaps most difficult was the pain of leaving home and loved ones; the sadness slowly ebbed away as the wagons rolled west.

Before 1849 nearly everyone headed toward Independence, the starting point for the Santa Fe trade and the fur caravans. In these early years most came by wagon across the settled hills of central Missouri, a third by steamboat up the Missouri River. The local economy of what would later be known as Kansas City boomed with the emigrant trade throughout the forties.[31] But Independence was south of the juncture of the Platte and the Missouri and necessitated a long trek north to the main highway. By 1850 Independence had relinquished its preeminence to other towns upriver; only local emigrants continued to use it as a jumping-off place.

The extension of steamboat service upriver to St. Joseph had drawn most of the emigrant crowd north, closer to the mouth of the Platte.[32] St. Joe was the center for the Gold Rush traffic in 1849 and 1850. With effective steamboat service, and in 1859 the first rail connection from the frontier to the east, St. Joe, of all the crossings, attracted emigrants from the greatest variety of states. From 1846 to 1863 over half the families who crossed at St. Joe arrived by steamboat or train, and of these 60 percent

were from states east of Indiana. The river traffic drew
wagoneers from the lower Mississippi and Ohio River valleys to
the St. Joe crossings.

Council Bluffs, another 160 miles up the Missouri, was not
connected by regular steamboat lines until the late fifties, and
rail lines creeping across Iowa did not link it with the east until
after the Civil War. But the Mormon base camp and ferries
established there in 1846 attracted many gentiles. The settlement at Kanesville (permanently renamed Council Bluffs after
the last Mormon exodus in 1853) was primitive and rough until
commercial lines came through. Nevertheless, nearly six out of
every ten emigrants jumped off from Council Bluffs after
1851. Nearly 80 percent of the Council Bluffs emigrant families
came from the northern Midwest; it was simply the most convenient crossing for the mass of emigrants with homes in Iowa,
Illinois, Indiana, and Wisconsin. In addition many emigrants
thought the north side of the Platte a better road and headed
for the northern ferries. The rudeness of Council Bluffs could
not compare with the Mexican color of Independence, the
diversity of St. Joseph, or the commercial prosperity of either
of those crossings, but this shabby outpost served the most
typical of the overland travelers throughout the fifties: run-
of-the-mill midwestern farmers, too poor for steamboats, who
traveled across Iowa by wagons provisioned, for the most part,
at home. If we were to pick one most characteristic jumping-off
place we would do best to remember Council Bluffs; its outward drabness was a reflection of the plain and sturdy character
of the farmer-emigrants.

Families drove to the Missouri in small groups, but few
families, especially in the forties, thought of setting out for
Oregon or California alone. Later, when the road was better
known and there were more trading posts and forts along the
route, some individual families ventured out, but in the first
year emigrants looked to large assemblages of people for support and protection. Over the whole period about half the
families traveled without trains, but from 1843 to 1848 almost
everyone traveled in organized wagon trains that set out to
journey together to either Oregon or California.[33]

The great trains of the forties were in the tradition of the caravans of the American Fur Company and the Sante Fe traders. Trans-Mississippi wagon travel had begun with the trade between Missouri and Sante Fe, New Mexico, in the 1820s. As we have seen, in the early thirties wagons began also crossing the continent to the north, carrying furs and goods up and down the Platte River plain. To maximize efficiency and safety, these commercial trains organized militarily. The leadership set a line of march, reconnoitered for water and camp, watched for Indian signs, and generally kept the train together with a code of discipline.[34]

The first emigrants followed in this tradition. Independence, the home of the commercial trade, was a natural starting point for their journey. During April, emigrants gradually assembled in spring camp, a few miles into Indian territory, waiting for the sprouting grass to ripen into forage. Usually in early May they set out, following the well-defined wagon tracks across Indian country to the Platte and beyond, guided by the experience and the scouts of the commercial trains. Likewise in the tradition of the earliest trains, emigrants usually settled on a semimilitary form of organization. An election among the male heads of household was held for a slate of officers, often from general right down through colonels, captains, lieutenants, and sergeants.[35] The ranking officers then divided the train into platoons or companies of armed men to apportion responsibility and set a rotation for defensive duties.[36] Unlike the commercial trains, however, the emigrant trains were composed of family units, each of which assumed nearly all responsibility for routine work. Emigrant trains rarely attempted to collectivize any more than purely defensive obligations. Some early trains placed minimum requirements on the size of a family's provisions, but the regulation was intended to guarantee, not undermine, the essential self-sufficiency of each unit.

The trains were more than simply functional affairs, however, for the emigrants' concern about Indians and accidents was equaled and in many cases overpowered by their anxiety about the absence of civil authority. How would they handle themselves when the constraints of civilization were loosened?

Mary Medley Ackley, remembering her trip of 1852, wrote; "When we set foot on the right bank of the Missouri River we were outside the pale of civil law. We were in Indian country, where no organized civil government existed."[37] Randall Hewitt, traveling to Washington Territory with his uncle's family ten years later, echoed her: "To the westward civil authority practically ceased; everything was in an unsettled condition, and where emigrant parties had joined for security and combined for their own protection each company was a law unto itself. In a region without law are apt to be lawless and troublesome characters."[38]

The wagon train had to be a surrogate society, "a fully equipped American community," in John Minto's description, "with all the incidents of orderly community life."[39] Full societies necessitate a complex organization, and in spring camp the emigrants turned their attention to the form of their temporary society. The earlier the emigration, the more complicated the organization. The huge trains of 1843, '44, '45, and '46 drew up constitutions and bylaws, elected officers, and tried to enforce an overall train discipline.[40] Their adopted rules and regulations specified flat punishments for specific crimes, but more importantly their codes tried to plot a moral direction for the organization: "Every man to carry with him a Bible and other religious books, as we hope not to degenerate into a state of barbarism."[41]

We have been left a view of these trains shaped more by what emigrants wanted them to be than what they actually were. Jesse Applegate's classic, "A Day with the Cow Column," which depicted daily life in a portion of the 1843 emigration, was colorful and picturesque, but in its portrayal of harmony and efficiency Applegate's was an inaccurate account of trail operation. Even at the time, the image of the train was highly romantic, the facade hard to penetrate. James Henry Carleton, on the trail as second lieutenant of the U.S. Dragoons, was beguiled by this image as he observed an 1845 train from a distance: "It was really a beautiful sight to see this company while on the march. The white topped wagons—the long line of cattle—the horsemen upon each flank, with their long rifles—the drivers with

their big whips—all moving so regularly forward, that when
viewed from a distance it seemed as if they were united and
propelled by the same power."[42]

But upon closer inspection the picture of unity dissolved. At
their best these little communities stumbled along. Once the
fears of Indian attack had been dispelled, for example, the
military posture became burdensome. With experience, Carleton shed his earlier illusions; he later complained about a train
captain who "made not a few pretenses of having all manner of
duties performed with a method; and where ever there was an
opportunity for the introduction of military discipline, and
military commands, he was sure to improve it. He was . . . what
in the army would be called a martinet. Hardly a yoke of oxen
could be permitted to drink without a command."[43]

Anxious about the wilderness, emigrants empowered a
leadership which soon conflicted with their inherent indi-
vidualism. Samuel Tetherow recalled the work of his father
Solomon as captain of one of those 1845 trains Carleton had
observed: "My dad was a pretty good man. He was capable as
well as popular. . . . But if you think it's any snap to run a wagon
train of 66 wagons with every man in the train having a different idea of what is the best thing to do, all I can say is that some
day you ought to try it."[44] Men argued about how fast or slow to
move, where to camp, how many guards to post, whether or not
to hunt. Any difference was a potential cause of heated argument during the frustrating journey. All these trivial conflicts
and more became pretexts for splitting the unmanageable
trains into smaller companies.

Parkman provided a glimpse into this disintegration:

> It was easy to see that fear and dissension prevailed among
> them; some of the men—but these, with one exception were
> bachelors—looked wistfully upon us as we rode lightly and
> swiftly by, and then impatiently at their own lumbering
> wagons and heavy gated oxen. Others were unwilling to
> advance at all, until the party they had left behind should
> rejoin them. Many murmuring against the leader they had
> chosen, and wished to depose him; and this discontent was
> fomented by some ambitious spirits, who had hopes of

succeeding in his place. The women were divided between regrets for the homes they had left and fear of the deserts and savages before them.[45]

The splintering could not be stopped, for the trains were never able to effect any meaningful discipline. The inherent discipline of the company–worker relationship stabilized the fur caravans; in these groups disobedience on the plains was tantamount to mutiny. The Santa Fe traders were tied together by the expedient of protecting their goods; even so, each proprietor was likely to counteract the orders of the elected captain, especially as the train neared Santa Fe and the premium shifted from safety to competition for the best stall at market.[46] Emigrants were even less successful. In the early trains there were some attempts to enforce the collective regulations, and discussions of punishments for infractions of the rules can be found in the record.[47] But there is a striking gap between the elaborate sets of regulations and punishments and their actual enforcement. Even for serious crimes, the most common punishment was banishment. This tacit admission of the inability of the trains to govern themselves reflected their lack of unity, a situation that made the elaborate formal organization meaningless.[48]

Emigrants would have had more incentive for maintaining a developed, albeit temporary, society if they had not soon discovered that there were few trail tasks which required efforts beyond the ability of a single family. The family could meet even unexpected exigencies with ad hoc arrangements. Written evidence of the spontaneous cooperation of many people is abundant. Fording rivers, for example, was a task that required great effort and much manpower. "In case of difficulty all helped," wrote Edward Allen on his way to Oregon in 1852 without a train; "in fording the rivers and creeks no sooner was one team over than all went to the aid of the remainder."[49] Unacquainted emigrants worked together for as long as it took to complete a task: "The emigrants that are here, all join and make a bridge," Henry Allyn noted in his 1853 diary.[50] Noah Brooks, also of 1853, remembered that "the cheerfulness with which these emigrants, total strangers to one another buckled to the work, never leaving it until all were safely over, was beautiful to behold."[51] Such cooperative behavior was typical in scores of different areas of work.[52]

Another reason the emigrants soon found trail organization somewhat irrelevant was the dissipation of their concerns about civil authority. There were no sudden outbursts of incivility once established law had been left behind, and in general the emigrants found that society as they knew it pretty much continued in the simple company of other travelers. The big trains nearly all splintered and many dissolved completely after South Pass, not because people decided to go it alone, but because circumstances did not require train organization. By the early fifties travel seemed so much more possible that most people were content simply to fall in and out with each other along the way; indeed, at times the trail was so crowded that they longed for a little family privacy. During the late fifties and sixties parties formed loose trains because of the perceived Indian threat on the Plains, but with some exceptions these later trains were much more limited affairs.

During the forties most emigrants traveled as members of trains, but within the caravans nearly half of all the emigrants traveled with only their conjugal families, including parents and children (with perhaps a hired man or two) but no other companions. Households simply packed up and headed for the spring rendezvous, expecting to take their place in an organized wagon train.

Peter and Harriet Burnett traveled that way. Burnett was an up-and-coming lawyer-politician from the raw western Missouri country. He had stumped all the winter of 1842–43 to organize the first substantial emigration to Oregon. In the spring the Burnetts and their six children moved to the rendezvous some distance outside Independence where Peter continued to pour his considerable energies into the organization of the train. His reward was election on May twentieth as captain of a most unwieldy train of at least 1,000 people, organized into perhaps as many as a hundred distinct parties, along with some 3,000 cattle and other livestock. The inevitable tensions of the march, exacerbated by the diversity of the group, soon made the well-planned organization a mockery, and Burnett resigned after only two weeks. The train divided, ostensibly into two administrative units but actually into a long meandering line of march in which the real solidarities were among kinship and neighborhood groupings. The Burnetts were without permanent associates, and although there were always people close enough with whom to share their extraordinary burdens, it was a lonely trip for Harriet, solely responsible, as she was, for the six children.[53] The same thing must have happened to hundreds of other families who found themselves alone, without kith or kin, on the trail.

Throughout the history of the trail some families—about a third of them—continued to embark on the trip without any company. The instability of train organization could have proved disastrous for them if casual associations had not made up for train failures, although later generations have exaggerated the dangers they faced. There were many accidents, but serious injuries were probably no more common on the trail than on the farm. Cholera was a terrible problem during the epidemics of 1849, '50, '52, and '53, but the complaints of most years were certainly no more fearful than the Mississippi malaria which many were fleeing.

Indians presented few real problems for the emigrants; the toll was great in incessant worry and anxiety, but even this was partially overcome by the exotic and colorful presence they lent to the experience of those emigrants who encountered them. The majority of emigrants, in fact, saw very few Indians along the route. In the 1840s and early fifties the ones they did encounter were a trial but not a serious danger, demanding tribute in sugar, coffee, or whiskey in exchange for free passage through Indian territory, or simply begging. Through the forties and early fifties there were no war parties directed at emigrants, although occasionally a group of braves might steal stock, a kind of plundering that resulted in a few killings on both sides.

It was when settlers began seriously to encroach on the plains and mountains after 1854 that Indian resettlement, broken treaties, and finally the growing Indian awareness that white farmers would soon lay claim to all the western lands resulted in a more hostile and aggressive attitude on all sides. In the late fifties and sixties the emigrants had to be more vigilant, especially in the regions beyond South Pass, on the routes to southern Oregon and northern California, where 90 percent of all armed conflict took place. But even in those years and regions most people got through with little or no difficulty. Over the whole history of the trail, emigrants undoubtedly killed and injured more Indians than Indians did emigrants, although there were provocation and aggression on both sides. More important at the time was the assistance Indians provided to emigrants down on their luck, by ferrying wagons, guiding lost parties, and sharing food and drink. In general families traveling alone fared reasonably well.[54]

Nonetheless, most emigrants were not content to travel with only the company of their immediate families. Emigrants of the fifties were less likely to travel in large wagon trains but more likely to make arrangements before the trip to travel as a member of a party—a group of individuals and families bound together by agreement, prior acquaintance, or kinship for the duration of the trip. While the emigrants themselves used the terms "train," "party," or "company" imprecisely and interchangeably, "party" as it is used here refers to larger-than-family traveling associations based on personal connections, distinguished from the usually larger and more formal "trains."[55] Parties were mobile and efficient and did not suffer the structural weaknesses of the lumbering trains. Most importantly, parties guaranteed people the company of other travelers. Because the trains broke apart easily and quickly, families like the Burnetts were thrown upon their own resources for social contact; for many this was an isolating and lonely experience. The social needs of the emigrants—a companion for the long walks, company outside the conjugal circle, a place to share a smoke or enjoy a bit of crocheting—could be met in the day-to-day associations of the trail party.

A quarter of the parties were voluntary associations, sometimes composed of acquaintances of the road or spring camps, but more commonly friends and neighbors from back home. In 1846, for example, Charles Imus, an early settler along the Apple River in northwestern Illinois, organized a party of

neighbors to emigrate to California. Included in the company
were Imus's nephew, the families of Joseph Aram, Adna
Hecox, Charles Isbell, his brother James Isbell, the Savage
family, and several single men. All twenty-two members had
lived within a few miles of each other and knew each other
before the trip.[56] Isaac G. Foster, a prosperous farmer of
Plainfield, Illinois, a township thirty miles southwest of
Chicago, organized a similar company in 1854. In addition to
Foster's family the party included the Burrell clan—Edward and
Louisa Burrell, his mother and sister Mary, Mary's fiancé Wes-
ley Tonner, Louisa's parents the Hannibals, and a cousin—the
Silas Wrightman family, and five hired men, twenty-two in all.[57]

The most common organizing principle for the party, however, was kinship. Close to half of all the emigrant families
traveled in larger-than-family parties based on kin. In a few
cases, kinship parties were composed of distant relatives—an
uncle with a nephew and niece, a conjugal family with a couple
of cousins.[58] But most often the kinship party was a version of
an extended family: an association of direct descendants and
siblings. Frequently a full three-generation family would make
the trip together. The Belshaw clan, for example, left their
homes in Lake County, Indiana, for Oregon in 1853. Five of
George and Elizabeth's seven grown children, two with families
of their own, accompanied their parents. The Parsons and
three of the McCarty brothers, all in-laws, also took up with
them for Oregon. Counting the cook and three unrelated
travelers, there were twenty-six people in the party.[59] The Barlow party of 1845 was smaller: Samuel and Susannah with their
teenaged and older children, married daughter and her husband, and grandchildren.[60]

Sometimes the first generation was too old, too ill, or too
settled to make a move of such consequence; sometimes grandparents were no longer living. But many families were held
together by strong sibling unity. Kinship parties were often
groups of siblings with their spouses, children, and sometimes
in-laws: Jesse, Charles, and Lindsey Applegate together with
their families moved from the Osage River country of Missouri
to Oregon in 1843;[61] Gustavus, Jeddadiah, and Harvey Hines
left for Oregon from Oswego, New York, with their families ten

years later.[62] Usually these sibling parties included sisters as well
as brothers. In 1852 Harmon Davis of Mahaska County, Iowa,
headed a party for California which included his family and
those of his brother and two sisters.[63] That same year, sixty
miles to the southeast, Stuart, Eliza, and Caleb Richey, their
spouses, and ten children left for Oregon after burying their
father.[64]

Both the voluntary and kinship parties afforded the emigrants the security and comfort of numbers, even in the almost
inevitable event of a train's collapse. Extended family groups,
indeed, could be quite large. The Zumwalt clan, the brothers
Jacob and Joseph with their wives, children, children's spouses,
and grandchildren, for example, totaled thirty-seven persons.[65]
On the road to Oregon in the same year (1853) was the Stearns
family: the Reverend John Stearns, an elderly widower, his
three married sons, two married daughters, nineteen grandchildren, plus ten more unrelated people, the forty of them
occupying ten wagons.[66]

Although the wagon train has been the most enduring image
of the overland experience, in fact the most salient social feature of overland emigration was its predominant family cast.
The emigration was for many a final severing of family ties and
the liberation, for better or worse, of the conjugal family from
the bonds of parents. But for nearly half of the family emigrants, the move was undertaken by and with a large network of
close kin, with the effect of pulling kin together even though
they might previously have lived quite some distance apart. The
quest for something new would take place in the context of the
very familiar.

In the days of the fur trade, the cross-continental traffic had
been predominantly male. The beginning of family emigration
in the 1840s completely changed the sexual composition of trail
travel. Until 1849 (judging from the available figures for 1843,
1844, and 1846) women constituted 15 to 20 percent of all
emigrants.[67] Probably only a few women traveled outside
families; in fact, there is only one extant diary of a woman
traveling without either husband or kin, that of Rebecca
Ketcham who traveled along the trail in 1853.[68] Family parties

sometimes employed female cooks and servants, but hired hands were integrated as part of the working family unit, and if children are counted as well, we see that the 1840s were years of farm family emigration.[69]

The Gold Rush marked a second fundamental shift in the character of the western emigration. The Army command at Fort Laramie kept a register of passing emigrants in the early 1850s; while some people must have shunned stopping to record their names on the ledger, the emigrants' penchant for leaving their names carved on rocks and cliffs suggests that people might well have been eager to sign up for posterity. Unfortunately the register was lost in a fire in the late fifties, but luckily some cumulative figures were noted and recorded by passing journalists, giving us some figures on the sexual and age composition of the 1850, 1852, and 1853 emigrations.[70] Not surprisingly, the Gold Rushers were overwhelmingly male. Yet in spite of the tens of thousands of single men the absolute number of families on the trail was probably not significantly lower than in previous years. The estimated number of children in 1850, for instance, is in the same range as previous years.[71]

Thus the steady flow of farm families continued through the Gold Rush. In fact it increased dramatically from 1850 to 1852, by a factor of ten judging by the number of children on the trail. A correspondent for the *Daily Missouri Republican* noted the change from previous seasons: "A marked feature of the emigration this year is the number of women who are going out by the land route."[72] It was probably the opening of California as a region of wide economic opportunity that was responsible for the increase in family emigration in these years, along with the liberal provisions of the Donation Land Act of 1850, which granted families twice the land of single men in Oregon.

By the early fifties, then, two groups were moving along the trail together, miners and farmers, single men and families, respectively.[73] There are no direct statistical data on the relative size of these unattached male and married populations. For our purposes, however, we can assume that nearly all adult women were married and accompanied by their husbands, and take the percentage of women as a rough index to the number of married couples; consequently the excess of men over women would be a rough estimate of the percentage of unattached men in the emigration.[74] By that standard, the percentage of married people in the total adult population must have fallen from around 50 percent in the 1840s to 20 or 30 percent in the 1850s, while the percentage of single men had doubled as a consequence of the mining boom.[75] For 1853 the statistics have the added dimension of distinguishing between Oregon- and California-bound emigrants, showing that over 85 percent of the single men on the trail were on their way to California, but only 66 percent of the families. The composition of the 1853 Oregon emigration was more nearly like the movements of the 1840s.[76]

Nonetheless, in contrast with the forties, there was a strong and at times predominant male character to the emigrations of the fifties and sixties. Many of these otherwise unattached men, however, traveled within the family system. While the majority of families who left written accounts traveled without hired help, some employed two or three men, so that on the average there were about nine family-hired men working for every ten families on the trail. If this ratio was typical for the emigration as a whole, a fifth of all the unattached men traveled with family parties.[77] The diaries and recollections of men who emigrated to the Pacific Coast without wives, parents, or other kin provide a second perspective.[78] Of 115 accounts by single men, over a third of the writers (37.3 percent) hired into family parties. These rough statistics, meant only to indicate the broad boundaries of the situation, suggest that between 20 and 40 percent of all single men traveled with families if the male-dominated Gold Rush is excluded.[79]

Forty parties, over a third of those reconstructed, employed single men to drive the wagon, the cattle, or generally to help out with the daily labor of the march. They worked in exchange for board, transportation for their personal outfit, and mutual assistance over the long haul. Essentially this same situation prevailed on the farms at home. In all agricultural areas young men, frequently new arrivals without property, were employed by farm families as occasional or seasonal workers. Probably about 20 percent of the mid-century agricultural work force were wage-earning farm laborers. While the percentage would rise dramatically during the next three decades as midwestern farming shifted to a solid commercial basis, farm labor itself remained within a continuing tradition.[80] Nearly all hired hands lived with individual farm families for the duration of the working season, April to November, and many resided with the families in the crude and cramped frontier accommodations year-round.[81] As recent studies of household composition indicate, boarding among families was a common, even normative situation in nineteenth-century North America.

Some farm workers may have chosen to accompany a family when a decision was made to emigrate. The four hired hands of the Burrell family, for example, seem to have worked for Mrs. Burrell on her Will County, Illinois, farm. Samuel and Jasquay Hall, who traveled the southern route to California with their children in 1853, brought along four hired men from their ranch in addition to their former female slave Delia. Traveling with the Reeds of Sangamon were three hired men, Milt Elliot, James Smith, and Walter Herron—each of whom had worked for Reed in one capacity or another before the trip—the family cook, Eliza Williams, and her brother Baylis. Other men hired on especially for the trip. Reed's friends, Jacob and George Donner of Springfield, placed a help-wanted ad in the *Sangamon Journal* just a few weeks before their departure:

> Who wants to go to California without costing them anything? As many as eight young men, of good character, who can drive an ox team, will be accommodated by gentlemen who will leave this vicinity about the first of April. Come, boys![82]

More typically, however, single men would approach a family or party leader with an offer of assistance in exchange for board. In 1844, for example, John Minto and Willard Rees were hired on by Robert Morrison of Andrew County, Missouri. Early that year twenty-two-year-old Minto had left his coal-mining family in Pittsburgh and headed west for adventure and fortune. On the steamboat to St. Louis he was attracted by the Oregon talk, but having spent his meager savings for transportation to the frontier and an outlandish set of weapons, he was unable, like so many others, to finance his own trip. A friend, however, introduced him to the means of getting passage: "There are men with families and means who need help, and will furnish board to single men for their work."

Morrison and Minto agreed to a simple, direct contract: "I can furnish you," Minto remembered his employer saying, "bed and board, and have your washing and mending done; and you shall give me your help as I require, to get my family and effects to Oregon. I have four guns, and two wagons, and after we are fairly started my oldest children will be able to keep up the loose stock; so that one of us can be spared to hunt every day if we choose, and you shall have your turn at that." Minto was, in other words, accepted as a male family member, almost as a son. By midpoint in the journey Minto's feelings for the family had developed significantly: "The old and the young of the family seemed already something like father and mother and brothers and sisters to me"; he called his party "our traveling family of ten."[83]

Hired men commonly became quite attached to and loved by others in the party. Virginia Ivins was a young wife of twenty with a small child and an infant in arms (born on the trail) in a family party that included her husband, guardian aunt, and uncle traveling to California in 1853. Mr. Ivins was a sober and silent husband, and Virginia came to depend on the five young hired men for conversation and companionship during the trip. The boys, in their turn, each became attached to the small group, to the children and especially to Virginia. Finally, outside Sacramento, came the time to part ways. "The men seemed loathe to say goodbye," Virginia recalled later, "but by nine oclock next morning all were gone except Louis, who lingered to go into the city with us and say goodbye there. At ten oclock we were again on the road, Louis driving my wagon to be with me a while longer, to tell me all his hopes and fears, and how much he loved us. My tears would come for I had learned to look upon the noble boy almost as a brother. When we reached the city he left us with a sorrowful face, and I never saw him again."[84]

The hired men were largely accepted and trusted as members of the household circle. Years after the trip, Mrs. J. T.

Gowdy, a nine-year-old girl when she emigrated with her father and mother, Riley and Mary Kemp, remembered that "our family consisted of my father, mother, eight children and three hired men, 13 in all."[85] Of course there were also instances of argument, of hired men deserting or quitting mid-route. Jessey Quinn Thorton's driver, Albert, without whom the patrician Thorton was quite helpless, tried unsuccessfully to abscond with a yoke of his employer's oxen at Fort Bridger. But examples of such petty contractual relations can be matched with displays of heroic loyalty. Charles Stanton, a bachelor traveling with the George Donners, was one of the few in the Donner party to make it safely over the Sierra pass and into Sutter's Fort when the majority remained stranded in the early snows. But despite his lack of family ties to the emigrants, Stanton returned twice through Sierra blizzards to assist the Donner rescue, finally perishing on his third trip out.[86]

The affective relations between single men and the emigrant families remind us that single men hired on not only for economic but for social reasons as well. Unattached men could and did group themselves into all-male companies, but many men preferred the well-understood and accepted divisions and unities of the family. These men, like John Minto, were attracted to a place where they could find "bed and board" and have their "washing and mending done" in exchange for masculine contributions to the family economy. This was a family, a place of hunting and sewing, a meeting place for men and women. In a move where so much would change, elements of stability were at a premium. The family was the most accessible unit of social organization.

2

The Midwestern Farming Family, 1850

Farming in the antebellum Midwest was part of a way of life that stretched back through the centuries, a way of life on the verge of a fundamental reordering. Families were at the center of this rural political economy; working lives were regulated principally through families. Work was organized by a domestic division of labor, roles and routines were set by family patterns, production decisions determined by a calculus of family needs. This traditional way of life was very different from our own, and we would do well to base our understanding of men and women emigrants on a detailed look at their lives on the farm.

American farmers were not peasants. They enjoyed a freedom of movement which set them off radically from their European peasant contemporaries.[1] Mobility was a prime fact of their lives, a tradition inherited from the first century of settlement in North America. The social and economic pressures of rapid colonial population growth (itself mainly the result of improved life and fertility chances in a more healthful environment) and the vast acres of arable land to the interior combined to make the search for new lands an imperative social and personal goal by the mid-eighteenth century.[2]

Westward emigrations of men and families reduced demographic pressures in many parts of the East (indeed some sections lost too many people) and opened the way for structural changes in farming. As the eastern seaboard became more a part of the Atlantic market, a new regional division of labor occurred, and commercial centers provided lucrative markets for farm products. Seventeenth-century opinion had stressed and valued self-sufficient farming and the closed circle of family labor. Farmers clung to these old attitudes tenaciously, but commercial values stressing economic rationality in market terms were more salient under the changed circumstances.

Farming moved increasingly toward commercialization and specialization to meet the market demands of nascent urban communities. The view of farming as a business rather than a way of life was ascendant, if not dominant, in the Northeast by the first years of the nineteenth century.[3]

Those who emigrated to the geographic and social periphery of the nation, on the other hand, met a different set of conditions. The move itself usually required some years of rather primitive living, but even after the early hunting-farming stage of pioneering had passed, the dominant fact of life in the Midwest was the isolation of farmers from the commerce of the East. Full entry of midwestern agriculture into the growing urban-industrial economy required effective transportation links with urban markets. The absence of transportation and market demands, R. Carlyle Buley notes in his seminal history of the early Midwest, "contributed to the practice of a self-sufficient domestic economy which in many regions by 1840 reached a high degree of development."[4]

The notion of farm self-sufficiency should not conjure up images of isolated, impoverished farmers, out of economic and cultural touch with their peers. There was a good deal of social intercourse in the Midwest. In all but the rawest frontier regions there was an important social division of labor. In the first place, farm families could not produce all their necessities at home; husbandry and domestic arts had to be supplemented by the trades and crafts of the small villages and towns. In this way it was "possible for the skilled and enterprising settler to achieve a standard of living high in proportion to his wealth as measured in cash values."[5] Moreover, the need of the Midwest for effective local administration, particularly in land and law, and the development of a local cultural apparatus (education, the press, the arts) further precluded pure subsistence and demanded the exchange of products and services.[6]

Midwestern life had as its cultural context a capitalist economic system in which the principal regulator of economic affairs was the market, but it existed in relative isolation from that market. These facts had important consequences. In the first place, nearly every farmer's son hoped to make his entry into the commercial system and better his lot, and to this end he

tried to turn a profit on whatever surpluses he could squeeze
out of his farm. By the second quarter of the nineteenth century few men wished to remain subsistence farmers for long;
economic society had other, more prosperous goals for its participants.[7] Largely laboring under commercial hopes, settlement was under way in the four principal home states of the
overland emigrants—Indiana, Illinois, Iowa, and Missouri—by
1825, and the opening of these areas was completed after the
Black Hawk War of 1832.

But entrepreneurial aspirations alone were not sufficient to
make a capitalist revolution in midwestern agriculture. There
were structural problems to be solved. The takeoff into commercial growth was stymied by midwestern isolation and poor
transportation; even enterprising farmers were frustrated by
prohibitive farm-to-market distances. Occasionally a farmer
with easy access to a river would load up a raft or flatboat and
float his produce down to the Mississippi and thence to St.
Louis or even New Orleans. Such interregional trade along the
Ohio and Mississippi river system fostered the growth of river
towns; a similarly hopeful trade on the Great Lakes contributed
to the prominence, exuberance, and growth of Chicago before
1850. More commonly, however, farmers bartered their
dressed hogs, bacon, or wheat for goods at the general store or
for the services of local craftsmen, and shopkeepers in turn,
shipped the produce to agents down the river. The farmer
rarely collected specie or accumulated savings, for his transactions were in credit or exchange for use. In this way, most
midwestern farmers were excluded from the benefits of the
market. Such a situation, in which local merchants played the
roles of middlemen, was inevitable under conditions where
farmers themselves could not make direct connections with the
market.[8]

During the second quarter of the century the hopes and
expectations of midwestern farmers paved the way for the
changes introduced by the railroads; these finally solved the
transportation problem and brought the Midwest fully into the
market. The decisive moment of change came in the mid-
1850s.[9] As far as future developments were concerned, the
nascent commercial trends and structures were unquestionably

the most important aspects of the years before 1850, and historians emphasize them most. But we are concerned here with the actual way of life of the majority of farm families in the Midwest. Until the Civil War (and the period of overland emigration to the Pacific Coast was mostly antebellum), most midwesterners lived by the traditional means of family self-sufficiency, whatever their aspirations. Before the Civil War, as Paul Gates observes, most midwestern farmers were isolated from commercial opportunities and practiced diversified, home-consumption farming.[10] With some exceptions the overland emigrants were coming from an essentially self-sufficient agricultural system.

The general shift to commercialism that began in the Midwest during the 1850s was accompanied by a revolution in farm technology. The steel plow, drill, reaper, mower, and thresher, although inventions of the 1830s, became commonly available during the fifties and were only fully utilized in response to the huge market demands, labor shortages, and high prices of the Civil War.[11] This technology facilitated commercial production by cutting labor costs and shifting farming to a capital-intensive basis, allowing for specialization in highly marketable grain crops, and incidentally facilitating agriculture's entry into the credit market, since most farmers were forced to borrow heavily to finance their investments in machinery.[12] The interdependence of commercial production and improved technology reminds us that until the Civil War the self-sufficiency of midwestern farmers was in large measure a feature of the means of production: hand power did not provide the average Midwestern farm family with enough productivity to turn to strict commercialism.[13]

The technology of most midwestern farms, then, was a traditional force, tying men and women to the hand-power heritage.[14] The essential tools of the farm—the ones the overland emigrants carried in their wagons—were the chopping ax, broadax, frow, auger, and plane.[15] Farmers used these tools to manufacture their own farm implements—hoes, rakes, sickles, scythes, cradles, flails, and plows—resorting to the blacksmith for ironwork.[16] Except for the cradle, which came into wide use west of the Alleghenies during the mid-1830s, the home production of these same hand implements had been a constant of farm life for centuries.[17]

Hand technology set upper limits on the number of acres that a family could cultivate in a season; the only way productivity could be increased beyond that limit was by adding field hands. Working at maximum output, a farm family with two economically active males could utilize perhaps fifty acres of growing land with the traditional technology.[18] Of these, perhaps one acre was devoted to the home garden, a score to small grain crops, the remainder to corn. In order simply to survive, a family required at least half an acre for the garden, the same for grain, and some ten acres in corn. Corn was the most essential; according to one observer, "it affords the means of subsistence to every living thing about his place."[19] Before the 1850s the majority of midwestern families fell between these limits: most families lived on farms with forty to fifty improved acres.[20]

As to livestock, an ox, or preferably a yoke of oxen, was essential, although when first starting out some families made do working a cow. Cows were necessary for milk and its products, however, and working them as draught animals negatively affected dairy production. A few sheep of mongrel breeds were necessary for wool, but mutton was almost never eaten. Geese and ducks were sometimes butchered, but they were valued most for their down. A family's meat supply was provided by the ever-present brood of chickens and the herd of swine, a dozen or more being necessary for a medium-sized family.[21] These animals were frequently unsheltered, although on the better farms cattle might have a lean-to shelter for winter. As late as 1850 farmers throughout the Midwest were reportedly in the habit of letting cattle and hogs forage on available grass and mast. When butchering time came hogs were rounded up for the kill.[22]

A farm family could gradually increase its level of consumption by clearing, draining, and preparing more land, and by increasing the size and improving the breed of its livestock. Then there came a limit, when the level of technology was a fetter on further expansion without resort to hired labor.[23] The limit came, however, after the level of consumption had been raised to the level of contemporary comfort. "A backwoods farm," wrote an English observer, "produces everything wanted for the table, except coffee and rice and salt and spices." To the list of supplementals could be added occasional dry goods, shoes, and metal for farm implements.[24] A self-sufficient family could produce enough for its annual table, along with a small trading surplus, but the task required the close attention of men and women to the needs of the land and the demands of the seasons.

The dominant paradigm of farm life was the cycle: the recurrence of the days and seasons, the process of growth and reproduction.[25] Hand-power technology did not deceive men into thinking they could overcome nature; their goal was to harmonize man's needs with natural forces as best they could. The length of the working day, for example, was largely determined by the hours of sunlight. Candles and grease lamps were common but expensive, and the hearth's flickering light was too dim for more than a little work after dark.[26] So most work was largely confined to daylight: up and at work by dawn, nights for sleeping. And in keeping with this daily round, midwesterners told time by the movements of the sun, not the clock. There was a variety of time phrases so rich they nearly matched the clock in refinement; the hours before sunrise, for example, were distinguished thus: long before day, just before day, just comin' day, just about daylight, good light, before sunup, about sunup, and, finally, sunup. Each period of the day was similarly divided.[27]

The seasons imposed the same kind of rule as the sun. The farm's work demands were primarily shaped by the seasons, each quarter calling upon husbandman and housewife to perform appointed tasks. The farming year opened in mid-March when thaws called the tenants outside. Land had to be cleared, drained, manured, and plowed, fields sown, gardens planted. Sheep, grown woolly, needed washing and shearing, geese plucking. In the hardwood stands farmers might spend a few days collecting and rendering maple sap, or searching out and hiving bees.

As the sun approached summer solstice, the work load increased with the day's length. The corn needed cultivation and hilling until it was strong enough to compete successfully with the weeds and "laid by" till harvest. There was hay to make, garden crops to nurture, gather, and replant, and often a winter wheat crop to harvest and thresh. In August, with the corn laid by and harvest coming, men took the opportunity for a respite; these were the dog days when "onery" farmers took long naps and "progressive" farmers mended fences. But August was soon overwhelmed by the frantic pace of September's harvest. Summer grain had to be cut, bound, and shocked within a critically short period, the corn picked, the last round of garden vegetables safely packed away in cold storage while still fresh.

Days continued to shorten, but after harvest the pace of work slowed as well. Still the grain needed threshing, the corn husking and cribbing, there was perhaps fruit to pick, dry, or preserve in a variety of ways, possibly pickles and kraut to make. These and other activities prepared the way for the winter: sowing the winter wheat, making firewood, daubing the cracks in old cabins, barns, and outbuildings, banking dirt around foundations to keep out some of the cold, and butchering enough hogs for salted and smoked meat until the spring again provided a larder of milk, eggs, and poultry.

Summer's activity was counterbalanced by winter's leisure. The daily chores of the farm—tending livestock, hauling wood and water, the domestic routine—continued. There were also numerous tasks to keep an industrious farmer busy: fences to mend, manure to haul and spread, trees to girdle and later fell, roads to maintain. But there was comparatively little opportunity for productive activity in the winter, aside from work in the woodlot. So winter months were occupied with general farm repair and improvement, visiting neighbors, trading the surpluses that summer's labor had produced. In late winter farmers would begin to plan the plantings of the next season, setting out planting dates in traditional fashion by carefully determining with the farm almanac the timing of the phases of the moon and the rising and falling of astrological signs.

Encouraged by their subordination to the natural world, the people of the Midwest held to a traditional animistic conception of the universe: the inanimate world was infused with will, feeling, and spirit.[28] "The world was a huge kaleidoscope, whose bewildering pieces fell by the twist of analogy or contrast into beautifully logical patterns of form, direction, texture, quality, process—patterns to cover everything that might happen, from evening to evening and from spring to spring."[29] As William Oliver, an English visitor and resident of Illinois in the 1840s, wrote, "There is a good deal of superstition or belief in witchdraft, omens, lucky times, etc."[30] The world could be best understood by analogy (if an animal disturbed the afterbirth, that baby would take on some trait of the beast) or contrast (cold hands, warm heart) or the rule of "firsts" (if a woman cries on her wedding day she will cry throughout her married life). Many of the beliefs were employed in a half-embarrassed way, perhaps pulled out only in times of emergencies like sickness, death, disaster; others were the stock-in-trade of midwestern life.[31]

The cycle of the seasons encouraged a traditional view of work as well. Work was the expenditure of human energy to meet given tasks. When wheat was ready for harvesting, for example, men would readily work fifteen-hour days to bring it in before the precious grain was shed on the ground. On the other hand, when seasonal demands slackened, as in winter, a man might quit early without qualms, and few worried when a winter storm closed in the family for a few days. The persistent pace of modern labor, measured not by natural cycles but by the clock, was almost unknown to midwesterners. By the same token, work was understood not as the opposite of leisure but as life's requirement for all creatures, regardless of sex or age. Men, women, and children would share life's burdens. "The rule was," William Howells remembered of his farm life, "that whoever had the strength to work, took hold and helped."[32]

The common work of the farm was, then, divided among family members, but the principal division of work was by sex. Men and women worked in different areas, skilled at different tasks, prepared and trained for their work in different ways. In an economy based on the family unit, women and men in midwestern society achieved common goals by doing different jobs.

Sex and gender is a foundation of individual and social identity in all human societies.[33] As Michael Banton
puts it, gender roles "are related so closely to the perfor-
mance of most other roles that the sex of a party can be
concealed only in the most restricted situations."[34] The
differences of sex are the starting place for gender roles:
each person is given a polar label, either man or woman.
Sex implies general natural potentials and limitations, to
be sure, but the biological distinctions alone have never
been sufficient social determinants of distinctive gender
roles; sex differences have always had to be elaborated by
patterned cultural forms. "Natural features are never translated directly into social ones. They are always dressed in
cultural clothing."[35]

If gender roles are essentially cultural constructions, it fol-
lows that the notion of what constitutes the masculine and the
feminine will vary greatly from one culture to another and
from one time to another. Men and women play their gender
roles according to a cultural script outlining the appropriate
activities and tasks (the sexual division of labor) as well as the
attitudes and personality (the character) of the two sexes.[36]
People appear most obviously in society and history as players
of their gender roles.

For historians (as well as other social scientists), the proper
place to begin an understanding of gender roles is by reconstructing and examining the customary ways in which men and
women divided the work of society among themselves.[37] This
priority makes methodological sense if for no other reason than
because outward behavior is what historians can best determine, and broad areas of behavioral uniformity suggest the
presence of roles.[38] These patterns then establish a context of
human action for the evaluation of what men and women
thought.[39] Such an approach employs an active, concrete concept of gender roles: gender roles are social regularities observed in what men and women do and the ways they think and
feel about what they do, as well as how and why they do what
they do. In this study both behavioral and attitudinal facts must
be derived from the same subjective sources—the diaries and
recollections. But even with such documents of personal ex-

perience the behavioral regularities are readily exposed and pieced together to form a whole pattern.

The functional principles of the general divisions of work by sex on the midwestern farm were quite clear and quite strict in application.[40] In only a few areas did the work of men and women overlap. Most clearly, men were occupied with the heaviest work. First, they had responsibility for work with the broadax. If the family was taking up new wooded ground—as many Oregon emigrants would be doing, for example—the land had to be cleared. Frequently a farmer would gird the trees with his ax the first season to kill foliage, felling trees and removing stumps in the following winters. Logrolling, when the men of the neighborhood joined together to clear a field belonging to one of them, was a common late-winter social event for men. Construction, including making fences, was also a male job, as was the ongoing work in the family woodlot. Wood was chopped, hauled and stacked, or dumped near the house.

Men also controlled work with the plow. For new land a breaking plow, drawn by several yoke of oxen, was often needed, especially in prairie sod. Working improved acres was easier, but still hard, heavy work. And within the limitations of available labor and marketability, men were usually itching to put new land to the plow, so the plow was associated with work of the heaviest sort and understood to be male. Work in the cleared and plowed fields, where grain or corn grew, also fell to male control and supervision. Men plowed in spring or winter, sowed their wheat broadcast (until the 1850s), and planted their corn in hills. Men and boys harrowed and weeded until harvest, when they picked the corn together and cooperated in bringing in the wheat, men cradling and boys binding. Fieldwork kept men extremely busy. Two mature men on fifty acres of corn and wheat land spent three-quarters of the whole growing season plowing, planting, and harvesting, exclusive of any other work.[41]

There was plenty of other work to do. Men were responsible for upkeep and repair of tools, implements, and wagons and care of the draft animals, the oxen, mules, or horses. Hogs and sheep, both pretty much allowed to roam, were herded, fed, and tended by men and boys. Finally, men were responsible for cleanup and maintenance of the barn, barnyard, fields, and woodlot. This meant ditching and trenching, innumerable repairs on all the things that could—and did—break, laying down straw and hay, and hauling manure.[42]

Less important in fact, but work which nonetheless played an important role in male thinking, was hunting. For the early pioneers game provided most of the protein in the family diet. By mid-century those pioneer days had passed in the Midwest. But the rifle remained in its central place over the door or mantle long after the emergencies that might call it out had gone the way of the forests. Hunting remained, if only as an autumn sport or shooting match, a central aspect of male identity. "Even farmers," says Buley, "at certain seasons felt a peculiar restlessness."[43] The hunting legacy had one practical consequence for male work loads: men had primary responsibility for slaughtering and butchering large farm animals. Indeed, when hogs ran wild, they were sometimes picked off by rifle shot. Hunting was the male activity that most embodied men's self-conceived role—keystone of the hearth, defender of the household, and main provider.

In fact, women were more centrally involved in providing subsistence for the farm family than men. Nearly all the kinds of food consumed by farm families were direct products of women's work in growing, collecting, and butchering. An acre or so of improved land near the house was set aside for the domestic garden. After husbands had plowed the plot, farm women planted their gardens. Housewives began by setting out onions and potatoes in early April, following up later that month by planting lettuce, beets, parsnips, turnips, and carrots in the garden, tomatoes and cabbages in window boxes indoors. When danger of late frosts had passed, the seedlings were moved outside and set out along with May plantings of cucumbers, melons, pumpkins, and beans. Women also frequently laid down a patch of buckwheat and a garden of kitchen and medicinal herbs—sage, peppers, thyme, mint, mustard, horseradish, tansy, and others.[44]

The garden required daily attention. At first the seedlings

needed hand watering. Then crops required cultivation, and the everlasting battle against weeds began. Garden harvesting could commence in late April and was a daily chore throughout the summer, supplying fresh vegetables for the family table.

Wives and daughters were also traditionally responsible for the care of henhouse and dairy. After a dormant winter poultry came alive in the spring. The farm-wise woman carefully kept enough chickens to produce both eggs for the kitchen and to set hens for a new flock of spring roasters. From late spring to late fall the family feasted regularly on fresh-killed rooster, selected and usually butchered by the housewife. Daughters and young boys gathered the eggs that were another mainstay of the summer diet. Women's responsibility for the henhouse extended even to cleaning out the manure by the bucket load.[45]

Cows were sheltered in whatever served as a barn, and men's general supervision there relieved women of having to shovel the stalls. But women milked, tended, and fed the animals. The milking and the manufacture of butter and cheese was one of their central tasks. Cows were milked first thing in the morning and the last thing at night; housewives supervised the milking but parceled the job out to children as soon as they were able. Boys, however, with their father's sanction would rebel from milking; "the western people of the early days entertained a supreme contempt for a man who attended to the milking."[46] Making good butter was a matter of pride among farm women. The churn had to be operated with patience and persistence if the butter was to come.

> Come butter, come;
> Come butter, come;
> Little Johnny's at the gate,
> Waiting for his buttered cake.
> Come butter, come.[47]

The meter marked the up and down of the churn. When it had come, the butter was packed into homemade, hand-decorated molds, and pounds of it consumed each week. Cheesemaking was less general; ripened cheeses were the product of a minority. Nearly all women, however, were trained in the manufacture of cottage cheese and farmer's cheese. Dairy production was especially important to the household and central to the definition of women's work. In 1839 a Springfield, Illinois, newspaper reprinted with horror a report that New England women were pressuring their husbands to take over the milking.[48]

There were some areas of food production where women's and men's operations overlapped, but these were the exceptions. When hogs were butchered in fall, men from several farms might work together; it was mainly when it became necessary to supplement the meat supply that women helped men to slaughter and dress the animal. In any event, women were always a part of the butchering, there to chop the scraps and odd pieces into sausage, prepare the hams for curing, and cook the ribs immediately. At other social and almost ritual occasions of food preparation—making cider or apple butter, rendering maple sugar—men and women regularly worked side by side. All of the work of the orchard was often a joint project.

The sexes also sometimes combined their energies during planting. If not preoccupied with field planting, men might help to set out garden seed. More likely, however, field planting would fall behind the schedule set by zodiac or moon, and men called their womenfolk out to help. Women most often assisted in the cornfield. "Tarpley made a furrow with a single-shovel plow drawn by one horse," Iowa farm woman Elmira Taylor remembered of the 1860s. "I followed with a bag of seed corn and dropped two grains of seed each step forward."[49] A farmer with no sons worked his daughters in the fields at planting time without a second thought.[50]

Food preparation was, of course, women's work, and by all reports midwestern men kept women busy by consuming great quantities at mealtime.[51] Wives were responsible for preparing three heavy meals a day; most farm wives spent their entire mornings cooking and tried to save afternoons for other work. Included in the daily midwestern diet were two kinds of meat, eggs, cheese, butter, cream (especially in gravies), corn in one or more forms, two kinds of bread, three or four different vegetables from the garden or from storage, several kinds of jellies, preserves, and relishes, cake or pie, and milk, coffee, and tea. Making butter and cheese were only two of the innumerable feminine skills needed to set the farm table.

Corn, for example, was served fresh, softened with lye and fried (hominy), parched, preserved as a relish, ground green and cooked in a pudding, or ground into meal from which mush, flapjacks, johnnycake, pone, or corn bread were prepared. Bread baking, whether with corn or wheat, was a daily task. Pork was salted and packed, brined and smoked, or pickled. Chickens were roasted, fried, or stewed. Vegetables were boiled fresh or pickled for storage, cabbage was salted down and cut fine or made into kraut, peppers and spices were dried, fruit was dried or preserved.

Women cooked on the open hearth, directly over the coals; it was low, back-breaking work that went on forever; a pot of corn mush took from two to six hours with nearly constant stirring.[52] Cast-iron, wood-burning cook stoves were available in Illinois in the mid-1840s, and by 1860 most midwestern women had been given the opportunity to stand and cook.[53] The next great improvement in domestic technology was the general introduction of running water in close proximity to the kitchen. But throughout the antebellum Midwest, water had to be carried to the house, sometimes from quite a distance, and that invariably was women's work. Domestic work—housecleaning, care of the bedding, all the kitchen work, in addition to responsibility for decorating and adding a "woman's touch"—was a demanding task under the best of circumstances, and farms offered far from the best. The yard between the kitchen and barn was always covered with enough dung to attract hordes of summer houseflies. In those days before screen doors kitchens were infested; men and women alike ignored the pests. In wet months the yard was a mess of mud, dung, and cast-off water, constantly tracked into the house. A cleanly wife had to be a constant worker.[54]

A farmer was said to be a jack-of-all-trades. But women's work outdistanced men's in the sheer variety of tasks performed. In addition to their production of food, women had complete responsibility for all manufacture, care, and repair of family clothing. During the first half of the nineteenth century, domestic manufacture gave way to industrial production of thread and cloth, but in the Midwest, from 1840 to 1860, while home manufactures declined, they remained an important ac-

tivity for women. On the Taylor homestead in southeastern
Iowa, for example, the assessed valuation of household manufactures declined from $73 in 1850 to $50 in 1860, but this
marked a decline, not an end to the use of the wheel and loom:
in 1861 Elmira Taylor spun her own wool, took it to a mill to be
carded, and wove it into cloth throughout the winter on her
mother-in-law's loom.[55]

Midwestern homespun was mostly of flax and wool, supplemented by a little homegrown cotton or purchased cotton
thread. A few sheep and a quarter-acre of flax were enough to
supply the largest family. Farm wives sowed flax in March,
harvested it in June (replanting immediately with a sterile-soil
crop like potatoes), and prepared it that summer by soaking
and sun-drying it to rot the outer coating.[56] Men lent a hand by
crushing the flax on the flax break to remove the inner fibers
and washing and shearing the sheep, but from that point it was
a woman's operation. Spinning wheels were in universal use;
each household required separate wheels for wool and flax.
Wheels were precision tools, but families could get them rather
cheaply from the wheelwright, and according to William Oliver,
"spinning wheels and a loom are very general items in a
farmer's establishment."[57] Wool had first to be carded into lean
bunches, then spun on the great wheel; the spinner paced back
and forth, whirling the wheel with her right hand, manipulat-
ing the wool and guiding the yarn on the spindle with her left.
Two miles of yarn, enough for two to four yards of woven wool,
required pacing over four miles, a full day's work. An excellent
spinner, sitting at the smaller flax wheel, could spin a mile of
linen thread in a day.[58]

The yarn was woven into wool and linen cloth or more
commonly combined into durable linsey-woolsey on homemade
looms. If cotton was available it was woven with wool warp to
make jean. The giant loom dominated cramped living quarters
when in use; it was knocked down and put away when weaving
was completed.[59] The cloth still had to be shrunk and sized
(fulled)—a job usually put out to the fulling mill if one were
nearby—and dyed, sometimes from home dyes, but increasingly
with commercial dyes bought at local stores. Nearly all farm
clothing was cut from this cloth. Coarser tow cloth, made from

the short-fiber, darker parts of the flax, was used for toweling, bandage, menstrual cloth, rags, or rough field clothing. Pillows and mattresses were made of tow and stuffed with the down women collected from the geese and ducks in their charge. The finest homespun, the pure linen bleached scores of times till it reached its characteristic color, was reserved for coverlets, tablecloths, appliqué, and stitchery. For their annual clothing a family of four would require a minimum of forty yards of cloth, or at least two full weeks at the wheel and loom for an experienced housewife. This work was, of course, spread throughout the available time, and one could expect to find women spinning or weaving at almost any time of the day, at every season of the year.[60]

Itinerant weavers first made their appearance in the Midwest during the 1840s, their Jacquard looms offering what seemed incredible detail in patterns. For most farm families, however, everyday cloth remained home-produced until the general availability of low-cost factory-produced dry goods. It was during the commercial shift in midwestern agriculture that family looms and then wheels gave way to cheap commercial cloth. Until the Civil War, however, a good deal of all midwestern clothing, and most clothing on emigrant backs, was homespun.[61]

Every wife was a tailor, fitting and cutting cloth for her own slip-on dresses and those of her daughter, her son's and husband's blouses and pantaloons, and the tow shirts of the younger ones. If there was "boughten" cloth available—cotton or woolen broadcloth, gingham or calico—it was used for dress-up clothing, home-tailored of course. Socks, mittens, and caps were knit for winter wear, but every adult went sockless and children barefoot in summer. Underclothes were not manufactured or worn, for they were considered an unnecessary extravagance.[62]

Women were personally involved in clothing manufacture, from sowing the flax seed to sewing the garment. Homespun "could not be lightly cast aside after so much toil and patience, on account of being slightly or considerably worn."[63] So worn pants and shirts were continually mended, garments too worn to be used saved for patches, and every scrap of every kind of cloth that passed through the house was saved for that special purpose it would one day find. As an old Kentucky woman remembered,

> You see you start out with just so much caliker; you don't go to the store and pick it out and buy it, but the neighbors will give you a piece here and a piece there, and you will have a piece left every time you cut out a dress, and you take what happens to come and that's predestination. But when it comes to cuttin' out why you're free to choose your patterns. You can give the same kind o' pieces to two persons, and one will be a *Nine Patch* and one'll make a *Wild Goose Chase* and there'll be two quilts made out o' the same kind of pieces, and jest as different as they can be, and that is just the way with livin'. The Lord sends in the pieces, but we can cut 'em out and put 'em together pretty much to suit ourselves.[64]

Sewing was the consummate feminine skill, a domestic necessity but one practiced and refined until in the hands of many it achieved the status of an art form. Girls were taught to sew before they were taught to read, and started on a four- or nine-patch quilt cover as soon as they could hold a needle. Coverlets, counterpanes, crocheted samplers, and most especially the elaborate patchwork or appliqué front pieces for quilts were the highest expression of the material culture of women. With patchwork, appliqué, and quilt stitchery, utility was a secondary consideration; these were primarily modes of creative artistry for women. One farm woman testified to the importance of this avenue for her: "I would have lost my mind if I had not had my quilts to do."[65]

On a more mundane level, clothes had to be washed, and women made their own soap for both the clothes and the family who wore them. Women loaded hardwood ashes into the ash hopper, poured water over, and collected the lye in the trough below. They boiled kitchen fats and grease, added the lye, and if everything was going well the soap would "come" after long, hot hours of stirring. They poured the hot soap into molds or tubs and stored it. Soapmaking was a big, all-day job, done only

two or three times a year.[66] Monday, by all accounts, was the
universal washday. Rainwater was used for washing, or alternately a little lye was added to soften well water. The water was
heated in the washtub over hearth or stove, soap added, and
clothes were pounded against a washboard, then rinsed, wrung
out by hand, and hung. The lye, harsh soap, and hot water
chapped and cracked the skin; women's hands would often
break open and bleed into the tub. In the winter, the clothes
were hung outside where sore, wet hands would freeze painfully, or inside, draped over chairs or lines, steaming up the
windows and turning the whole place clammy.[67] Ironing and
mending were also allocated one day each week.

To women fell a final task. Women bore the children and
nursed them for at least the first few months, and in this they
worked completely alone. Even after weaning, farm women
remained solely responsible for the supervision of young children; both boys and girls were under their mother's supervision until the boys were old enough to help with the fieldwork,
at about ten years, at which time they came under their father's
guidance.[68] Girls, of course, remained apprenticed to the
housewife's craft. Farm mothers put their charges to work
"almost as soon as they could walk," and although they could
not contribute materially until they were five or six, the correct
work attitude had by then been instilled.[69] There was plenty
that children could do around the garden, dairy, and
henhouse; they watered, fed the animals, collected eggs,
milked, hauled water, weeded, and performed innumerable
other chores that housewives could never have finished but for
the work of their children.

Midwestern farm mothers had relatively large families. The
mean family size in the Midwest in 1850 was 5.7.[70] Mean family
size of the overland emigrants in this study was a little less, 5.0,
mainly because there were so many newlyweds; otherwise the
size of emigrant families was very typical of the population at
large. The mean size of emigrating families in their full
childbearing phase was 7.6. In her lifetime, then, a farm
woman could expect to raise five or six children of her own.

These children helped significantly with the burden of farm work, but not without the expenditure of a great deal of physical and emotional energy by their mothers.

To determine the full occupations of women, their total work load, we must consider the social effects of childbearing as well as childrearing. Miscarriages, stillbirths, birth accidents, and infant mortality took a terrible toll on the energies and spirit of women. Counting infant deaths alone, one in five children died before its fifth birthday, and prenatal losses were at least as high.[71] Childbirth certainly was a central experience for farm women. It was no occasional or unique event but occurred with demanding regularity. To assess women's reproductive burdens fairly we can measure women's fertility.[72] The mean age of marriage for emigrant men and women was 25.1 and 20.5, respectively. Some women, of course, married earlier than the average and were pregnant before their twentieth birthdays. The peak childbearing years were from age twenty to thirty-five, during which time emigrant women bore over four out of five of their children. Fertility declined precipitously after thirty-five as a combined effect of lowered male and female fecundity, although some mothers continued to bear children into their late forties.

Let us translate abstract fertility into the real terms of farm women's lives: childbearing had to be a dominant fact. Over half the emigrant women gave birth to their first child within their first year of marriage, another quarter the second year, and fully 98 percent by the end of the third. Thereafter a mean of 29.0 months intervened between births throughout a woman's twenties and thirties.[73] For their most vital years farm women lived under the dictatorial rule of yet another cycle, a two-and-a-half-year cycle of childbirth, of which nineteen or twenty months were spent in advanced pregnancy, infant care, and nursing. Until her late thirties, a woman could expect little respite from the physical and emotional wear and tear of nearly constant pregnancy or suckling.

Given the already burdensome tasks of women's work, the additional responsibilities of the children were next to intolerable. Women must have searched for some way of limiting the burden. It is possible that mothers introduced their babies to supplemental feeding quite early and encouraged children's independence in order to free themselves from the restrictions of nursing, which had to seriously limit their capacity to work.[74] There is almost no mention of child-feeding practices in the literature, but there are some indirect indications that babies were soon consuming "bread, corn, biscuits and pot-likker" right along with their parents.[75] On the other hand, there was a prevalent old wives' notion that prolonged nursing was a protection against conception. To achieve a twenty-nine-month cycle without practicing some form of self-conscious family limitation, women would have had to nurse for at least a year.[76]

Short of family planning, there was no easy choice for women in the attempt to reduce the burden of child care. Other groups had practiced family limitation before this time, but the need for labor may have been a mitigating factor here. It comes as no surprise, then, that as soon as it was possible, children were pretty much allowed and encouraged to shift for themselves, to grow as they might, with relatively little parental or maternal involvement in the process. We will find children little mentioned in overland diaries and reminiscences.

By no means were men the "breadwinners" of this economy. Both women and men actively participated in the production of family subsistence. Indeed, women were engaged in from one-third to one-half of all the food production of the farm, the proportions varying with regional and individual differences.[77] Of the farm staples—meat, milk, corn, pumpkins, beans, and potatoes—women produced the greater number as a product of their portion of the division of labor. Women were also likely to be found helping men with their portion at peak planting time. To this must be added the extremely important work of clothing manufacture, all the household work, and the care of the children. To be sure, men and women alike worked hard to make their farms produce. But one cannot avoid being struck by the enormousness of women's work load.

In 1862, in its first annual report, the Department of Agriculture published a study by Dr. W. W. Hall on the condition of farm women. "In plain language," Hall proclaimed, "in the civilization of the latter half of the nineteenth century, a farmer's wife, as a general rule, is a laboring drudge. . . . It is safe to say, that on three farms out of four the wife works harder, endures more, than any other on the place; more than the husband, more than the 'farm hand,' more than the 'hired help' of the kitchen."[78] In his recommendations for improvements in women's condition, Hall's report supplements our view of farm work. The practice of many farmers of letting their wives cut the firewood and haul the water, especially in the cold of winter, needed correction. Men should be responsible for providing a root cellar for potatoes and other vegetables, otherwise wives were compelled to go out in the cold "once or twice every day, to leave a heated kitchen, and most likely with thin shoes, go to the garden with a tin pan and a hoe, to dig them out of the wet ground and bring them home in slosh or rain." Equally perilous for women were the extremes of heat and cold encountered in washing and hanging the winter laundry; men were stronger and should take that job. "The truth is, it perils the life of the hardiest persons, while working over the fire in cooking or washing, to step outside the door of the kitchen for an instant, a damp, raw wind may be blowing, which coming upon an inner garment throws a chill or the clamminess of the grave over the whole body in an instant of time." Men should make sure that women had ample time to produce the clothing needed for the coming season, or at least not hold their wives responsible when because of overwork they fell behind. By the same token, women should be allowed to purchase cloth for an adequate winter dress; too many women were underdressed, principally owing to their husband's niggardly attitudes.

Hall lamented the lack of attention to women's needs and recommended to men that they adopt a more sympathetic attitude. "There are 'seasons' in the life of women which, as to some of them, so affect the general system, and the mind also, as to commend them to our warmest sympathies. . . . Some women, at such times, are literally insane. . . ." Husbands had to be patient and affectionate or risk driving their wives to a "lunatic's cell." In addition, a man should realize that his wife loved finery and beauty and should supply her "according to his ability, with the means of making her family and home neat, tasteful and tidy." Hall reminded the farmer that "his wife is a social being; that she is not a machine, and therefore needs rest, and recreation, and change." If hands were to be hired perhaps help in the kitchen was worth considering. Women should be allowed to get out of the house once in a while to do a little visiting with other people; in fact, it was a good idea for both husband and wife to dress up and step out for the day now and then.

More comprehensively, Hall insisted that women be given full authority within their domestic sphere. As the husband was master of the fields, so the wife must be mistress of the household. Husbands should not contradict a wife's domestic authority but must "make the wife's authority in her domain as imperative as their own." Most important "let the farmer never forget that his wife is his best friend, the most steadfast on earth; would do more for him in calamity, in misfortune, and sickness than any other human being, and on this account, to say nothing of the marriage vow, made before high Heaven and before men, he owes to the wife of his bosom a consideration, a tenderness, a support, and a sympathy, which should put out of sight every feeling of profit and loss the very instant they come in collision with his wife's welfare as to her body, her mind, and her affections. No man will ever lose in the long run by so doing."

Hall's report was a mixture of constructive suggestions and temporizing platitudes; it is unlikely that many farmers or farm women ever saw, let alone heeded, its advice.[79] In the end it is more important for what it suggests concerning the working relations of husbands and wives than for its proposed reforms. Hall implicitly leveled a harsh indictment against farmers: that they were insensitive to the work load of their wives and drove women past reasonable limits; that they did not comprehend the natural or psychological needs of their wives; that they refused to give women the respect and authority that was their due. Hall attributed the problem to calculations of profit and loss which ignored social and emotional needs (although he made his appeal to men on the very same basis: "no man will ever lose in the long run").

The report adds depth to what we have thus far seen and suggests that the division of labor was structured in favor of men, that it exploited women, and that it was perpetuated, in part, by a masculine attitude of superiority. Daniel Drake, who visited the Midwest in the late 1830s, concluded that the farmer's wife was one who "surrounded by difficulties or vexed with hardships at home, provided with no compensation for what she has left behind, pines away, and wonders that her husband can be so happy when she is so miserable."[80] The true inequity in the division of labor was clearly expressed in the aphorism, "A man may work from sun to sun, but a woman's work is never done." The phrase has a hollow ring to us today, but it was no joke to farm women, who by all accounts worked two or three hours more each day than the men, often spinning, weaving, or knitting late into the dark evening hours.[81]

There are some areas of women's participation in farm life that suggest a higher status. Cross-cultural studies indicate that the responsibility for exchanging goods and services with persons outside the family tends to confer family power and prestige. "The relative power of women is increased if women both contribute to subsistence *and also* have opportunities for extra domestic distribution and exchange of valued goods and services."[82] In the Midwest, the products of dairy, henhouse, garden, and loom were often the only commidities successfully exchanged for other family necessities. Powder, glass, dyes, crockery, coffee, tea, store cloth, metal utensils, and sugar were bought on credit from the local merchant; butter, cheese, eggs, vegetables, homespun, and whiskey were the main items offered in trade to pay the tab.[83]

However, while it was true that women traded, the proceeds were not credited to them individually, but to the family in general.[84] Commodity exchange in corn and grain surpluses, on the other hand, was most frequently used for male economic pursuits: paying off the farm mortgage, speculating in new lands, and as innovations in technology became available, experimenting with new farm equipment. Men's product was for male use; women's product was for the family. It has been claimed that "there was no doubt of her equality in those days because she showed herself equally capable in all the tasks of their life together, and she was proud to know that this was true. Her position and dignity and age-old strength was that of the real help-mate in everything that touched the welfare of the family and the home."[85] From a modern perspective equal work may seem a first step toward sexual equality, but the question of power is not only a question of what people do but also of the recognition they are granted for what they do and the authority that recognition confers. There is little evidence to suggest that men, for their part, gave women's work a second thought. That it was a woman's lot to work that hard was simply taken for granted.

Indeed, one theme of midwestern folksongs was the lament of the husband wronged by the wife who refused to perform her appointed tasks.

> Come all you wary bachelors,
> Come listen unto me
> Come all you wary bechelors,
> Who married once would be.
>
> Before my wife was married
> She was a dainty dame.
> She could do all kinds of cunjer work,
> Like butter, cheese an' cream.
>
> She'd weed her father's oats an' flax,
> And milk the cows I know;
> And when she would return at night
> She could spin a pound of tow.
>
> But since my wife got married,
> Quite worthless she's become.
> An' all that I can say of her
> She will not stay at home.
>
> She will wash herself, an' dress herself,
> An' a-visiting she will go;
> An' that's the thing she'd rather do
> In place of spinning tow.[86]

One looks in vain for evidence of songs that sang the praises of women's diligence. Even the woman accomplished at all of her duties was likely to fall short in male estimation.

She could wash and she could brew,
She could cut and she could sew,
But alas and alas! she was dumb, dumb, dumb.

She could sweep with the broom
She could work at the loom,
But alas and alas! she was dumb, dumb, dumb.

She could card and she could spin,
She could do most anything,
But alas and alas! she was dumb, dumb, dumb.

She was pretty, she was smart,
An' she stole away my heart,
But alas, in the door she was dumb, dumb, dumb.[87]

Men and women were locked into productive harmony. The farm could not exist without the cooperative labor of both sexes. Yet men gave women minimal recognition for their work. Women, fully equal in production, were not granted the status of equality.[88]

Despite its interdependence, the character of men's and women's work was essentially different. Woman's work was dominated by the omnipresent awareness of the immediate usefulness of her product, be it milk, cabbage, eggs, or flax. Whatever processing was required she herself performed. Her view was inward, to her household and family. For them she was not simply to provide food and clothing and keep up the house, but to do these things with imagination and care: by gardening industriously, by preserving, drying, and storing to overcome the limitations of nature, by preparing the season's fare with distinction, by dyeing, bleaching, and cutting clothes in ways to please, and by keeping not only a clean but a well-appointed house. The joys of women's work lay in the satisfactions of accomplishment—of bread well made, butter nicely molded, quilts intended for heirlooms—and in the variety of skills each woman had to master. Women who worked up to this standard were good wives; those who failed on these counts were cast in male folklore as improvident slatterns.[89]

Men, for their part, worked long, monotonous, solitary hours at a single pursuit in the fields, plowing row after row, hoeing

hill after hill. Hamilton remembered work in the cornfield:
"Usually you cultivated the corn with a hired man or two. But
you each had your own 'land,' maybe two dozen rows each was
working on, a row at a time. So you did not pass close as the two
or three crossed and recrossed the fields, stopping, uncovering
corn, pulling cockleburrs."[90] Such work would produce, it was
hoped, quantities of staple grain great enough to sustain the
family and provide a surplus, but there was little satisfaction in
the immediate labor. The flavor of male work was quantitative:
acres, fields, bushels—all measured a man's work. Neither the
corn nor the grain was immediately consumable but required
processing;   the   connections   between   production   and
consumption—the full cycle of work—was not embodied in a
man's own activity. The cyclical nature of farm women's work
might allow her to see in a flowering field of blue flax the linen
for next summer's chemise. For men the fields would yield not
usable, tangible articles—bread or hominy—but bushels; quantities, not things.

On the self-sufficient farm, or farms approaching self-
sufficiency, the character of men's work was a powerful link
between the field and the house. The housewife converted the
corn to hominy, the grain to bread, while the farmer looked on:
only woman could realize the product of man. But the somewhat abstract nature of men's work enabled them to envision
another mode within which they were not dependent upon
their wives to fulfill their labor. The market could connect
men's work to a larger social process and renumerate them in
the tokens of commerce. In order to qualify as social labor,
work had to have this characteristic: to be able to reach out and
connect the family to the larger social world. Woman's work,
always cyclical, always looking inward, did not qualify; it was
hidden by domestic draperies. Men's work, even in the precommercial Midwest, encouraged a kind of economic vision
women could not ordinarily achieve.

3

Men's and Women's Work on the Overland Trail

The routines of farm life and the sexual division of farm labor were translated smoothly into the work of the trail. By contrast, in all-male parties the assignments of trail duty were a source of conflict. As Noah Brooks remembered,

> At the onset none knew who should drive the oxen, who should do the cooking, or whose ingenuity would be taxed to mend broken wagons or tattered clothing. Gradually, and not altogether without grumbling and objection each man filled his own proper place. . . . Indeed, the division of labor in a party of emigrants was a prolific cause of quarrel. . . . We saw not a little fighting in the camps of others who sometimes jogged along the trail in our company, and these bloody fisticuffs were invariably the outcome of disputes over the divisions of labor.[1]

Likewise Rebecca Ketcham, traveling without family in a volunteer party of men and couples, noted after almost two months on the trail and considerable shifting of jobs, "I believe the day's work is pretty regularly laid out now."[2]

For family parties this division of labor was more easily accomplished; it was assumed that men would drive the oxen and mend the wagons, that women would cook and sew. We might expect that the extraordinary conditions of the trip would have disturbed the standard patterns, but as both men and women recorded in the diaries, journals, and reminiscences of the emigration, from the preparations for the journey right through to arrival on the Pacific Coast, responsibilities were apportioned in strict adherence to the traditional sexual division.

As far as the preparations were concerned, the first necessity was raising the cash for the outfit. The first task, then, was men's: the sale of the farm property. Although a cash sale might not realize the farm's full value, demand for midwestern farm property was high enough that nearly all emigrants were able to sell their farms without much difficulty. William Thompson, a boy of ten in 1852, remembered years later that "in February a gentleman came to our house and after dinner he and my father rode over the plantation. The next morning they rode over to Bollivar, the county seat. Returning in the evening my father announced that the plantation was sold."[3] In nearly all accounts women are absent from this process. Frequently men sold the farm equipment and household effects as well.[4] Since very little could be taken, the object was to liquidate the property and accumulate all the cash possible. Reverend Neill Johnson spent several weeks circulating among his Mount Pleasant, Iowa, parishioners collecting outstanding debts to supplement his stake.[5] Men then had to procure the necessary provisions from town. If after purchasing the necessary supplies there was a little cash to spare, they might convert it to cattle or sheep to drive to the coast; this was an investment they determined would pay off handsomely at inflated Pacific prices. At any rate most men wanted good, fresh yokes of oxen to pull the wagons. After lengthy haggling over prices and numerous trips to town, there were wagons to build or modify, running gear to make ready, storage boxes to construct, and oxen to break to wagon load and yoke.[6]

January, February, and March were normally quiet months on the farm, but now they bristled with activity as family members readied themselves for the move. As Mary Ellen Todd remembered,

> After we decided to go to Oregon we found there were many things to be thought about and done in order to prepare for such a journey. As time went on I noticed that father was not taking his customary five or ten minutes just before mealtime for reading his favorite books; and I did not get my lessens quite so regularly, nor commit so much of Bobby Burns or other poets. . . . Sometimes father and mother were calling to me at the very same time. I heard, first, "Mary Ellen, bring me the saw, or the hammer, or

take this to mother," or "Help the baby down, or take this
little bucket and get some water"; again from mother,
"Mary Ellen, won't you finish this churning while I get my
soap to boiling: we'll need a lot of soap you know; also I
must finish spinning all those rolls that we have been
carding, as we just must take with us plenty of yarn."[7]

Soapmaking was an important preparatory task. A family of
four required at least ten pounds of washing and body soap for
the trip. It was, however, clothing manufacture that most
preoccupied women in those days of preparation. The family
needed appropriate clothing for the strenuous work of six long
months, during which time there would be no chance for manufacture and only incidental opportunities for mending.
Weight limitations, of course, required that clothing like everything else be restricted to a minimum, and some clothes,
already made, could be packed. Nonetheless, a great deal of the
family's clothing had to be made especially for the trip. The
standard wardrobe included two or three changes for each
person. Men needed cotton or linen shirts, gathered at the waist
by a broad leather belt, coarse and roomy fustian or linsey-
woolsey pantaloons, heavy stockings, certainly an overcoat of
jean or fustian and perhaps an India rubber poncho, and
rough cowhide boots. Women required two or three dresses,
usually of dark gingham, calico, or heavy wool, with perhaps
one or two petticoats of linen, aprons and shoulder kerchiefs, a
warm shawl, and perhaps a coat. Like men, women wore
cowhide boots. Many women also packed in at least one good
dress, often a feminine heirloom. Children over six or seven
dressed like their parents; a small child might be fitted in a
simple chemise, called a wannis.[8] To protect themselves from
the sun, it was necessary for all to wear something on their
heads. Men donned floppy, big-brimmed felt hats, or wheat-
straw hats to match those the children made for themselves;
women wore the inevitable sunbonnets, made from heavy calico
stretched over wire frames.[9]

Spinning, weaving, and sewing, regularly accomplished bit by
bit throughout the year, now in the final weeks before departure had to be compressed: six months' work in two. During all

of February and March 1852, the women of the Thompson
family

> were busy spinning and weaving. Every article of wearing
> apparel must be made at home. "Store clothes" were out of
> the question in those days. Wool must be carded and spun
> into thread for Aunt Ann's old wooden loom. The cloth
> was then fashioned into garments for clothing to last a year
> after we should reach our goal far out on the Pacific shores.
> The crank of the old wooden loom was almost ceaseless.
> Merrily the shuttle sang to an accompaniment of a camp
> meeting melody. Neighbors also volunteered their services
> in weaving and fashioning garments for the family. All was
> bustle and hurry.[10]

The home-manufactured clothing for women and children
was frequently inadequate for the volatile weather on the trail.
Thunderstorms along the Platte drenched the emigrants, and
on the mountain plateaus and passes the summer could turn
suddenly cold, with unexpected night freezes. Men nearly always had coats, but women and children were generally underdressed in their shawls and jackets. "The great and sudden
change of the temperature connected with the heavy fall of rain
last night, completely drenching everything exposed to it,"
Edwin Bryant noted on June 1, 1846, "is exceedingly distress-
ing to the women and children, who generally are thinly
clothed and unprepared to resist the efforts of exposure and
atmospheric eccentricities."[11]

Clothing accounted for most but not all of the preparatory
sewing. Wagon covers and tents too were made by the women.[12]
For sleeping each person would require at least two blankets,
and sometimes this meant additional weaving.[13] Blankets were
the only protection from the summer night's chill for most of
the emigrants, unless one counts the cover afforded by the
bottom side of a wagon. About a third of the families, however,
took tents in which the young or female children and old folks
slept. Husband and wife most commonly enjoyed the privacy of
the wagon, where, if they were lucky, they slept on a feather
mattress laid atop the provisions. "William and I have slept in
the light wagon lately, as Ma came into the tent, and we pre-

ferred a place to ourselves. But it's very crowded in the wagon, and I have to lay baby across our heads. But we'll still try to make it answer." Infants invariably slept with their mothers.[14]

In addition to sewing, women had to make careful plans for the family's diet. The weight limitations demanded simple meals, but wives tried to add variety by including some home-produced foods in the wagon larder. Virginia Ivins spent her winter evenings "putting up such preserves, pickles and other delicacies as could be kept to become most acceptable when afterwards compelled to partake of cold meals as we often were throughout our trip."[15] Allene Taylor's mother and aunt "baked as much as they could that would keep well. Mother made a large fruit cake and it was to be a surprise to the men folks after we had gone on the journey for some time. I can remember I was in a hurry to have them surprised."[16] From the large quantity of staples, women had to measure out daily portions; a few days of overabundant cooking at the first of the trip would be balanced by days of scarcity at the end. So women practiced cooking with camp staples before they were actually on the road, trying to perfect the amounts. As Louise Rahm wrote in her diary two days before they packed the wagons, she set up a campfire, "was browning coffee and got dinner for the men just to see how it would go."[17]

Husbands built a "grub box" and attached it to the end or the side of the wagon; wives filled it with their cooking utensils. "In ours," Helen Carpenter entered in her diary, "there is a Dutch oven, a camp kettle, frying pan, and coffee pot—these with some tin plates, tin cups, tin spoons, knives and forks; a rolling-pin, bread pan, milk can and a smoothing iron, constitute my entire kitchen furniture."[18] Add a small coffee mill and a length of chain on which to hang the pots, and this could well be the average kitchen inventory for a traveling family. The well-appointed farm wife, even on the frontier, certainly had accumulated many more implements than this in her kitchen. Caroline Kirkland, in her contemporary view of frontier farm life, for example, found that even backwoods women displayed their china tea sets proudly on their hewn-log tables.[19] Leaving items like this behind must have been a disappointment. "But for my part," Margaret Frink wrote in her first days out, "I

was satisfied to do as other immigrants did, and if it was the
fashion to drink out of tin, I was quite content to do so."[20]

Packing was the final and perhaps most difficult job, for here
was finally revealed how little families could take. Husbands
and wives worked together packing and deciding what could
and could not be taken.[21] Filling the few pounds of space left
after the food, arms, kitchen utensils, bedding, clothing, and
tools had been packed was a matter of contention between men
and women. Wives argued for household items and furniture;
husbands might want a few pounds of trade goods to placate
begging Indians. A temporary compromise was generally
negotiated which allowed women to pack some of their precious household possessions at the risk of overloading. "Along
the sides were long boxes like window gardens where were kept
sewing materials and various odds and ends dear to the housewife's heart," Virginia Ivins recalled.[22] Charles True wrote
home the first day out that "in the hind end of the wagon are
what things Elizabeth could not possibly give up."[23] And
Frances Peabody remembered that "although my father often
said that many necessities could be found in Denver, my
mother clung to familiar things." The couple finally agreed to
tie her rocking chair on the back of the wagon, and Frances,
years later, could still recall her mother "sitting in that chair in
the midst of the endless plains when we stopped for the
night."[24]

On the trail, men's work was narrowed to one principal
task—getting the wagons and the family safely through to the
coast. Thus men were concerned almost exclusively with transportation: the care of wagons and stock, driving and droving,
leadership and protection of the family and party. On a normal
day of travel the men of each family were up between four and
five in the morning to cut out their oxen from the herd and
drive them to the wagon for yoking and hitching. The wagon
and running gear had to be thoroughly checked over. After
breakfast the wagons pulled out, often in single file, but frequently drivers spread themselves out to avoid the choking dust
thrown up by the hooves and wheels to the front. Normally a
man drove each wagon. Since many parties had some addi-

tional loose stock, some men herded and drove the stock to the rear of the line. A good morning march began by seven and continued until the noon hour, when drivers pulled up, unhitched their oxen, set the stock to grazing, and settled down for the midday meal the women produced. After an hour or so for lunch and rest, the men hitched up the oxen again and picked up the line of march.

Driving and droving were strenuous and demanding occupations. Some men drove their wagons while sitting on the wagon perch, but most drove by walking alongside the oxen; a few men owned horses they rode along the trail, but most walked. "Of course riding was out of the question. We had one horse, but he was reserved for emergencies, and nobody but a shirk would think of crawling into a wagon, loaded down as it was with the necessities of life, unless sickness made it impossible for him to walk."[25] Walking the fifteen or so miles of trail each day was, in the best of conditions, enough to tire any man. Conditions, of course, were not always the best. Soaring midday summer temperatures on the shadeless plains sapped the strength. The mornings, on the other hand, especially in the high plains and mountains, were sometimes frigid. " 'Tis dredful cold," Agnes Stewart scratched early on May 17, 1853, "Oh, the wind goes to a person's heart. I will shiver to death. I feel for the men gathering the cattle and yoking them up. It was so cold for them, and no warm breakfast."[26] Driving, and especially herding the cattle, meant eating large portions of dust. "It has been immensely disagreeable for the drivers today for a Northwest wind drove the dust in clouds into their faces, as they walk besides their teams. Am glad that I am not an ox driver."[27] The sun and wind decreed another common fate, painful chapped skin. "I feel well except my lips, they have been sore ever since I left Council Bluffs; but one half of the Emigrants share the same fate, something I had never heard of before."[28]

The most common obstacles were the rivers. By the 1850s many crossings were served by ferries, and as long as the emigrants could afford the toll, the only inconvenience was the wait. At other times and places, however, oxen and wagons had to be driven down steep embankments and across the flow, and the danger of quicksand bogs or rapid currents that could sweep away goods, stock, or men lurked in even the shallowest of streams. Consequently men took the greatest care at crossings. Women and children frequently shuttled over on horseback or raft.[29] Sometimes men labored to build rude bridges or ferries for the wagons.[30] Most often they double- or triple-teamed the oxen and drew each wagon across.[31] At any rate, it was slow, frustrating, demanding work. Along the road wagons could always break down; axles especially were prone to snap with all the jolting. Only a lucky man did not have to jerry-rig or abandon a wagon along the road.

By the late afternoon the normal demands of most days had so tired the men that sleep could not be resisted. "A drowsiness has fallen apparently on men and beast; teamsters fall asleep on their perches and even when walking by their teams, and the words of command are now addressed to the slowly creeping oxen in the soft tenor of women or the piping trebel of children, while the snores of the teamsters make a droning accompaniment."[32] "It is with the greatest effort we can keep awake. Even Mr. Gray sometimes nods with the lines in his hands," Rebecca Ketcham wrote in her journal. "We can all, as soon as we stop, lie down on the grass or anywhere and be asleep in less than no time almost."[33]

In the evenings the stock sometimes had to be driven a distance for grazing. "The men of the company divided into two bands. The elderly ones were detailed to stay with the wagons; keeping one or two horses with them while the others, taking with them the other horses, drove the cattle up the creek valley, searching for food."[34] After a hard day's drive in 1853, George Belshaw and some other men from his party "took the Cattle and Horses about one mile to feed and watched them all night. I fealt well but it is hard fateage loosing so much rest and Driving the teams through the Day and to manage so large a company and get them along as fast as I can."[35]

Belshaw was, as he noted, captain of his train. For those men in the advance guard there was added responsibility. George complained in a letter to his brother, Henry, "They have elected me captain. I have taken them across one stream and it keeps me very busy all the time to pick the camping places for them and attend to everything, besides, and lead them along, as you know some of them are very slow so I have to urge them up. I do not get to bed until ten or eleven, and have to be up at daylight. I have my hand full, but you know I will persevere for a better climate."[36]

Guard duty was another responsibility that fell to men. The duty rotated, two or three men splitting the night's watch, protecting the stock from wolves or Indians, preventing a sudden stampede. Guard duty was probably the most hated male chore but one—chasing lost stock.[37] A slipshod night's watch could halt a party for days as the men roamed the prairie, often unsuccessfully, in search of the stock. Men measured their success in units of forward progress: the mileage they calculated and noted in their daily journals. A setback of days because of lost stock was, in these terms, a frustrating failure.[38]

There was a distinctive dialectic to men's work on the trail. The heads of household had overall responsibility for movement. It was men who had made the decision to move, it was men who determined the route, direction, and speed of travel, it was men who would make the sometimes fateful decisions to turn back or move on, it was men upon whom fell the burden of repairing faulty or broken equipment. In short, it was men who provided the leadership for the emigration: men would take the credit, and they had to accept the blame.[39] This responsibility bore heavily upon husbands and fathers as they led their wives and children into hardships they had not fully anticipated. There is, of course, no way to measure their burden; we can be sure, however, that it took its toll of energy, vitality, and good humor.

The physical work of men was organized so as to provide compensations for this heavy burden of responsibility. While the wagons were rolling, men worked at peak capacity. Time and again in men's accounts of their trips, they took spiteful aim at the few shirking able-bodied males who dared to hitch a ride on one of the wagons.[40] A man worked the trail from the time the oxen were yoked in the morning until they were herded in the evening; a person who did not work at this full capacity and with this constancy was simply not a man. But when the wagons were parked once more, the oxen and cattle set out to graze, and the guard was posted, men were off duty. There were occasional jobs to be done, of course, and men were still in command, to be sure, but in the evening they acted out their responsibilities at a leisurely pace, intermingling work with the pleasures of food, relaxation, and company. Men bore final responsibility, but they enjoyed a rhythm of long periods of hard work punctuated by periods of rest.

Women's trail work was structured around the men's: women were the working support of the trail's labor system. In the first instance, women enjoyed little overall responsibility for the direction or outcome of the emigration. They were not called upon to participate in making the critical decisions; indeed, a wife had probably played almost no role in the decision to emigrate in the first place.[41] The lack of overall responsibility, however, was accompanied by a demanding work schedule that made adult women the most fully and materially responsible members of the family. The men's work schedule required that a woman tend to the needs of her family when the wheels stopped turning for the day. The need to work did not disappear when the men went off duty; work merely changed its character.[42] Randall Hewitt put it most bluntly: "Having ladies do the 'housework' everything went along smoothly."[43] Amelia Knight confirmed this view from a distinctively feminine perspective. Her husband was upset at having lost three hired hands who had decided to pack through alone; Amelia saw it differently. As she confided in her diary, "I am pleased, as . . . I shall have three less to wait on."[44]

On the other hand, in contrast to men, women were not at liberty to relax while their opposite numbers worked. After all, who could relax while bumping and jogging along in a wagon? More to the point, during the hours of travel women were either working or on call, available to lend a hand, do a critical job, or take over for an ailing male. When the overriding principle of the trail was to "keep moving," could an able body simply stand by? Women's work, then, was a reflex of men's: a rhythm of long hours on call to substitute and supplement the work of men, punctuated by shorter periods of intense activity.

First we shall look at work that belonged distinctively to

women. They regularly began the trail day by getting up around four, an hour to half an hour before the men, to stoke the fire and put up kettles of water to begin breakfast.[45] If there was a cow along, wives milked her before breakfast.[46] James Clyman arose early one morning to write in his journal as the women prepared breakfast and noted that other than the breakfast bustle there was no other activity "except Sleeping which is performed by the male part of the camp to the greatest perfection."[47] By the time coffee had been boiled, bacon fried, beans warmed, and bread baked, all of which required a good hour's work, the men had arisen to hear the report from the last guard, brought in the oxen, and were ready for their meal.

Cooking in the open was a new experience for most women. As Lodisa Frizzell wrote, "it goes so much 'agin the grane' at first."[48] "Eliza soon discovered that cooking over a campfire was far different from cooking on a stove or a range."[49] "Two forked sticks were driven into the ground, a pole laid across, and the kettle swung upon it."[50] Pots were continually falling into the fire, and families soon became accustomed to ashen crust on their food.[51] In the absence of tables, all preparation was on the ground. This "requires me to stoop considerably. All our work here requires stooping. Not having tables, chairs or anything it is very hard on the back."[52] The weather rarely cooperated, especially in the early morning. "Everything was soaked with water and dry wood so scarce that our women could scarcely make coffee or fry meat."[53] "Rainy this morning; very disagreeable getting breakfast," Cecelia Adams complained in her dairy, and she noted a few weeks later that she "could not raise enough fire to cook breakfast."[54] James Clyman, ever an admiring observer of women, committed to his journal the story of "one young lady which showed herself worthy of the bravest undaunted pioneer of west, for after having kneaded her dough she watched and nursed the fire and held an umbrella over the fire and her skillet with the greatest composure for near 2 hours."[55]

After breakfast the women washed the tinware, stowed away the cooking equipment and food, and packed up while the men readied the wagons. After several hours on the road there was a brief stop at noon. Then, while the men relaxed, the women brought out the lunch, usually prepared the night before, and the party enjoyed a cold meal and a few minutes of rest. After the women had again packed up their gear, the wagons pushed off once more for the remainder of the afternoon.

By evening everyone was ready for camp. After one particularly rough day of moving their wagons across a cold stream, the Burns party moved into camp. "Our campfire was soon burning brightly and in a few minutes we sat down to a nice warm supper prepared by Mrs. W. P. Burns, which was eaten with relish."[56] For men, the evening was the reward for a hard day's labor; for women, who prepared the reward, unpacking the wagons was the prelude to four or five hours of sustained work. Rebecca Ketcham lamented these relentless demands: "To ride on horseback, rain or shine, tired or sick, or whatever might be the matter, then as soon as we get into camp, go to work!"[57]

The fire had to be kindled and water brought to camp. If the travelers were lucky, the camp was close by a spring. The fear of mosquitoes, unhealthy vapors, or hidden Indians, however, kept them away from the covered, low-lying river bottoms, so water had to be hauled, usually by women.[58] Collecting fuel for the fire was also women's work. Presumably if wood had had to be chopped, men would have done it, but there being no trees, women cooked with sagebrush, cottonwood twigs, or buffalo chips, which they gathered. James Reed, writing in his diary, noted that "the women and children are now out gathering 'Buffalo Chips' to burn in order to do the cooking."[59] Some women complained about having to handle and cook with dried dung, but necessity, of course, prevailed.[60] Because there was frequently not enough kindling in the vicinity of camp for both the evening and morning fires, women collected chips as they traveled. "We always had a sack of them hanging on the side of the wagon on the plains. We used to average about ten miles a day and I believe that I ran an extra five miles trying to gather feed for our toothless ox or buffalo chips for our evening fire."[61]

Despite the primitive surroundings, women continued to practice midwestern culinary arts. Judging from the diary notations of menus, women worked mightily to overcome the limit imposed by hauling weights. In addition to the basics—cooking bacon, beans, and coffee—women milked, made butter and cheese, boiled and mashed potatoes, made gravies, stewed dried fruit, made bread, biscuits, pies, and cakes, puddings of bread, rice, or cracker, and even prepared preserves and jellies from wild berries and fruit gathered along the way.[62] The cooking continued past the dinner hour and into the late evening as food for the next day's breakfast and lunch was prepared: "Everybody is in bed but Agnes and myself i believe and we would be there to but we have wait til the apples are stewed enough."[63]

Camp was just like home in one respect—there was plenty of housework. After dinner the beds had to be made up, wagons cleaned out, and provisions taken out to air to prevent mildew. There were always clothes to mend or socks to knit. "I visited the tents of our fellow-travelers and found the ladies busily employed, as if sitting by the fireside which they had so recently left. . . . Mrs West, a lady of seventy, and her daughter Mrs Campbell, were knitting."[64]

Except for rinsing out a few garments in the evening, however, the family washing piled up; women waited for a day when the wagons might stop over near an ample supply of water. Washing "was not done always on Monday to the annoyance of our excellent housekeepers who at home had been accustomed to thus honoring 'blue Monday.' "[65] The wagons made frequent, unavoidable stops for one reason or another, and women invariably used these occasions to wash. "Came to a creek so high we could not cross, camped, the women to washing and the men to examining their provisions." "It is agreed to stay in this camp until tomorrow to rest the cattle. Water and grass are both fine. The women are going to wash. It is the best chance we have had for a long time, wood and water are plenty and convenient." "One of the company broke the axletree of his wagon, then camped, the women washed." "Still at Bridger. Here we have a good time for washing, which we women deem a great privilege."[66] For parties that had agreed to "rest" on Sundays, the day was turned to washing, but under the pressures of time few parties could observe the Sabbath strictly.[67] If there had been no occasion to stop over for two or three weeks, women demanded a chance to wash; or, as George Belshaw put it, "the women ruled and would wash."[68] In most parties women spent a full day washing about every two weeks.[69]

Washing began early. "The banks of the small rivulet was lined at an early hour after breakfast with fires, kettles, washtubs, and piles of unwashed linen, showing conclusively that a general lustration was to be performed by the female portion of our party."[70] If there was fuel to spare, water was heated, but generally women had to be content to suds their harsh soap in hard, cold water. A day of sun, wind, soap, and water could be a painful combination. "Camilia and I both burnt out arms very badly while washing. They were red and swollen and painful as though scalded with boiling water. Our hands are blacker than any farmer's, and I do not see that there is any way of preventing it, for everything has to be done in the wind and sun."[71]

With all this, there were the children to be watched, although the burden of other responsibilities made child care a relatively low priority. Notes on children are rare in the accounts of men and women, and when they do appear, children are the accompaniment to other work. "In getting up a steep bank after we had forded a stream I had to carry a heavy stone to block the wheels . . . , and carry and pull along the children at the same time."[72] "Descending the mountain, which was steep and difficult, the men having to steady the wagons down while we women carried and led our children."[73] At most times children fended for themselves, the older boys working with the men, the older girls appointed as nursemaids to the younger ones. The ultimate responsibility, however, resided with the mothers.[74]

In parties with more than one able-bodied woman, women divided up their responsibilities just as the men did. Women would commonly take turns cooking.[75] However, as Helen Carpenter complained to her diary, even with help from sisters and children

> the plain fact of the matter is *we have no time for sociability.* From the time we get up in the morning, until we are on the road, it is hurry scurry to get breakfast and put away the things that necessarily had to be pulled out last night—

while under way there is no room in the wagon for a visitor, nooning is barely enough to eat a cold bite—and at night all the cooking utensils and provisions are to be gotten about the camp fire and cooking enough done to last until the next night.

Although there is not much to cook, the difficulty and inconvenience of doing it, amounts to a great deal—so by the time one has squatted around the fire and cooked bread and bacon, and made several dozen trips to and from the wagon—washed the dishes (with no place to drain them) and gotten things ready for an early breakfast, some of the others already have their night caps on—at any rate its time to go to bed.

In respect to women's work the days are all very much the same. . . . Some women have very little help about the camp, being obliged to get the wood and water (as far as possible), make camp fires, unpack at night and pack up in the morning—and if they are Missourians they have the milking to do, if they are fortunate enough to have cows.

I am lucky in having a Yankee for a husband, so I am well waited on.[76]

Most women, of course, were from Missouri and its midwestern environs and had the worst of it by Mrs. Carpenter's description.

Indeed, despite Mrs. Carpenter's disclaimer for Yankee men, men assisted in only the most unusual of circumstances. In some parties men did the cooking during storms and very bad weather.[77] And most husbands, like Jessy Thornton, took over when their wives fell sick; Thornton only asked that Nancy "not scold me for my blunders."[78] There were other instances where husband and wife both hired into a party to do the cooking,[79] or where women were relieved of cooking when a man hired on as trail cook.[80]

Men, however, made inept domestic helpers. The experience of single men again places the family experience in perspective.

"How do you like it overland?"
His mother she will say;
"All right, except for cooking,
Then the devil is to pay.

> For some won't cook, and others can't,
> And then it's curse and damn;
> The coffee pot's begun to leak,
> So has the frying pan.[81]

John A. Johnson was one of the many who followed his heart to the goldfields in 1849, leaving his wife Almire and their children behind. In a rich series of letters written home, he discussed among many other things the cooking arrangements in his party of five men.[82] "It would no doubt be interesting to hear how we manage matters in camp as to cooking, etc.," he wrote. "All of us seem to understand cooking as well as our wives and are anxious to try their hands." A few weeks later he added: "We have, as I said before, several excellent cooks in our company. Some crack on making one thing and some another and really we get along very well in this respect. Today each mess made a pot-pie; I had the honor of officiating at our mess; it was good of course."

Perhaps inspired by his success at Sunday dinner, his confidence was building; a week later he wrote that

> yesterday our mess . . . proposed that if I would act as cook on the road I would be relieved from every other kind of work and further that I need not stand guard at night. I said *I would do it* and it was unanimously agreed to; so that I need not harness or touch a mule, or do any other work on the road, save preparing the food, which to me, you know, will not be burdensome as I have a rather natural taste for that kind of work and they all think so. . . . The beauty of my berth is that I can walk, ride in the wagon or on a mule all day as I please and after supper go to bed and *sleep all night* while others have to watch or stand guard two hours every other night and are consequently exposed to danger if there be any dangers at any time for Indians.

A friend of the family traveling with the male party wrote to Johnson's wife as if to address her suspicions about her husband's newfound capacity for the wifely role: "He is decidedly the best cook in the camp. He goes about it rather awkwardly but really I don't think his wife can beat him at making bread."

Johnson's tenure as trail cook was all too predictable. A week later he wrote home again: "I have given up the office of chief cook and take my turn with the rest and my portion of other duties. I had rather do so as it is more slavish work than I had anticipated and by far the hardest post to occupy. I found I was working all the time during our halts while others were at least a portion of the time resting. I could not get time to write a letter or a note—as for guarding, my turn will not come oftener than once in two and perhaps three nights and then only two hours at a time with some eight or ten others."

Where families, not single men, made up the parties, women were only too glad to replace men at the campfire. Men's clumsiness with domestic details was an object of feminine scorn. "Mr Gray does most of the cooking," Rebecca Ketcham noted, "and it is most amusing to see some of his operations."[83] Lucy Cooke traveled all the way to Salt Lake with a hired male cook but went on to California the next season without male domestic assistance: "It's so nice to have women folks manage the cooking; things look so much sweeter."[84] "We are in a camp tonight with a small company of emigrants among whom are several ladies," Frances Sawyer wrote. "These, like myself, were engaged in helping to cook supper, and I have no doubt, but that they all enjoyed it heartily as I did."[85] She was, undoubtedly, correct. Camp housework was "more slavish" than even experienced farm women might have expected. It was "by far the hardest post to occupy" but accepted by women, nonetheless, as their responsibility.

What about the work women did during the hours of travel? The picture that emerges from men's and women's accounts is fuzzy and indistinct, reflecting a confusion as to what was normative in the actual situations that developed out on the trail. Men were supposed to be the drivers of the wagons and stock, and clearly the leaders of the march; women were to enjoy the privilege of riding in the wagons. Both men and women agreed on this division of labor, and during the early weeks on the trail most people conformed to this ideal. Certainly men rarely rode the wagons, and women frequently did. This distinction between riding and walking was so basic that it came close to a role-defining division between the sexes.

Mrs Ridgley said that her back ached riding all day in a wagon that jolted you to pieces every time you hit a stone. She didn't see how that poor woman in the wagon in back of the deacon's could get along, with a cross baby. And if one was a man one wouldn't have to sit cramped up all day and every day.

In mild defense of his sex Mr Ridgley would reply that it wasn't exactly easy to walk halfway across the continent alongside of a team of oxen with a yoke of steers in the center that you had to keep watching continually. At which his good wife would smile a little wearily. *She* knew who had the hardest part of the bargain, etc.[86]

If there was a formulaic quality to this conjugal debate it was because this behavior was taken to be standard for men and women. Essentially the haggling was about the respective virtues of the sexes themselves.

In fact, this was not the full picture. Women walked too, and many women walked most of the time. We have already noted women gathering fuel as they walked. As the emigrants matured with the march, they could see how every extra pound lessened the distance a team could haul, so "the women would walk to lighten the load" and even "would push to help the poor teams up the hills."[87] There is cause for believing that by the time the journey was well under way women walked as a matter of course. The difference remained that women could ride when they tired of the walk, while men could not.[88] When they did choose to ride, women busied themselves with mending or knitting.[89]

When teamsters fell sick or were otherwise incapacitated, women, of course, substituted.[90] Emergencies—stranded wagons, prairie fires, Indian scares—also called on women to carry out male duties.[91] This is not surprising. More unexpected, perhaps, is that many women took a regular turn at driving both the wagons and the stock. As we have seen, men only rarely took over the women's work. Women, however, regularly performed certain details of what were men's responsibilities. "Mrs Burnett and myself drove and slept alternately during the day," Peter Burnett recalled.[92] "I drive a great deal now, as I am very fond of handling the lines," Frances Sawyer wrote in her journal.[93] In their diary accounts women were more likely than men to note women's work with the stock; fewer than a fifth of the men's diaries mention women driving, compared to a full third of the women's. Yet women themselves seemed a bit reluctant to admit this discrepancy in the conventional division of labor. "The two-horse spring wagon was our bed room and was driven by the Major," Margaret Haun wrote, and then added "and in good stretches of the road by myself."[94] Susan Angell declared that their mule-drawn wagon was "driven by my husband"—certainly a clear statement, except that later, in passing, she added the important qualifier that she "took turns in driving the mule teams during each day."[95] These women stated the normative as if it were the actual situation; the truth only came out in elaboration. Their values prevented them from writing simply, "My husband and I drove the wagon." These indications suggest that the work of women during the traveling hours violated normative standards of work.

There was, of course, a social life in the camps. Young people frequently got together for singing and sometimes dancing around the campfires. "The young ones of our party are all assembled around a blazing fire, from which sounds of mirth and hilarity come floating on the evening breeze."[96] Special occasions, like the Fourth of July or a stopover at Fort Laramie or Fort Bridger, might generate an evening of merrymaking.[97] But women were mostly just too busy for evening entertainments. If they were able to end their domestic duties a little early, women too gathered around the campfires, but mostly in feminine groups. "High teas were not popular but tatting, knitting, crochetting, exchanging recepts for cooking beans or dried apples or swapping food for the sake of variety kept us in practice of feminine occupations and diversions." For their part, the menfolk spent their evening hour "lolling and smoking their pipes and guessing, or maybe betting, how many miles we had covered during the day."[98]

Quite simply, women had little extra time, although men found time for a variety of leisure activities. Fishing and swimming were common at the rivers and occasional ponds.[99]

Randall Hewitt remembered men producing "greasy, well-thumbed packs of cards," and games of euchre, old sledge, and pinochle were "something for amusement constantly."[100]

The most popular male pastime, however, was hunting. Nearly every man hunted whenever he could. When the wagons stopped for a wash day, men would hunt. "We shall not move today. The women will wash and the men will hunt," John Zeiber wrote in his diary.[101] The captain's order for the day in one 1844 train was "a rest for the cattle, wash day for the women, and a day to hunt for the men." Although captains' orders in general soon fell out of favor, the priorities remained the same.[102] Moreover, despite expert advice as to the folly of stopping the march for a hunt,[103] men who otherwise stressed the importance of continual movement above all else would stop their wagons, saddle all available mounts, and head out for the kill at the slightest sign of a distant buffalo herd. When the cry "Buffalo!" was raised, excitement pulsed from one man to the next; Minto's captain, "General" Cornelius Gilliam, "called loudly for his horse. . . . He slung himself into the saddle, and turning his face to the train called in a raised voice, 'You boys with the teams camp where there is wood and water, and you that can get horses and guns mount and follow me.' He did not speak to any particular officer, and in the ardor of the hunter seemed to have forgotten the responsibility of the general."[104] When the buffalo appeared, many men left their responsibilities behind with the women. As her party moved across buffalo country, Cecilia Adams noted in her diary that "our boys are on the chase most of the time."[105]

Men had this opportunity for play, and play it was. The amount of usable food produced by these masculine sorties was dismally low. Edward Parrish recorded that his comrades had killed buffalo enough for 40,000 pounds of meat but left nearly all for the birds; the hunters had neither the time, the equipment, nor the inclination for butchering. "God forgive us for such waste and save us from such ignorance," Parrish pled.[106] Burnett offered sound advice: "When you reach the country of buffalo, never stop your wagons to hunt, as you will eat up more provisions than you will save."[107] Hunting could not, then, be justified as a working activity. Nor did very many men seem to feel, as Parrish did, that it required such a justification. Most simply felt as George Belshaw: "Fine sport was this for all the Boys."[108]

There was no comparable play activity for women outside of their working time. Hunting was but a glaring example of the contrasting ways in which men and women employed their time on the trail. Men worked within a pattern of activity/inactivity geared for functional efficiency; periods of maximum exertion were matched by periods of rest and relaxation. This pattern was in literal accord with the principal function of the trip; indeed, men could and did see themselves as the motive force itself, since it was principally men's labor that drove the wagons. In addition, men had the prerogative of leadership, including the option of stopping the train. Women's work, on the other hand, was at the mercy of the march and its male leadership. Unable to rest during the long hours on the road, often called upon to lend a crucial hand during the day, women finally shifted into high gear in the evenings, precisely when the men and the wagons lay still.

Hunting well illustrates a second characteristic distinction between the work of the sexes. In their roles as leaders of the march, men had to work together with other men. As we have seen, cooperation, whether in trains or informally, was at a premium for the length of the march. It was during the moving hours that cooperation was most in demand: agreeing and holding to the line and pace of the march, agreeing to a camping time and place, assisting one another in the difficult stretches. Men were the representatives of the parties and families, and security was dependent upon their ability to communicate and cooperate. Collective games, storytelling, singing and dancing—all shaped mainly by the male participants—were important ways of building and sustaining social cooperation. Hunting together was another important way. The buffalo hunters returning from their successful (albeit wasteful) foray, Minto remembers, "made a jolly party going back to camp, as the man who led the way, walking beside his mule, Joseph Watt, started us singing"—an archetypal scene of male camaraderie.[109] Women's work confined wives to the family circle. There was little chance, as Helen Carpenter said, to visit while traveling, and in the evening women were all but bound to the domestic fires.

These distinctions could ordinarily be contained by family dynamics habituated to the everyday differences between men's and women's work. Women, as we have seen, were used to working beyond the boundaries of "sun to sun." There was a difference on the trail, however, which produced some significant conflict. On their simple farms, men and women were engaged in common work with an internal character. Here on the trail the work of men and women diverged: men fixed exclusively on outward goals—the stock, grass and water, mileage, the destination, future planning—compatible with their working goals. Women, because of the repetitive features of their work, found it more difficult to achieve this outward perspective.

Phoebe Judson articulated this divergence of the sexes:

> During the week our men had been very busily employed. . . . Saturday night found them very tired and much in need of physical rest, so they lolled around in the tents and on their blankets spread on the grass, or under the wagons out of the sunshine, seeming to realize that the "Sabbath was made for man." But the women, who had only been anxious spectators of their arduous work, . . . not being weary in body, could not fully appreciate physical rest, and were rendered more uneasy by the continual passing of emigrant trains all day long. . . . To me, much of the day was spent in meditating over the past and in forebodings for the future.[110]

Reams of testimony could be marshaled to demonstrate the physical exhaustion of women, so we can only assume that Mrs. Judson's memory was faulty. The anxiety she remembered feeling, however, was real enough and pervaded nearly every woman's account of her experience. The immediate source of this anxiety was the divergent goals and work patterns of men and women on the trail. On a deeper level, however, these divergences themselves were part and parcel of significant cultural distinctions between men and women. The conflict between sexual styles we see revealed in the analysis of the division of labor found more fundamental expression on the level of values, beliefs, expectations, and emotions.

4

Masculine Men and Feminine Women

Everywhere they looked, midwestern people saw men and women performing essentially different tasks calling upon different skills and routines: men worked the fields and were responsible for tools, animals, and produce; women toiled in and about the household and yard, with responsibility for reproducing the ongoing life of the family. And people expected that for much of the time men and women would inhabit separate spaces. Men were away from the household, in the fields; women were called out only when needed, and then on men's invitation. Beyond the fields were woods or prairie, distinctly men's territory, a place for hunters, fighters, traders, and alongside the hidden stills, for drinkers. Women were confined to the household, much of the time to the kitchen. (In southern Illinois the word "cook" was another term for "wife."[1]) These domestic spaces were more or less under feminine control. This sense was so strong that even at the trail campfire the presence of a woman was enough to make a man feel clumsy and awkward cooking his beans or boiling his tea.

One kind of work and space for men, another for women: this lesson was impressed on children no less than on adults. Barbed male jokes about boys doing "women's work"—milking, churning, or feeding the hens—were like spurs urging sons to their fathers' sides in the fields. A boy's masculine identity was called into question by continued association with the domestic spaces of women. For that matter, neither did mothers want their sons caught doing women's work. The same process occurred on the trail, where circumstances demanded that boys make the leap to manhood under the added compulsion of necessity. "Willie is taking his first lesson in watching," Harriet Ward wrote when her eleven-year-old son volunteered to drive the loose stock. Two weeks of hard travel later she confessed that her son, who had left Wisconsin that spring, her "little Willie," now "does the work of a man" and Will was no longer seen around the wagon during the day.[2]

On the trail children played at being little men and women. Irene Dunham remembered that in one typical game, "we would fish and have our campfire. The boys would clean the fish and we girls would cook them and set our own table and get the supper often."[3] Most frequently, however, the child's day separated boys and girls just as the working days of men and women were largely spent in different ways and places. Boys were expected to watch the stock, a demanding job, and to be available for father-assigned chores. Boys were sent to the rear of the wagons with the stock; girls were kept around the wagons. "Mother would make me get into the wagon and amuse little Frank. . . . I would feel myself very much abused, preferring to walk."[4] In the evenings, while daughters helped their mothers with the domestic duties, "the boys were marching around playing soldier, led by a youthful drummer, who pounded with might and main upon a small specimen of that warlike symbol."[5]

Children learned not only the sexual division of labor, but also a comprehensive set of cultural rationalizations about gender. Midwestern farm folks, along with the rest of the American people, believed the sexes to be as characterologically different as the work they performed. Upon the behavioral differences between the sexes were constructed the elaborated distinctions of gender roles. These cultural beliefs about the nature of the sexes added up to composite character types: masculine and feminine. These basic character types were perceived as God-given, immutable as the physical distinction of male and female.

In their writings emigrants frequently revealed their thoughts and feelings about sex-specific qualities, usually through the way they showed people acting in selected situations. More rarely a writer turned her or his attention directly to the supposed qualities and characteristics of the sexes. For example, an essential difference between the sexes, Peter Burnett offered, was strength. "When anyone could shoulder a bag of corn, he was considered a man, and to stand in a half-bushel measure and shoulder a bag containing two and a half to three bushels was considered quite a feat. I heard of a woman who could do so, but I never saw her and can not say that the statement was true."[6] Strength versus weakness was perhaps the most prominent of several bipolar sets of ascribed sexual attributes.

Emigrants believed, however, that male strength was more than a physical characteristic. Men were strong in all ways; the ideal masculine character was stalwart and unshakable in the face of adversity. The responsibility of men on the trail placed a premium on this kind of self-assurance and certainty. When Harriet Ward heard "startling reports of the horrors of the route," she confessed that "were there none more courageous than myself in the company I think we might possibly take our homeward way again." She might feel this way without jeopardizing the trip, for "our gentlemen paid but little heed to all the stories," and the party moved on.[7] This scene is repeated time after time in the diaries and remembered by many in their recollections. According to the emigrants, men were naturally less afraid, gifted with more courage, and were more willing to head straight into the difficulties ahead.

Women, on the other hand, were portrayed most often as constitutionally fearful and cautious. In his diary George Bel-Belshaw, to take one example, consistently presented women in that guise: the men had to "run the waggons across [a stream] by hand. Women very much frited. . . . Deep creek and had to swim out. Cattle got the teams over safe. Women verry much frited. . . . We met some Indians yesterday and I went to them shook hands with them, but the women was very frightened especially some of them."[8] "It was deemed taking dangerous risks for a man to be far from his party while in the mountains, unless well armed," Randall Hewitt wrote. "Much more was it extra hazardous for a young woman."[9]

Women assented in their writing to this notion of feminine weakness but saw it generally as something they could overcome. "I was always timid," Margaret Hecox remembered. "A bug could frighten me into a spasm. I couldn't stand idly by, however, when danger threatened and my services were needed. I knew that if I couldn't shoot straight I could at least sound the alarm. . . . I put on my husband's hat and overcoat, then grasping our old flintlock between my shaking hands I went forth in the darkness."[10] About a similar situation Mrs. Benjamin Ferris exclaimed, "Did I not act bravely: By all ordinary rules I would have screamed."[11] Andrew McClure capped the discussion: "It is sometimes necessary that women would assume a degree of firmness wholly masculine."[12]

It is likely that men too were secretly disturbed and frightened by the dangers of the trail. Men, however, had learned to spurn those "weak" feelings, to discipline themselves to their perceptions of choice and necessity. While women could admit to their fears and even laugh at themselves a little, masculine determination demanded that men live with their feelings enclosed by heavily buttressed walls. William Keil, setting off in St. Joseph, bumped into an old friend not seen for years. "The pleasure of seeing our brother M. Schaefer again was great," he wrote home, "but as usual I was master of my feelings."[13] To be the master of your feelings—this was a definitional male assignment. If emotions were allowed free reign the stalwart character might succumb to the fears and insecurities of the moment. On the trail, where the advantages of self-confidence were patent, men were described as tight-lipped, silent, brooding, even truculent; they allowed themselves to open up in only the most restricted circumstances.

Crying, an emotional display absolutely foreign to the notion of masculinity, defined the outer limits of accepted masculine behavior. It was not that men never cried, but they bitterly remembered their few tears and marked the experiences as traumatic and identity-shaking. Thomas Chambers told of the time he lost some of his family's precious store of flour when the raft on which he was transporting their provisions down the Columbia was overrun by the swift currents. "I thought the family would starve. I was twenty years of age, but in my anxiety I cried. This was the first, last and only time I cried while crossing the plains."[14] Chamber's trauma is evident in his syntax: "But . . . I cried . . . the first, last and only time." Basil Parker's hour of trial came when he lost his cabin to fire in 1852. He absorbed the blow like a man and with his neighbors

built a new house for his family, but the loss of his previous
labors began to eat at him. When soon after he was obliged to
bed down a visiting uncle on his puncheon floor, the outer
veneer of masculine strength dissolved as he bitterly remembered the beds he had built into his old cabin. "I broke down
and stepped out on the porch so none of them could see my
crying. It made me mad to think that a strong man like I was
should cry like a baby, and I made up my mind to leave the
country."[15] Parker's shame at his "weakness" became the central
psychological motive for his emigration; unable to face the
scene of his distress he turned instead to a trek across the plains
that would affirm his masculinity.

The male horror of tears was well founded, for cultural
consensus about masculine strength and feminine weakness
meant that a public display of sentiment might mark a man
indelibly.

> A man named Smith had a wooden rolling pin that it was
> decided was useless and must be abandoned. I shall never
> forget how that big man stood there with tears streaming
> down his face as he said, "Do I have to throw it away? It was
> my mother's. I remember she always used it to roll out her
> biscuits, and they were awful good biscuit." He had to leave
> it, but they christened him "Rolling Pin" Smith, a name he
> carried to the day of his death.[16]

The canon of femininity, on the other hand, allowed women to
relieve their frustrated needs and pent-up emotions with frequent crying. Women's tears were a recognized part of their
identity.

Men's most common emotional displays were of an altogether different mode. The frustrations of hard travel and
responsibility found ventilation in forms that the women in
their turn rejected. Swearing, for example, was a convenient
way of expressing frustration and peppered nearly every man's
conversation. The Hecox–Aram party was invaded en route by
a horde of beetles. "The children cried, . . . the women scolded
and the men swore. I never did hear men swear as they did that
night. I think Father swore, also, and he a preacher! But they

were having a dreadful time to keep the cattle from stamped-ing."[17] Lavinia Porter recalled that her male fellow travelers were "the champion swearers of the world. They swore at their horses, at each other, at the wind that blew, at the stones in the road. The air was constantly filled with their curses."[18] The trail experience, indeed, seemed to encourage swearing, much to the women's consternation. The first day out of Missouri, the Cooper party came to Spring River, but despite insistent urging the team refused to cross. "In the nick of time a burly fellow came down on the other side and said 'throw me that whip' and presto! that whip began to pop like a volly of musketry and the woods fairly roared with the oaths he rolled out, and those oxen lined up on that bank as if they meant to cross the plains that day. The man handed back the whip with the remark, 'You don't know how to drive cattle. You must swear at them.' "[19]

At home swearing was probably prohibited in the domestic circle; men's more worldly attributes were confined to male spaces. But on the trail the spheres of men and women were merged enough, perhaps, to disturb and trouble women. At any rate, feminine complaints about male vices were legion. "What dreadful swearing! I think they might do without that, sinning their souls away for nothing. How plain we are told 'thou shalt not take the name of the Lord, thy God, in vain.' And yet one would think there was no hereafter, or no God to serve."[20] "We hear nothing but bitter oaths that an all wise and over ruling God our father and our Creator forbade us to take. Such as makes sober and rational people shudder to hear."[21] To most women, swearing was not only blasphemy but an unchar-acteristic way of dealing with tension. Sarah Cummins told the story of a traveling companion whose Dutch oven kept falling into the fire. Finally a hardened westerner who had been watching the scene commented, " 'Well you are not a swearing woman or you would have been using some sort of swear words alright.' . . . the lady smiled and by her look of patient perse-verence showed the folly of any rash speech as a remedy for the many trifling and annoying occurances of everyday life."[22]

Another male emotional release—a way of relaxing tired mus-cles and jangled nerves—was liberal recourse to the whiskey cask which was, by nearly all accounts, strapped onto almost every wagon. Some wealthier farmers and businessmen, like James Reed, could afford to stock the recesses of their wagons with bottles of brandy and champagne, which they brought out to celebrate the Fourth, the crossing of the continental divide, or other special occasions.[23] But most men were content to cask up a few gallons of the local brew. Lavinia Porter complained that their family wagon had become a traveling saloon because "while my husband was a temperate man, yet he was socially and hospitably inclined, and many of the emigrants, taking undue advantage of these qualities, would too frequently for their own good and my peace of mind visit our camp. I knew it was useless to complain or interfere."[24] In St. Joseph, Agnes Stewart found "brick houses and plenty of whiskey. Every man I meet looks like an ale cask himself"; and when the next day four men drowned crossing the Missouri, Agnes naturally attributed it to their drunkenness.[25] Lavinia Porter, by the way, was not as resigned as she claimed, for as she told the story, "One day when no one was around, I quietly loosened the bung of the barrel of whiskey and by nightfall there was nothing left of the precious stuff, save the empty barrel and the aroma of its spilled contents."[26]

These worldly masculine traits were one side of a second set of sexual ascriptions. Women defined their own propriety in terms of masculine worldliness.

> I know we are much nicer
> Than ugly horrid men,
> We do not chew tobacco,
> We do not cuss like them;
> We do not drink cheap whiskey,
> We don't get on a bust,
> The boys don't have to watch us,
> For girls will do to trust.[27]

No, men did not have to watch out for women's conduct; on the contrary, they agreed to the proposition that women were society's moral guardians. "Our company were 'a band brought close together,' and humanized and refined by the presence among us of women—God bless them."[28] The discriminating feminine sensibility was defined in opposition to clear devia-

tions from propriety, female as well as male. Mariett Cummings
one evening camped with some emigrants from the Carolinas.
"They knew about as much as so many Arabs. They were eating
their suppers. The women sat flat on the ground and turned
their backs to us, peering occasionally from under their awful
old dirty bonnets at us as though they had never seen a civilized
person before, which I presume was the case."[29] Lavinia Porter
recalled another group of "unkempt, soiled and bedraggled
women, most of them lean, angular and homely, nearly every
one of them chewing on a short stick, which they occasionally
withdrew and swabbed around in a box containing some black
powder, while a muddy stream oozed from the corners of their
polluted mouths."[30] Images like these defined what women
should not be—namely, like men.

Nowhere was this divergence between men and women more
clearly evidenced than in the dispute over the Sabbath. The
question of whether or not to observe the day of rest was one
that divided trains and parties, but even more was it a question
that divided men and women. For women Sundays were an
essential day for renewal; in the rigorous working routines of
both farm and trail the Sabbath offered women a lone chance
for pause and recreation. Beyond this practical necessity was
the notion that keeping the Sabbath was a bulwark of propriety,
a barricade against the encroachments of male barbarism and
irreligion. Men's routine, as we have seen, allowed periods of
daily rest; furthermore, from the responsible male point of
view, a regular weekly stopover was simply too costly in time. So
on this issue men and women frequently came into conflict; it is
a measure of the weak social position of women that in this
instance, despite institutional and (as it were) divine support for
their position, they usually lost out to male practicality.

Early in the trip, when time pressures were less well perceived, women's wishes were more easily met. "Sunday—a nice
day; here, we stop for the day to rest ourselves and teams, and
think of our dearest friends, at this time attending their
churches."[31] "Once we made a mistake," Nancy Hunt recalled.
"Thinking it was Saturday, we were washing when some traders
came along, from whom we learned that it was Sunday. We
quickly put away the washing for that day."[32]

Soon, however, the necessities of the trip became more imposing, as these Sabbath entries in Helen Stewart's diary show.
May 22, 1853: "It was not our intention to travel on the Sabbath
but we find that we do more harm by stopping than moving
on." June 5: "Oh dear me, I did not think we would have abuse
the Sabeth in such a manner. I do not see how we can expect to
get along, but we did not intend to do so before we started."
July 3: "I think it is hardly right to rest two days and then start
on this day but we are all so wicked that we do far more harm
when we are stopt than when we are going." July 10: "I do not
think it is the best way. Some of them is washing today, but I do
not think [it] right. . . . I would rather wash at night when we
stop than do it on the Sabbath day."[33] These lines convey the
troubled spirit of a woman whose assumptions were being
tested. "Tomorrow is the Sabbath, but oh, how unlike it!" Harriet Ward echoed.[34] Rebecca Ketcham concluded that "it requires a great effort to live as a Christian should on this journey. . . . There is no time nor opportunity to pray except as
they travel along."[35]

The loss of Christian assembly, of social worship, was another
part of women's lament about the Sabbath. At the end of their
trip Maria Belshaw noted in her diary that "Sabbath day has
again rolled around and yet no worshiping assembly have I
seen and have not had the privilege of seeking one for we are
still traveling."[36] Randall Hewitt sympathetically recalled a
young woman sadly singing the words to Robinson Crusoe's
song one Sunday evening:

> The sound of the church-going bell
> These valleys and rocks never heard;
> Ne'er sighed at the sound of a knell,
> Or smiled when a Sabbath appeared.[37]

One gets the sense that had women been able to roust the men,
they could have managed a service; when the wagons did happen to lay by on a Sunday, it was the absence of men from
feminine-organized worship that most troubled the women. On
board a steamboat taking her family to Independence, Lucy
Cooke was pleasantly surprised to hear hymns in baritone
voices: "It rejoiced my heart to look over the guard[rail] down

to the deck and see a company of men singing from hymn books and then engage in reading a portion of scripture."[38] But a day of rest on the trail was more regularly put to leisure uses by men. Samuel Francis, one of the few men who was actively concerned about the Sabbath, complained to his diary one Sunday that "most people do not regard this at all. If they do not travel, they hunt, fish, or anything to pass away the time."[39] Elizabeth Keyes likewise complained that "the men, dreadful to tell, tried fishing, but said they did no sin as they caught nothing to speak of."[40] Nancy Bradley wrote that she and her party "lay over Sunday here. . . . The other Elk Horn Boys camped with us last night, but moved this morning ½ mile to where R. Green was, for the purpose of playing cards without any restraint we suppose."[41]

What was dominant in the projected and perceived views of the emigrants on this issue was the difference between masculine self-indulgence on the one hand and feminine self-denial on the other. Swearing, drinking, and the good times of hunting, fishing, and cardplaying were all marks of an indulgent type. Patience, propriety, morality, and godliness—seemingly the virtues of women—were a counterpoint to male worldliness. The two sexes held contrasting values and placed themselves on different sides of this characterological divide.

The contrasting images of feminine propriety and masculine egotism might suggest that the trail experience emphasized the worst in the male character. Indeed there were those who believed it. "If there is anything in this world that will bring to the surface a man's bad traits, it is a trip across the continent with an ox team," Enoch Conyers swore.[42] Echoing him, Mary Powers wrote home to her mother that "if there is anything that make a brute (yes and worse than a brute for I have seen them lick one another and show sympathy for each other) of man, it is a journey from Council Bluffs across the Plains."[43] Edwin Bryant added his own heavy prose: "The pugnacious and belligerent propensities of men display themselves on this prairie excursion for slight causes and provocations. The perpetual vexations and hardships are well calculated to keep the nerves in a state of great irritability."[44]

On the other hand, as we saw earlier,[45] cooperation was also a prominent feature of the emigration. "I do not believe there is any combination of circumstances that will unite people as closely as are the members of a train, after weary, heartbreaking efforts to surmount obstacles that seem unpassable—months of privation, unending toil, dangers and hardships."[46] Edward Jay Allen wrote home that "there was a friendliness of feeling and a community of interest pervading, that was delightful to witness, and there is no place 'under the cannister of Heaven' . . . where the converse of this would be so sensibly felt, and where the necessity of self-reliance yet at the same time mutual dependence, is so necessary."[47] Katherine Dunlap expressed a balanced view when she noted in her diary that "we see many instances of manly generosity on the Plains. There is no place in the world where the qualities of a man will show themselves sooner than crossing the plains, let them be good or bad. I have met with men and women who were like brothers and sisters to me."[48] Thus while men were perhaps stripped of some social pretense, their basic character emerged undistorted.

At first sight of the emigrant men, observers were impressed by their barbaric and rough appearance. Margaret Frink, somewhat removed from the frontier farming milieu by virtue of her eastern origins and middle-class up-bringing, observed that the men, "a woe begone, sorry looking crowd, with long hair and matted beards in soiled and ragged clothes, covered with alkali dust, have a half-savage appearance."[49] This was in 1850, a predominantly male year, but views from other years substantially agree. Most men were wont to costume themselves as if for battle and consciously cultivate an aggressive and competitive pose, as did John Minto, the one who spent his modest grubstake to arm himself elaborately. "Yesterday we had our Daguerrotypes taken to send back to our wives," John Johnson wrote home. "I had mine taken for Sarah in full California rig. . . . I got me a new revolving pistol that will shoot six times in ten seconds and knife and dirk and hatchet."[50] This was standard male costume and had been since the first days on the road. Elkanah Walker, a missionary emigrant of 1838, described himself as "mounted on a black horse with a white hat, with a leather belt around me, with a knife

laying before, with a powder flask hung to the side, with bullet
mold attached to it."[51] If their intended effect was an imposing
appearance, emigrant men were successful. "The men were
well armed—each one having a rifle, and many in addition to it,
had a brace of pistols and a large knife, which they wore in their
belts," J. Henry Carleton observed admiringly. "The fact of
their moving to such a distance, and by such a route, is in itself a
sufficient proof of their enterprise and courage, though they
are abundantly able to show a stronger one to whoever may
have any curiosity of testing the point."[52] Women, on the other
hand, were more likely to share Lucy Cooke's cynicism: "Our
men are all well-armed. William carries a brace of pistols and a
bowie knife. Aint that blood-curdling? I hope he won't hurt
himself!"[53]

The aggressive male self-image was certainly fully compatible
with the male preoccupation with the hunt, of which we have
seen something already. Hunting had a strong ego-supporting
function for men; a true test of manhood was to bring down a
species of big game. Minto, loaded down with his firearms,
"under a news tip, left camp alone early, his burning desire
being to kill an antelope."[54] However, the hunt was usually
pursued by several males in a group. These hunts helped establish the friendly relations among the men that were essential
for trail cooperation, although this was accomplished by having
them compete against one another for highest shooting honors.
"We had killed a few antelopes along the road . . . and were
fired with the resolve to secure a still greater luxury in which we
had not yet indulged. . . . So I selected Ivan Watt, a crack shot,
by the way, as my companion, and with bright hopes and spirits
high we started to bring in some buffalo meat and thus prove
our skill as hunters from the Hoosier State."[55] Another pair of
successful hunters not only relished the savory wild game but
also "the satisfaction of observing signs of jealousy on the part
of the other men who had never killed a buffalo."[56]

James Reed elaborated on his and his comrades competitive
urges:

> We have had two Buffalo killed. The men that killed them
> are considered the best buffalo hunters on the road—
> perfect "stars." . . . I came to the conclusion that as far as

> buffalo killing was concerned, I could beat them. Accordingly, yesterday I thought to try my luck. . . . Before we left, every thing in camp was talking that Mr. so and so, had gone hunting, and we would have some choice buffalo meat. No one thought or spoke of the two Sucker hunters, and none but the two asked to go with us.
>
> And now, as *perfectly green* as I was I had to compete with old experienced hunters and remove the *stars* from their brows; which was my greatest ambition, and in order too, that they might see that a Sucker had the best horse in the company, and the best and most daring horseman in the caravan.

Reed successfully outshot his cohorts that day.

> An hour or two's ride found us safely among our friends, the acknowledged heros of the day, and the most successful buffalo hunter on the route. . . . Mrs R. will accompany me on my next buffalo hunt, which is to come off in a few days.[57]

If Mrs Reed went hunting with James, and we have no record of her doing so, she was one of the very few women who expressed an interest in the hunt. Margaret Frink remembered that "the animation and excitement of the moment beat anything I ever saw, and I would not, for a good deal, have missed the sight of that great chase over that grand plain," but she was for the most part alone in her opinion. More typical were Harriet Ward's cynical comments:

> [June 12] The young men of our party . . . went out this morning for the purpose of hunting buffalo. They soon discovered a herd of a hundred and fifty, rushed into their midst, fired their guns without effect and finally succeeded in capturing a cow. . . .
>
> [June 16] This morn some excitement prevailed in our company on account of the discovery of some buffaloes on a high bluff near us. Several of our gentlemen seized guns and ran at full speed, when, Lo! the imaginary buffaloes proved to be holes in the land with weeds growing upon them.[58]

Agnes Stewart also expressed negative sentiments: "Two antelopes were coming toward the camp and two of the fellows took guns and chased them, but did not get any and I was very glad, for the poor things were at home and we were the intruders."[59]

Aside from hunting, men's aggressive attitude was most apparent in their frequent fights with each other. By both men's and women's accounts, there was a lot of fighting on the trail; nearly every diary recorded at least one incident somewhere along the road when a male party member got into a fistfight. Indeed, fighting among the men was one of the best noted trail phenomena. Arguments inevitably occurred, and when they did, male tempers flared, and men were suddenly at each other's throats, although the disputes were usually of little consequence. Scenes like this took place daily, within everyone's sight. Most often these fights ended quickly, one man knocked to the ground, the other retiring, but the smoldering bitterness only needed rekindling to burst into the open again. Sometimes the fights were not so restrained, and men had to be kept from augmenting their fists with knives or guns. "Ed had a fight this morning with Bob Parish. Both men started for their guns but were restrained."[60] "After some words Taylor struck at Jim with a drawing knife he had in his hand, then both men rushed for their Guns. But friends rusht in and settled the fuss without Bloodshed."[61] In the Reed–Donner party, just such a flare-up ended with the competitive James Reed mortally wounding another man.[62]

Women had little power to stop the fighting, but they established their independent sensibility by thoroughly disapproving. "Fred and his man quarreled about striking some loose cattle," Agnes Stewart wrote. "Fred struck him with his hand, and then knocked him down with his whip stock. A mean low dirty trick of his. I feel so mortified about it." A week later, "Tom and as usual Fred, came to blows. Tom and Fred are always quarreling about something. I do wish they had not come with us, but it cannot be helped now. Tom is impudent and Fred is overbearing and arrogant, and between the two we have a sorry time. But Fred will repent of this some day, dearer perhaps than he thinks."[63]

Sometimes the women dared to intervene, as did Mrs. Medley when she tried to restrain her husband from thrashing a thieving hired man.[64] On other occasions the mere presence of women inhibited open male conflict. Andrew Chambers recalled that one night his horse was stolen and he, his brother, and a man named Smith doubled back the next day to find the thief "and do something terrible." "Smith," he added, "wanted to kill an Indian." A few miles back they spied their horse, mounted by an Indian who had been hanging around the camps; surging with adrenalin and self-righteous anger the three men jumped the thief. "Immediately Smith insisted on shooting the Indian," but some nearby emigrants quickly intervened. "They urged us to make the women in camp feel easy by releasing the Indian. After consulting for some time, we agreed to let the Indian go."[65] The drama was entirely male, but the feminine sensibility made its influence felt. Violence was avoided by appealing to male pride in the role of protector of women, which was rationalized as having priority over revenge. After a false Indian scare Harriet Ward complained that "after all the excitement I think the gentlemen were somewhat disappointed that they had not *even seen an Indian*."[66] Men were anxious to test themselves against these dangers, but as Catherine Haun noted, the presence of women "extended a good influence, as the men did not take such risks with the Indians and thereby avoided conflict."[67]

Men prided themselves on their strength and steadiness of character, yet outside the circle of family and kin, they characteristically assumed a slightly suspicious and antagonistic posture toward others. To be sure, competitive skills and attitudes were highly valued in the culture of the nineteenth-century United States.[68] But people considered these competitive values to be part of the definition of masculinity itself; competition as a means to a social end had been transformed into a character type, a psychological trait. Competitive attitudes, in short, were a habit, a style, without reference to the pursuit of any particular goal. Hunting illustrates one facet of these attitudes: the intense competition among and between men for prestige and rank. The two masculine themes—strength of character and competitiveness—do not quite fit together; true strength of character does not require a defensive set. The pervasive sense of man pitted against man suggests that men felt insecure and feared their own weaknesses, that male strength was a defensive pose. Weak ego development is, in general, characterized by a lack of fellow feeling and a basic hostility toward and suspicion of other people. These midwestern men seemed to suffer from underdeveloped capacities to identify with other people, possibly owing to insecurity or uncertainty about their essential selves.[69]

There was, for example, a striking absence of male empathy for women. Observers such as James Clyman or Randall Hewitt, both of whom had notable powers of empathy, were certainly exceptions. Andrew McClure paid women the kind of compliment they could typically expect from men: "Much praise for the success of this enterprise is due to our women. Their indefatigable exertions have always contributed to our success and when our program has depended upon their movements they have ever been active and perservering."[70] In other words, women were appreciated, but few men were able to put themselves in their wives' boots.

Balancing even these few appreciative remarks about women were some particularly offensive and insensitive ones. "However much help your wives and daughters have been to you at home, they can do but little for you here—herding stock, through either dew, dust, or rain, breaking bush, swimming rivers, attacking grizzley bears or savage Indians, is all out of their line of business. All they can do is to cook for camps, etceteras."[71] There is no need to retrace here ground already covered concerning women's contribution to the emigration; it should be clear that the remark is most important for what it reveals about the male perspective and the lack of male empathy. It was perhaps just this kind of male insensitivity that convinced Sarah Royce, in her own recollections of the trip west, deliberately to emphasize and defend the role and contribution of women. "Without exception," she asserted, women were "seen doing their full share of the work."[72]

Indeed, men so disregarded women that in male diaries and recollections women were practically invisible. Samuel Hancock's narrative of his 1845 overland emigration is typical in this respect. Hancock traveled to Oregon in a predominantly family train, hired on as a driver in a family party.[73] In his account of the emigration he wrote using the collective second person plural throughout. Nonetheless not only did he express his perceptions exclusively from the male viewpoint (we can certainly allow him that much), he at the same time showed an almost total lack of awareness of the female participants, who in his train constituted close to half of all the emigrants.[74] The few times women did appear in his narrative were in response to the actions of men. During an early Indian scare, "quite a confusion ensued, the females of our company being quite frightened." When the emigrants found water after several bad dry days and the company was overcome with joy, he observed "the women and children clapping their hands and giving other demonstrations that they too were enraptured." Hancock himself called attention to his disregard of women, "for which the reader will doubtless pardon me, when assured they comprised decidedly the most interesting portion of our company."[75] This kind of equivocal appreciation is reminiscent of Tocqueville's claim, late in his second volume, that despite his preoccupation with things masculine and inattention to things feminine, "if anyone asks me what I think the chief cause of the extraordinary prosperity and growing power of this nation, I should answer that it is due to the superiority of their women."[76]

In dramatic contrast, the general sensibility of women was marked by empathy, a process in which the subject attempts to adopt the other person's outlook and situation for the sake of better understanding and communication.[77] Helen Carpenter illustrated this capacity when she wrote, "It has been immensely disagreeable for the drivers today for a strong Northwest wind drove into their faces as they walk beside their teams. Am glad that I am not an ox driver."[78] When their party was forced to travel through the desert at night to find a decent watering and grazing spot, Harriet Ward observed, "The gentlemen were in no very pleasant humor, for all these things try their patience, and indeed I sometimes wonder that it is not entirely exhausted."[79] Agnes Stewart actively empathized with the men: "The men is all very tired. We are to ford. We had to run and put blankets round them all whenever they came out of the water and drenched them all with ginger tea and boiling coffee."[80]

Men saw the overland emigration as a male enterprise and ignored the women; women saw it as a male enterprise too (there was no way they could ignore the men), but through their own particular field of vision. Men were insensitive to women's active part in the enterprise. These differences in perceptions were characterological. Masculine lack of empathy, competitiveness, wordliness, and strength were facets of a male character which men and women alike saw as part of the male condition. Likewise, feminine empathy, propriety, and gentleness were seen as inherent to women. To a large extent these characteristics were evident in the behavior of men and women: men were rough, aggressive, and egotistic, women more sensitive to manners, morals, and the feelings of others. Yet notwithstanding the feminine character, women were demonstrably strong, assertive, hardworking, and more than able to pull their own weight.

"The terms *masculine* and *feminine*," Simone de Beauvoir writes, "are used symmetrically only as a matter of form as on legal papers. In actuality the relation · of the two sexes is not quite like that of two electrical poles, for man represents both the positive and the neutral, as is indicated by the common use of *man* to designate human beings in general; whereas woman represents only the negative, defined by limiting criteria, without reciprocity."[81] We can go just so far uncovering characterological symmetries before we confront the cultural power employed specifically to regulate the options for women.

Perhaps the most obvious regulation was the female costume itself.[82] Men dressed in sturdy homespun and decorated themselves with aggressive accoutrements; their costume was at least functional. Almost as soon as women got on the road, however, they confronted the obvious inappropriateness of the traditional clothing they had manufactured for themselves. Dresses reaching to the ground were clumsy enough around the farmyard, but trail travel made them impossible. "In jumping off the horse alone today, I caught my dress in the horn of the saddle and tore almost half of the skirt off. That I must mend tonight. I have had no dress on since the day we came to Westport but my palm leaf muslin delaine. I mean to stick to it

as long as I can. It is very dirty and has been torn nearly if not
quite twenty times, but another would look nearly as bad in a
day or two."[83]

Most women suffered through it, but others took the bold
step of shortening their skirts or regularly wearing "wash
dresses," those with shorter hemlines designed not to drag on the
wet, wash-day ground.[84] In 1852 a large number of emigrant
women adopted Amelia Bloomer's reformed dress style as a
more sensible traveling costume. "A good many ladies on there
way to California dressed in Bloomier," Solomon Kingerly
wrote home from Kanesville (Council Bluffs), in April 1852.
"Short dress, pantaloons, Hats & Boots. A good dress to travel
in. They look quite handsome."[85] Arriving in Kanesville the
next month, Lucy Cooke noted in her diary: "I wear bloomers,
as do most of the women folks in the different companies."[86]
Frances Sawyer confided to her journal a few days later that "I
think it is a very appropriate dress for a trip like this. So many
ladies wear it, that I almost wish that I was so attired myself."[87]

Almost, but not quite. Mrs. Sawyer, despite the obvious advantages of the bloomers, did not embrace dress reform. It had
a flurry of popularity in 1852 and 1853, and a few women wore
a modified bloomer costume in later years, but dress reform
was not very successful even on the trail, where the irrationality
of the traditional garb was painfully apparent.[88] It was difficult
to deviate from fashion, connected firmly as it was with sex-role
norms. We catch something of this in Harriet Ward's comment:
"We left encampment at an early hour and took a long walk
with Mrs Singletary, whom, not withstanding her bloomer
dress, we found to be a sensible pleasant woman."[89] Women's
concern for appropriate appearance was demonstrably an aspect of their consciousness on the trail. Rebecca Ketcham declared her disregard for appearance—"as long as I look as well as
the rest, I don't care"—but her disclaimer betrays adherence to a
social standard.[90] More typical was Virginia Ivins's recollection
of discomfort when she encountered a party whose women
were "tastefully dressed." "Really they were 'no end of swell,'
and the contrast worried me not a little."[91]

Shame over their inevitably dirty and disheveled appearance
was a consistent theme of the women's recollections if not of the

diaries.[92] "Dear me," a young Missouri woman exclaimed to another preparing to embark, "are you really going across the plains to California? . . . Are you not afraid of being burned black by the sun and the wind on the plains?" "Oh no," the other answered quickly, pausing and then continuing defensively, "and if I am, I can stay in the house until I am bleached out again."[93] At the other end of her journey, fifty miles above Sacramento, Luzena Wilson encountered a gentleman riding east. "The sight of his white shirt, the first I had seen for four long months, revived in me the languishing spark of womanly vanity; and when he rode up to the wagon where I was standing, I felt embarrassed, drew down my ragged sun-bonnet over my sunburned face, and shrank from observation."[94] Lavinia Porter described the trauma of encountering settled society in her dirty emigrant clothes:

> I had no opportunity or time to make a change in my dress. . . . We presented anything but a prepossessing appearance. I dreaded woefully to face the wife who knew nothing of the strangers her husband was ushering thus unceremoniously into her well ordered house. . . . She looked somewhat askance at our worn garb. My trunks were brought in and I unpacked some clean, fresh garments and after the luxury of a good bath and having removed the red dust of the road we gladly donned the garb of civilized society and looked and felt fit to be once more within the pale of civilization.
>
> Such is the power of good clothes, for the unkempt and soiled emigrants had blossomed out into really good looking people. . . . I had worn my shaker sun bonnet so closely and was always so vain of my white hands, never allowing myself to go ungloved save when cooking, that I bore no marks of the emigrant when I discarded my emigrant garb.[95]

Women's self-regulation in costume was encouraged by the sense that society expected, even demanded, conformity to a rigid feminine standard. Women's roles were also regulated by public censure of deviation. Loren Hastings, in 1847, saw a woman riding with a company of men, and "the woman rode with one foot on one side of her pony and the other foot on the other side. This is the greatest curiosity I have ever seen yet, it knocks everything else into the shade."[96] Men did not keep these opinions to themselves. When Harriet Ward mounted on a regular saddle, "a position not altogether compatable with the delicacy of an American lady," she was anxious enough. Then her husband, "who chanced to look back (for I will assure you I kept quite in the rear), burst into a roar of laughter and observed to Trow that he never expected to see his wife crossing the Feather River Mountains in that style. We were happy to abandon our horses and take our good sticks and make our way down [the mountain] as best we might."[97]

We have seen how women were called upon to both substitute for and supplement the work of men on the trail. Yet the women who were so compelled by necessity had to watch that they were not tarred with the brush of unwomanliness. Usually the social censure took mild, rather innocuous forms, heavy, however, in their cumulative effects. Agnes Stewart commented that "we present a sight watching the cattle with a whip"; it was, simply, an unfeminine position.[98] When a rambunctious pony broke loose, Harriet Ward's daughter Frankie "exercised her Yankee ingenuity and caught him" but was then victim "to the amusement of some of our company, who remarked that she should have been a boy."[99]

On other occasions the censure was more overt. "I had learned to drive an ox team on the Platte, and my driving was admired by an officer and his wife who were going with the mail to Salt Lake City. I heard them laughing at the thought of a woman driving oxen."[100] Mary Ellen Todd remembered her mother "always reminding Louvina and me to be ladies, but sometimes it seemed to me that the requirements were too rigid, for I also liked to run, jump and climb, yet I did try to keep from talking and laughing loudly." Mary Ellen was fascinated, as a child will be, with the wagon, and particularly with the whip that drove the oxen. "It was a weapon to be feared. When an experienced person cracked it, you might as well have thought it was the report of a gun." All along the trail she had played at driving the wagon but could not manage that big whip. Finally in Oregon she kept practicing "until I was fairly successful. How my heart bounded a few days later when I chanced to hear father say to mother, 'Do you know that Mary Ellen is beginning to crack the whip?' Then how it fell again when mother replied, 'I am afraid it isn't a very lady-like thing for a girl to do.' After this, while I felt a secret joy in being able to have a power that sets things going, there was also a sense of shame over this new accomplishment."[101]

Underlying male attitudes on the appropriate roles for women was a deeply rooted belief in the natural inferiority of the female sex. These attitudes do not surface in the men's diaries or recollections in a direct way; the sum total of male attitudes, however, certainly does suggest a comprehensive belief in female inferiority. The presence of misogynistic attitudes is suggested by this traditional snippet from central Illinois:

> A woman, a dog, a hickory tree,
> The more you beat them the better they be.[102]

Ralph Carlyle Buley concludes that although men generally prided themselves on their respect for women, "it appeared at times as though the menfolk depreciated the very existence of the women as somehow a manifestation of weakness in themselves."[103]

Midwestern society operated on the assumption that men and women were gifted with separate characters and capacities. Lives lived out on the assumption of such differences were bound to touch different bases, encompass different kinds of relationships, and develop separate rituals. The cultural classification of men and women into masculine and feminine was an aspect of the coexistence of two separate sexual worlds, which I shall examine in the next chapter.

5

The Separate Worlds of Men and Women

Midwestern society had a developed sense of gender distinction. The existence of a strict division of labor and separate cultural character models for men and women suggests that significant portions of men's and women's time were spent in the company of their own sex. Indeed, despite the importance of the family, midwestern society contained separate sexual worlds for men and women, each with its own separate bundle of behaviors and beliefs, each understood and appropriated by the right sex only.[1]

Women's work was in the household, the spaces of women were domestic, and women were expected to conform to a domestic ideal. The social keystone of the system of separate worlds, however, was the nearly total exclusion of women from public life. If we are to understand rural midwestern life we must first appreciate that this was a place and a time in which women played no part in public life. Cultural sanctions separating the spheres of masculine and feminine were so effective that women rarely tested them. Despite some feminist rumblings in a few prominent but distant places, this was by no means an age of open feminine protest. In the trail materials there is only occasional evidence of a woman overstepping customary bounds. When a man traveling in Rebecca Ketcham's party refused his stint at guard duty, his domineering wife approached the captain to obtain her husband's deferment. "Mrs Love had considerable to say in a quiet but earnest manner," but Mr. Gray chose to respond sharply that "he was not in the habit of consulting ladies about arranging night guard." That was the end of the matter.[2]

Another example of women's enclosure, this time with ironic consequences, occurred in the Hecox–Aram party as they completed the last leg of their journey over the Sierras into California in the late summer of 1846. Margaret Hecox, doing the family wash in a mountain stream, noticed that the riverbed was covered with golden specks. "I gathered my apron full of the shining specks and carried it to Mr Hexox, saying that I thought it was gold." Margaret was not welcomed with her discovery. "He laughed at me and seemed to consider it a good joke. This made me angry and I threw it away. I have always been sorry that I did not keep it and wait until I could have it tested. I am sure that it was gold. It was just like the dust they brought from the mines two years later. Besides, gold was afterwards discovered in that locality."[3] The gold awaited discovery by men, for women were not permitted to play that role. These kinds of stories are rare, however, not because men were hesitant to remind women of their proper places, but because women did not often challenge the status quo. Consequently, the diaries and recollections contain few evidences of the conflicts that generally signal social boundaries.

The general male domination of the leadership process, on the other hand, is obvious. Society, composed of men and women, was run by the men; women were allowed no formal roles. Jesse Applegate and Ezra Meeker both wrote that collective decisions of their train were made and enforced by a council of patriarchs; the idea of a formal council was probably something of an embellishment of their colorful imaginations, but it is indisputable that whenever decisions were made, they were made by men alone.[4] Other diaries and recollections mention more informal councils, and these were invariably all male: "Our gentlemen," Harriet Ward noted, "held a consultation and soon came to the conclusion that . . . ," and so forth.[5] At one point along the trail, the Hewitt party held a "council of war" to decide how to treat some local Indians, and because of the considered gravity of the meeting, Randall Hewitt recalled, "the ladies of the party were invited." But this exception proves the rule.[6] As Sarah Royce wrote, while the men met to organize their train, "the few women in the company were busy meantime in cooking, washing, mending up clothes, etc."[7] Parkman captured one scene in its stark sexual segregation, his shorthand diary notes conveying much more accurately than Ap-

plegate's or Meeker's heavy and formal nineteenth-century
prose the kind of "councils" the men held: "The Cap't threw up
his authority, such was the hurly-burly—women crying—men
disputing—some for delay—some for hurry—some afraid of
the Indians."[8] Women had a role to play, privately influencing
the men, but men made the decisions.

This situation on the trail was no different, really, from life at
home. The isolation of women in their homes was a social fact
introduced by the division of labor, but it was further reinforced by the settlement patterns of the Midwest. In 1840, in
the Sangamon River farming country of Illinois, for instance,
there were only about eight people per square mile, although
this figure is slightly deceptive because settlement was somewhat denser along the little creeks that fed the Sangamon. In
western fashion, however, the homes were not built in proximity to each other; each was isolated on its separate farm-
stead.[9] Between the creek-bank settlements, travel was calculated in hours; within the settlements a walking visit to
neighbors was not a casual affair but could take an entire
morning or afternoon.

This residential isolation severely limited the social opportunities for women. Men's responsibilities allowed them to lay
up their ploughs or hoes for the day and ride or walk out to visit
the neighbors or frequent the village store, but women, with
their more or less constant responsibilities at home, especially
the care of the children, could not be so casual. The single most
important distinction between the social and cultural worlds of
men and women was the isolation and immobility of wives
compared to husbands.

The public world, culture and society outside the family, was
the world of men. The Midwest was first and foremost a society
of farmers who for most of the year were locked into isolated
and solitary work on their family homesteads; at these times
public life was accordingly slow, almost nonexistent. But at
other times, and on other occasions, neighboring men came
together in cooperative work. February and March were the
traditional times for logrolling.[10] By late winter a farmer might
have completely timbered a new field, and as the thaw ap-

proached he would ride around to his neighbors and invite the men to "bring the old woman and the youngins" to the log-rolling "bee" or "frolic." "A life in the woods teaches many lessons," one observer wrote, "and this among the rest, that you must both give assistance to your neighbors and receive it in return, without either grudging or pouting."[11] As many as forty or fifty men from the surrounding countryside would assemble on the appointed morning to work the day hauling and piling the felled logs, perhaps burning them in a great bonfire, clearing the fields for plowing the next fall. This was work that one or two men just could not handle working alone.

Logrollings were a first chance for the neighboring men to get together after the winter and break the social monotony that had prevailed since the close of the previous hunting season. These were not only workdays but celebrations of male strength and physical prowess as well. "Each man vied with the other to show his strength. It meant much in those days to be considered the strongest man of the neighborhood."[12] Masculine accomplishment was tested at lifting the logs, rolling them onto four-foot dogwood pikes, and carrying the timbers to the pile, two to four men on each side. Any man "found reaching for the 'long end of the handpike' [the lighter end] was the butt of all jokes the balance of the day," one man remembered.[13] By the same token, one farmer would try to trick another into taking the short end with its extra weight. Sometime during the day one joker was sure to cover the end of a pike with cow dung and incite his fellows to raucous laughter as an unsuspecting bumpkin grabbed "the shit end of the stick."

Midday the host would call the men to tables "groaning under piles of eatables" prepared by the farm women, who often came with their men but worked together performing a separate ritual in the house.[14] After dinner the men continued working until they broke into late-afternoon wrestling, racing, and games of "pull 'em down" with the handpikes. The event sometimes included supper and an evening dance which joined men and women, but usually "just about sundown" the men departed one by one for their own farms and neglected chores.

Logrollings in the late winter marked the opening of the male social season; the harvest was the complementary

cooperative event in the early fall. In those days before me-
chanical reapers, neighboring men circulated to one another's
farms, bringing in the hay and wheat, cradling, binding, and
mowing in gangs. Campaigning for a seat in the Illinois legis-
lature in 1834, young Abraham Lincoln circulated the Sangamon farms at harvest. At one homestead "there were thirty
men in the field. . . . The boys said they could not vote for a man
unless he could take a hand." Lincoln, of course, grabbed a
cradle and led the way around the field, for as every enterprising politician knew, participation in the harvest was a community requirement.[15] A few weeks later one or more farmers
were sure to hold a cornhusking where the men worked into
the night with much rivalry, competition, and heavy whiskey
drinking. "No match at football or shinty was ever engaged in
with more uproarious animation," Englishman William Oliver
wrote. "The yells of defiance, mingled with whoops and yells in
Indian style, arose in one continuous medley and reverberated
far through the woods, whilst an unceasing shower of corn
streamed through the air towards the roofless crib. . . . There is a
plentiful libation of that most execrable of spirits, corn whiskey,
or of peach brandy. A red ear, which is now and them met
among the white flint corn, is always a signal for a round of the
bottle."[16] Occasionally men came together when needed for a
cabin raising, where much the same competitive and boisterous
spirit prevailed.[17]

Whiskey was the common ingredient of these male occasions.
The jug, one settler remembered, "was a thing of prime importance in the assemblages of all men—at log rollings, house-
raisings, huskings and elections. It was essential at all births and
even at funerals."[18] The drinking habit accompanied men on
their trips to the local village, where male social life thrived
between working celebrations, "enlivened by the unpredictable
conduct of men deep in their cups."[19]

One such hard-drinking village was New Salem, an altogether typical village of the subsistence-dominated Midwest;[20]
the midwestern farming frontier of the 1830s, forties, and
fifties was peppered with hundreds of little towns like this one.
At its high point in the mid-1830s, New Salem was a village of
twenty-five to thirty log structures, including a saw and grist

mill on the dammed Sangamon (the economic focal point of the surrounding farmland), a tavern and lodging house, three or four general stores, one with a post office, a grocery (the contemporary name for a saloon), the workshops of a cooper, blacksmith, tanner, wheelwright and joiner, cobbler, and hatter, a carding mill, a doctor's house, and a school. New Salem was served by an unimproved post road connecting the village with Springfield to the south and Beardstown and the Illinois River (with access to the Mississippi) to the north. Farmers of the surrounding twenty or twenty-five miles reached the village center from their outlying homesteads by riding across open country or following shallow trails; farmers from the east crossed the Sangamon at the New Salem ferry.

Men rode in to mill their grain or corn, to trade surpluses in corn or pork for goods at the stores, to have their wool carded or their skins tanned and made into shoes, to call on the craftsmen, and generally to meet their neighbors and socialize. The village was the hub of country life in northern Sangamon County, the little general stores the center of village life. "Throughout the day shoppers and gossipers came and went, or lounged on its porch, reading mail, exchanging news, or talking crops and politics."[21]

Recollections of village life mention women trading eggs, butter, and vegetables for goods at the general store, but women really did little more than pass through the masculine haunts of the village. Sangamon farm women sometimes complained that younger village men disrupted even these brief visits by poking fun at them as they ran their errands. The regular social life of the village was unmistakably male, "ultra-virile," as one historian suggests.[22] The village yawned during the week when the farmers were at home working their fields, but on weekends it awoke as they made their way to the crossroads to spend the day together. On Saturday afternoons country villages would fill up with " 'strapping big' fellows, bare footed and riding their three-year-old colts barebacked. On they would come with a dash, single file, whooping and yelling."[23] In New Salem a horse race came off regularly every Saturday afternoon, followed by a round of drinking, a few fights, and some hands of old sledge or poker.[24] During the mid-1830s, New Salem men spent their social time together cockfighting, bearbaiting, foot- and horse-racing, and gander pulling. A track at the eastern end of the village was reserved for the gander pulls: a goose was strung up by its legs, its neck greased, and as it screeched in horror, mounted men galloped beneath, grasping at the slippery neck until someone succeeded in yanking off the head.[25] Shooting competitions were very popular. "The rifle," Everett Dick tells us, "was the very center of frontier life." Each man would supply his own target, or they would compete at shooting to drive nails, split bullets, or snuff candles. On special occasions like Christmas, men would form a pool to "shoot for the beef"; the first four winners divided the quarters, fifth place took the hide and tallow, the sixth the accumulated lead in the target.[26]

Not the least of the competitive sports was wrestling and rough-and-tumble fighting, frequently in the "no holds barred" western style with its biting and gouging. The willingness to fight was an important social requirement. In his biography Benjamin Thomas tells us that Lincoln's 1831 fight with village champion Jack Armstrong "gave him the reputation for courage and strength that was so essential to success on the frontier."[27] When not engaged in what Everett Dick calls their "bloody, crude, barbarous and cruel" sports, men enjoyed quieter pursuits: ball games, billiards, pushpins, horse swapping, and storytelling.[28]

We can see how the movements of male social life and the cultural forms of male sociality conformed to the contours of the male gender role and character. The common denominator of the male experience was boasting and boisterous competition, the settlement of disputes by resort to force, and the promotion of the hail-fellow feeling that fostered necessary social cooperation.

We can see this male character at work in the public occasions of Midwest society. On the annual muster day for the local militia, all the men showed up for a so-called drill which was usually more a rowdy time of singing, wrestling, racing, gambling, and playing pranks than practice in discipline. One old Indianan remembered those days especially as the time when men came "to settle old disputes and grudges, and hand-to-hand fights were frequent."[29] Men elected officers by putting their candidates forward and lining up behind the man of their choice. The candidate with the longest "tail" was elected.[30]

Politics was perhaps the most refined of the common male pursuits, and the midwestern countryside "seethed with politics."[31] At the local level, politics and social life were woven from the same yarn, spun on the wheel of male social life. Talking politics, defining the important issues—nearly all of them of local significance—was a constant habit. On election day each man stepped forward at the polls as his name was called and shouted out his preferred candidate to the huzzahs or catcalls of his fellowmen. Election day was a local holiday; local Indians called it the day of the "big drunk."[32] "The men went to town, voted, drank whiskey, smoked, swore, wrestled and fought, all for a little fun."[33] All the heads of household in the community turned out, the grocery did a booming business, local candidates or shopkeepers might offer up a barbecue, and a carnival atmosphere prevailed. As with cooperative harvests, men conceived of themselves as part of a male community. To refuse to participate was to define oneself in opposition; no man could ignore the public patriarchy.

Politics tied the community of men together, despite differences between the partisans of Clay and the Democracy.[34] There were emerging differences of class as well. One old farmer later insisted that village life included men of a steadier character, shopkeepers, schoolteachers, and lawyers, who were unwilling to participate in the rowdiest games but instead formed reading circles and debating societies.[35] These were the future political and social leaders of the town, state, and nation; commercial development in the Midwest would swell their ranks with successful farmers, merchants, and politicians as well as create a new class of permanently unpropertied laborers and heavily mortgaged farmers, exacerbating the distinctions of wealth, social status, and power. But for the time being, the social fact of coexistence transcended the emerging differences. William Oliver believed that among all the ordinary rural men he met, "there is an ease and self-possession which is seldom seen, amongst what may be considered their equals" in England, who constantly deferred and kowtowed to their social betters.[36] In the precommercial village men "rubbed elbows" with one another regardless of social differences, and poor farmers, at least, liked to think of themselves along with shop-keepers and lawyers as members of a single male class. "Diverse types were represented in the groups that idled at the stores. Discussions in such groups brought out conflicting opinions and differences in points of view. Men learned what other men were thinking."[37]

The status provided by sex gave this social order its ideologi-cal homogeneity. Men were united by their common roles as heads of household and keepers of the fields. In their elections, male heads of household chose male representatives to make policy for, to administer, and to sanction the social and eco-nomic order of the midwestern patriarchy. The masculine state was the capstone of male control of the public world.

The social relations of men in the community created a capacity for public discourse among men that facilitated com-munication, education, and economic growth. The linkages between men outside their families were rapidly becoming the most important ones for the society of the Midwest, both objec-tively (measured by the progress soon to be made in institu-tional growth, the development of markets, and technological advance and innovation) and subjectively (measured by the increasing importance that public roles, as distinguished from private, family roles, would play in men's self-image). In this male-dominated public world, the culture of men was thought to be the culture of all the people. Indeed, there is good reason to accept male culture as the hegemonic culture of the Ameri-can nineteenth century, which saw itself as the century of prog-ress, construction and growth, all male notions.[38] The antebel-lum Midwest, however, was still a culture of heads of household and sons, men who saw only a glimmer of the greater things to come.

This male public world of cooperative farm labor, village social life, politics, and the state was a world from which women were absent. "Men had the hunt, the chase, the horse-race, foot-race, the jolly meetings at rude elections, school meetings, muster-meetings, cabin raisings, road making and road repairing, pitching horse shoes . . . quite all to themselves. Women of that day attended none of these rough and exciting sports of men."[39] At best women were allowed to be spectators at the milder events.

In most communities the Fourth of July was the social high point of the year, a day for families to come to town and assemble for a reading of the Declaration and a patriotic oration in the grand style. Nonetheless, sexual differences were obvious in the manner of participation. William Oliver, in Illinois for the Fourth in 1842, noted that the men and women filed into the public hall separately and sat, "the ladies on one side . . . , and the gentlemen on the other. . . . It would have been considered the very height of indecorum had one of the beaus offered his arm to any of the ladies . . . . The demeanor prevails at all the public meetings of the sexes, and is a national trait."[40] In the afternoon, after a barbecue of quartered beef and pork followed by pies and cakes served up on outdoor tables, the women would retire to conversation, while the men picked up the day's pace with games and competitions. New Salem men "nearly strained their gizzards out" each year competing to lift the heavy old cannon in the village square. The day's events often concluded with a dance.[41] The sense of the occasion was clearly male, from the flamboyantly patriotic oration to the competitions to the shooting off of cannon, small arms, and firecrackers.

The one public event that women claimed as their own was the religious meeting. Throughout much of Indiana and Illinois, churches were few and far between, so the few dedicated churchgoers met in schools or farmhouses. Annual camp meetings, a tradition through the thirties and forties, were a way to prevent serious backsliding. When it was camp-meeting time, work was put aside and a family might camp out for a few days of vacation. The simple cold meals freed women from most of their cooking chores, and it was one of the only times of the year when wives were free from housework. Women responded by getting into the thick of the meeting; it was often the women who were most prone to emotionalism, who would "get the jerks."[42]

But men were freed from work too, and many used camp

meetings as occasions for general rowdiness and recreation. One observer of the forties testified that at least a quarter of the men "never came on the camp ground unless it was to interrupt the quiet of the meeting." Peddlers set up whiskey wagons at the fringes, where men went "to run, jump, wrestle, play, yell, swear, talk vulgar, and in some instances, there is more mischief done to the morals of the youth of the land about these wagons, than there is religious good effected on the campground."[43] Even here, in religion, women's right to public roles was challenged by the mockery men made of the occasion. Men were free to exclude women from their events, but as this example shows, women's few public events were fully open to rowdy men.

Sexual segregation was the predominant feature of social life up to the Civil War. Buley concludes that "public relations between the sexes were characterized by extreme diffidence and stiffness. European travelers noted that at church, lecture, picnic, or rally the women sat congregated or marched separately, and there was lacking the freedom of relationships which would be expected in a country so proud of its freedom."[44] The rough old male patterns were coming to an end during the 1850s, however, as the gander pull and the horse race gave way to the more civilized pursuits of commercial farmers and civic leaders, a trend finally culminating in the tone and style of the postwar chautauqua.[45] But segregation of the sexes would remain as a rural tradition for the whole of the century.

Sexual segregation extended even to the language of midwesterners. Carl Sandburg wrote that "there were sayings spoken among the men only, out of barn-life and handling cattle and hogs; the daily chores required understanding of the necessary habits of men and animals."[46] We can reasonably suppose that male language was as earthy as the influences of the barnyard, grocer, and gander-pulling ground. We have already heard emigrant women testify that men could swear, yet at home this masculine language was carefully kept to male circles.

Almost no one at the time collected examples of male speech; even today folklorists are reluctant or unable to publish their earthier collections of folkspeech.[47] Some gleanings of late nineteenth-century Midwest vocabulary have come down to us, however, and they do suggest a sexual segregation in language.[48] The names for male animals—boar, stallion, bull, cock—were considered taboo words around women; a boar was known as a "male hog," a stallion as a "stable horse," bulls were "gentlemen cows," and cocks "roosters." By the taint of association no one referred to bull fiddles or bull rushes because of the sexual connotations. Similarly, to avoid the allusion, men stumbled through such contortions as I "pulled back both roosters" on the shotgun.[49] In southern Illinois bags were always "sacks" because the former was a male word for the scrotum; flowers were "blooms" or "pretties" because the female genitals were called by this name; and one never pricked but always "stuck" his finger.[50]

These contortions of the language have traditionally been considered a manifestation of American Victorian prudery.[51] But all other indications are that midwestern men were a bawdy and boisterous lot, and it is difficult to label the male life style "prudish" in most respects. Rather, in normal situations men tempered their language around women, partly in deference to feminine sensibility. More importantly, by shifting to a separate language, men were protecting their own cultural world from the moral scrutiny of outsiders—the opposite sex. Oliver, at dinner with a large Illinois family, found that "during the short time we sat, before and after supper, there were scarcely half a dozen words of conversation—quite characteristic of the people, when the sexes are met."[52]

In contrast to men, women's social relationships were mostly within their families. A certain number of family kin usually remained settled in one area, and for women the relationships among sisters and cross-generational feminine kin provided them with their social contacts. As we have seen, this critical family mass often set out for the Pacific Coast together.[53]

Documenting female social life on the farm is difficult. The male experience is relatively easy to trace since what we know about social life is after all mostly the product of male memories, on which movement and activity left the greatest impression. The defining characteristic of the men's world was action, denied to women by virtue of their gender. For this reason male recollections provide scanty evidence relating to women. That women did not partake of a social life as active as men's, however, should not lead us to conclude that their lives were impoverished—on the contrary, women's lives were rich in emotional and mental resources.

We must look then for a quieter kind of evidence, evidence of a specifically feminine culture. That evidence is to be found abundantly in the knowledge, lore, and superstition that formed the everyday culture of midwestern people. The American Midwest has not been the scene of great folklore collecting, but enough has been preserved to allow us a fairly close look at the cultural conventions of men and women from several midwestern areas in the mid-nineteenth century.[54] Folklorists, however, have not been especially sensitive to the distinctive contributions of men and women in the perpetuation of folk wisdom. Much of what people believed had to do with weather, crops, and animals, and in much of this there was little sexual bias. But great parts of the collected lore were clearly the exclusive property of women.

All women, in all societies, must relate to their own life processes, to the care of children, to courtship and marriage, and to details of the domestic economy. That these things were so exclusively the province of women was a characteristic of midwestern society, and the conventional wisdom, secrets, and superstitions about how they were accomplished were the bedrock of the midwestern woman's world, the things communicated within the kin family from mother to daughter, from sister to sister, or from "granny" and midwife to young wife, neighbor to neighbor. They included knowledge about the female life process—menarche, menstruation, contraception, abortion, pregnancy, miscarriage, confinement, delivery; knowledge about children—who will have a baby, how to determine the number of children, determinants of a baby's sex, birthmarks, nursing and weaning, the care of infants; folk wisdom about love and marriage, as seen from a woman's point of view; knowledge about household affairs, the kitchen, sewing. Thus was women's world structured around the intimate events of family and personal life, events experienced not alone but within the circle of feminine kin and neighbors. Women's world was marked by qualities of personal intensity and inter-subjectivity.

In Adams County, Illinois, the mass of advice directed toward the common problems of women reflected the sympathy women felt for one another. A girl entering her first period will have an easy time provided her "grandy rags" are handled with three fingers when washed. The more you change your cloths, the greater the flow. If you burn your rags instead of washing them you will get thin and weak because you are just burning up your life. Washing your head during the "monthlies" will bring on sickness; taking any sour food or drink during a period will cause tuberculosis. To cure cramps, drink the broth of a chicken, beaten to death.[55] To prevent conception, eat the dried lining of a chicken's gizzard; sleep with your menstrual cloths under the pillow for the first three days of your period; take gunpowder in small doses for three mornings, all the while thinking hard about the desired result. A woman who wants to put an end to her childbearing must throw the after-birth of her last baby down an old well or walk directly over the spot where the afterbirth was buried. Keep nursing your child, don't wean it early. If none of the contraception remedies work, rub gunpowder on your breasts each night, drink a tea made from rusty nail water, or rub your navel with quinine and turpentine morning and night for several days; each of these remedies can induce abortion.[56] The lists of helpful suggestions are as endless as they were ineffectual, but at the very least this feminine lore suggests that women were active in their search for a reliable means of limiting their fertility, and that nine-teenth-century rural women shared a casual attitude about abortion.[57]

Granny women or midwives were storehouses of this wisdom of the feminine life cycle and were consulted by community women in matters of contraception, abortion, and miscarriage as well as menstrual problems. Most important, grannies, and women in general, were holders of the secrets of birth and obstetrics. In rural Missouri a woman in the later months of her pregnancy was supposed to be in "confinement," attending to her wifely duties but not going out in public.[58] By the same token, men (the public) had almost no role to play in the elaborate feminine rituals of birth.

In New Salem country during the thirties and forties, "Granny" Spears, a midwife in her seventies, was said to have attended nearly half of all the births in the area.[59] Women may have preferred midwives over male doctors. One Ozark woman told Vance Randolph in the 1920s that "Doc Holton's all right, in case o' sickness, but I sure don't want no man-person a conjurin' round when I'm havin' a baby!"[60] Given the general sexual segregation of the midwestern social order, it is likely that such attitudes were widely held by nineteenth-century rural women as well. If a granny was not available, a couple of neighboring women performed the midwife's function and kept the men busy fumbling in the kitchen, boiling water.[61] Only women could provide the absolute support and understanding the expectant mother needed.

Women shared the experience, helping young mothers to understand what was happening to them; most important, perhaps, was the plain and simple encouragement, hand holding, and comfort women provided to each other. In addition to personal support, the granny brought her own bag of female folk wisdom about delivery. In Adams County some women believed labor pain could be "cut" in half by placing an ax or knife edge up under the delivery bed. A powder of dry sow bugs taken just at the onset of labor eased the pains and settled the nerves. More cynical grannies might advise a woman in advance of labor to crawl secretly over her sleeping husband, for that was sure to transfer some of the labor pains to him. Breech babies were turned, dilation advanced, stretch marks eliminated by the experience and superstitious wisdom of attendant women. After delivery the granny was able to read the signs—the number of knots in the umbilical cord, the presence or absence of a caul, the meaning of birthmarks—and thus give some reassuring predictions about the child's life. She was also able to advise on the treatment of the afterbirth: if burned, the baby's health might be endangered, if buried the mother was most secure, but the granny could advise on the advantages and disadvantages of the various courses.[62]

Women's culture also prescribed treatments for the many problems of motherhood. Among the many practical suggestions and folkways was a more animistic kind of wisdom: soreness of the breasts could be relieved by rubbing the nipples with some of the afterbirth; a woman having trouble drying up her breasts after weaning or the death of her infant might be advised to squeeze some of her milk on a hot stove lid, letting the steam rise up against the breasts for three successive mornings. Weaning itself was a practice dominated more by the prevailing spirit world of culture than by schools of child rearing; children ought to be weaned in the sign of the legs (Aquarius, the water carrier) for

> If you wean a baby in May
> You will wean it away.[63]

Until the role of healer was finally legislated into a masculine career, women took main responsibility for the health and care of the entire community, male as well as female.[64] The association in the popular mind of women's lore with health care is suggested by the use of a female kin name—granny—for the role of healer. "When sickness came," one farmer later recalled, "reliance was mainly upon nursing, and every neighborhood had its good motherly woman ready to go without money and without price, whenever called upon, and many an old settler can attest the tender soothing care with which they smoothed the aching brow, or administered the cooling draught."[65] Around New Salem, Granny Spears was more trusted and called upon for general health care than the village doctor. "Some of the old settlers will doubtless remember Granny Spears' salve and other medicines. She followed her calling till over 90 years of age."[66]

Women were much more self-consciously aware of the life and care of the body than were men. Women's personal lives, unlike men's, were shaped by passage through a series of character-defining life-cycle events of bodily change. The terrible toll of miscarriage, infant mortality, and maternal mortality certainly impressed mothers with the close conjuncture of death and the genesis of life. In addition, their responsibilities for infant care and the maintenance of family health made

women most conscious of the problems of health. On the basis
of such concerns women built an enormous lore concerning
health and health care. Midwestern farm wives continued in the
centuries-old tradition that placed women in the role of ad-
ministratrix of folk medicines. Given the state of the healing
profession even as late as 1850, it may have been a distinct
advantage that doctors were scarce in the Midwest. Home gardens included herbs for folk remedies, and women seemed to
know substantially more than men the value of wild plants and
Indian concoctions.[67] The principle was "every disease has a
herb that cures it."[68]

It was from these common bases—the experience of being a
woman, of childbirth and motherhood, of healer and nurse—
that a specific female culture took form. Just as men were
united in competitive action, women too shared a unique view
of the world, a common culture.

Moreover, this common culture was given meaning beyond
the family in the social relationships neighboring women enjoyed with one another. Although the opportunities for social
contact were severely limited in the Midwest, nonetheless
women had occasion to come together. There was a female side
to the work bees, for instance; at logrollings, cabin raisings,
cornhuskings and the like, visiting wives joined the hostess in
the kitchen to prepare the midday meal. "They would cook
cakes, pies and chickens. Oh there's so much they had to cook—
roast pigs and roast sheep."[69] Southern Illinois farm women
worked "for a day or two before hand with a most praiseworthy
and successful zeal to twist each article in the larder into the
most various and recondite shapes possible."[70] The ritual of the
kitchen complemented the male ritual of the field.

After dinner, while the men continued their work, the
women might join in a quilting. Frequently, quilting bees were a
distinctly autonomous event, independent of male plans: com-
pleting a trousseau, putting together a friendship quilt for a
departing friend, commemorating an event, or sewing a
mourning quilt for a grieving sister. A single woman would
complete the top appliqué piece, but a group would gather to
do the quilting; the piece was attached to a backing, cotton
wadding or an old wool blanket used as lining, and the layers

were connected with thousands of tiny quilt stitches. A quilting brought as many as twelve women together for an afternoon. We must guess at what women did with their young children, but probably they were underfoot. Women sat around the piece to be quilted, two or three to a side. As the work progressed, the sides were rolled up, shrinking the width of the material between the sewers, and as the women moved closer conversation, which might have begun general and cautious, would grow more and more intimate.[71]

Midwestern women, among the rural women of the whole nation, produced an amazing variety of quilt designs; collectively North American women practiced and invented nearly a thousand different designs.[72] These patterns were traded back and forth, carried from place to place, transformed, and passed from mother to daughter along with sewing skills. This wealth of design bespeaks a women's material tradition, much of which has gone unrecorded and is today forgotten, a handicraft culture concomitant with women's domestic responsibilities. Associated with this were the expected truisms, superstitions, and analogies: never patch an old garment with new cloth; she who sews before breakfast seeks disappointment; it is bad luck to quilt on Friday; sew on Sunday, stick the needle through Jesus' heart.

> See a pin and leave it lie,
> All the day you will cry.
> See a pin and pick it up,
> All the day you'll have good luck.[73]

To an extent, of course, men too possessed a lore that was theirs alone: signs of luck and fate in poker hands and horseflesh, or little wisdoms and superstitions about breeding, stock raising, and animal castration. Hunting certainly contributed its share of specifically masculine stories, lore, and language. But most of the great abundance of traditional agricultural and weather wisdom was without clear sexual orientation. Indeed, while conversation about cultivating crops might most directly interest men it certainly did not exclude women. In Adams County, Illinois, a farmer loitering about the village store wondered aloud to his cronies which was the right sign under which to plant corn. A bold and sassy farm woman trading eggs overheard the conversation and interjected, "I will tell you a good sign to plant corn. You go home, take down your pants, sit your ass down on the ground for five minutes, then get up, and if you don't take cold the next day, it is time to plant your corn."[74]

On the other hand, women brought their own unique perspective to events common to both sexes. Take the wedding night. Here a couple lived through the first of many solitary nights together, alone despite the fact that friends might still be reveling downstairs. Yet the cultural heritage had its way of sneaking in to join the loving couple. There were, for example, multitudes of future signs, many employing the rule of firsts: the first to get into bed or blow out the candle or fall asleep or turn over in bed would be the first to die. Many a couple must have spent their first night sleeplessly watching for signs as the candle burned itself out.[75] Men shared in this tradition of signs but brought with them few specifically male rites and rituals. The bride, however, entered the chamber her head a daze of feminine rules and advice, watching for signs and signals laid down by feminine conventions: she must carefully throw away every pin securing her wedding dress; she must not allow her new husband to hang his clothes in her closet for at least the first seven nights; she dare not sleep in her husband's arms that first night for it would augur an unhappy marriage.[76]

In the world of men such a guiding lore was largely unnecessary, for standards of conduct were actively articulated as a part of masculine social relations. For women, however, the absence of an active communal social life meant that aphorisms, sayings, and expressions of shared culture were needed to meet the many situations a woman had to encounter alone. Women's collective wisdom was oriented most frequently not to the community of women but to the individual. It was perhaps this specifically feminine lore that sustained women in their days of isolation.

Differences between the worlds of men and women are reflected in the emigrant diaries. Despite similarity in content, there was a notable difference in the style of men's and women's writing. Women usually wrote with a pervasive personal presence, most often using the first person. "I am now sitting on a hill side on a stone, a little distant from the camp," Rebecca Ketcham wrote in her diary late one afternoon. "After I commenced writing Mrs Dix called to me to come to her to see a beautiful bunch of verbena she had found. I went and looked about with her a little, then sat down again to my writing. Very soon Camela called to me to see how the wild peas grow."[77] Even in less fluently written women's diaries, the subjective "I" tended to be the ultimate standard of perception. "Met yesterday a very long and steep road coming out of Grande River bottom. I never saw as crooked a road in my life."[78] Men, on the contrary, typically employed the more impersonal "we."[79] Sometimes the referent of this pronoun is hard to specify, shifting with the context. Usually the "we" most clearly referred to the men as a group.

> [May 4, 1851] We traveled 16 miles this day over very hilly road.
> [May 6] This day we left camp at 8 o'clock and traveled 12 miles, camped where we found but little wood and poor water.
> [May 7] This day we gathered up and started after traveling five or six miles it commenced blowing and raining very hard. We all got very wet.
> [May 8] This morning some of our women washed. We gathered up afternoon and traveled ten miles and camped on an open prairie, where we had no wood and but little grass.[80]

The subject of these passages is not clear until the women are introduced; then the "we" seems to be masculine. Another man wrote, "We drove up and turned out our stock to grass while the girls go busy getting supper."[81]

Women diarists typically located themselves in relation to space and time—often taking care to note where they were sitting, what they had been doing, and what was going on around them as they wrote. "The sun is shining bright and warm, and a cool breeze blowing makes it very nice indeed, and it seems very much like home. . . . Oh, they are starting, so I must stop for today. . . . Trying to write walking, but it won't do."[82] Most women did not go into quite the detail Agnes Stewart included in this passage, but men, by contrast, were likely not to bother with any of these, content to assume that the fact of writing itself established a sufficient identifying framework.[83]

Men's writing was usually plain, unadorned, and terse.

> Fri 10 made this day 14 and encamped at the Willow Springs good water but little grass 3 Buffaloes killed the Main Spring 1-½ miles above
> Sat 11 Made this day 20 Miles to Independence Rock Camped below the Rock good water ½ way
> Sun 12 Lay by this day.[84]

Women, on the other hand, frequently employed a range of stylistic elaborations. They took care to identify names of people and places and specify dates and times, while men regularly left names out, neglected to record dates, and abbreviated their words and phrases, sometimes beyond recognition.[85] Most women used extended description: colorful adjectives, qualifying phrases, long passages of explanation and summary. Elizabeth Dixon Smith, who often wrote long passages, commented that "I would have written a great deal more if I had the opportunity. Sometimes I would not get the chance to write for two or three days, and then would have to rise in the night when my babe and all hands were asleep, light a candle and write."[86] It was a rare man, however, who regularly employed elaborating devices in his diary writing.[87]

In general, men and women were concerned with different orders of meaning. There was an almost inverse relationship in the way most men wrote about objects and things, most women about people.[88] The following two passages—both written somewhat more elaborately than the mode for either sex—illustrate the differences:

> [September 23, 1843] We went up to the ford & fastened our waggons to gether as we did at the upper crossing & drove over. This ford is better than the upper one, tho it is a bout 8 or 10 inches deeper than the upper one. Tho we

went strate a craws, & in camped on the bank. Grazing indifferent.

[September 24] We struck through the hill & struck a creek & in camped Grazing indifferent. Dist 12.

[September 25] We continued through the hills & struck a smawl spring in nine miles Grazing indifferent. Then we struck a nonther one in 5 or 6 miles. Tolerable incampement Then we struck a smallre branch at nite. Grazing indifferent. Distance 19.[89]

[June 16, 1853] Frank and a number of young friends are amusing themselves with the "Mansions of Happiness" and judging from their merry laugh, I should think they were enjoying it very much indeed. Father has taken his pillow under the wagon and is having his daily siesta. Willie is watching the horses and I am in the wagon, spending an hour with you, my dear children.[90]

These differences in writing style conform to the differences between the social and cultural worlds of men and women. Speech patterns, it is known, can reflect such cultural differences. "Different social structures may generate different speech systems or linguistic codes. The latter entail for the individual specific principles of choice which regulate the selections he makes from the totality of options represented by a given language."[91] In other words, groups enjoying different social and cultural relations but sharing the same language will make use of different syntactic and lexical selections for everyday communication in a given social situation; these language choices in use are known as codes.[92]

The connections between speech and written language are complicated, the latter mediated by formal conventions that do not apply to everyday speech. But as Arthur Ponsonby notes in his study of diaries, diary writing may be the closest of all written forms to speech. The effort to conform to a stylistic convention requires too much of a person making daily entries. "You have no time to think, you do not want to think, you want to remember, you cannot consciously adopt any particular artifice; you jot down the day's doings either briefly or burst out impulsively here and there into detail; and without being conscious of it, you yourself emerge and appear out of the sum total of those jottings, however brief they may be." The overland diaries fit Ponsonby's characterization precisely; lacking in formalities, they are probably good, though limited, representations of the speech codes employed by men and women.[93]

Basil Bernstein has distinguished between two general types of language codes in contemporary English speech that correspond remarkably well to the contrasting styles in the diary writings of these mid-nineteenth-century men and women. Men's diaries may be characterized by their use of a "restrictive" code, that is, a code drawn from a narrow range of choices: unelaborated prose, written in apparent haste, emphasizing the how rather than the why, with implicit as distinguished from explicit meanings. Such a code typically appears among people in close behavioral connection, sharing common assumptions and expectations. In this context group members can assume that their fellows understand without having everything stated explicitly. The "we" dominates the "I," because people assume a common identity. Restrictive codes are part of a communal situation; the communication of gesture, motion, and physical interaction often substitutes for language and discourages the development of expressive skills.[94]

Women's writing best fits the contrasting designation of "elaborated" code: the use of extended description, modifying words and phrases, and explicit statement. Elaborated codes are required in situations where social connections are weak or lacking and language is employed to bridge the gap between individuals. In these circumstances people cannot assume a common understanding but must use language quite explicitly to inquire and inform. Consequently rather less is taken for granted; clarification, elucidation, and discovery are the primary tasks of verbal communication. This code, then, takes as its subject not a group but individuals (the "I" and the other), places a premium upon empathy, and is in general most often associated with a people-oriented content.[95]

The analysis of the diary writing suggests again that essentially different social situations of men and women were associated with different cultural phenomena. The men's world was made of the stuff of action, a world of closely shared identifications, expectations, and assumptions. In the standardized and even ritualized behavior of men lay the ability to communicate without verbal expression. "The men generally," William Oliver reported, "are not very talkative."[96] For women, however, articulation was at the very heart of their world, for verbal expression could achieve an interpersonal closeness that was socially denied by the exclusion of women from the public world and their isolation at home. In contradistinction to his silent men, Oliver remarked that he had overheard women "unfasten the sluces of their eloquence, and fairly maintain the character of their sex."[97] A large part of women's rich cultural heritage was verbal—women's voluminous lore. And women were required to learn the cultural art of conversation and communication, including letter and diary writing, to make up for the social isolation of the farm.

Psychologically this analysis further suggests that the meek feminine character assumed that she needed to explain and elaborate her feelings in order to make herself understood. Women's empathy for others was the other side of women's concern that their true selves be truly communicated by taking time and care with language. Masculine characters, on the other hand, assumed that they were understood and saw no need to articulate things that seemed perfectly obvious to them. The face men presented to the world, however, was held rigid; no tears were allowed to soften the harsh exterior to reveal the emotional essence within. Men assumed that their public faces, silent and brooding, represented their true selves, but they were fooling themselves. Men hid their feelings from themselves, understood themselves in an incomplete way, but found comfort in the company of their similarly repressed brothers. These were men, in Avery Craven's well-chosen words, "with homely vices and virtues and with more than their share of half-starved emotions."[98]

In the context of these separate sexual worlds the experience of men and women on the trail looks very familiar. For men the trip was a continuation and extension of their social lives at home. The grand encampment outside the jumping-off place replaced the logrolling as the opening social event of the year. Men reproduced their own experience when they organized the trains and parties, so the society of the trail most resembled local militias and local politics. Electioneering for trail office was complete with the panoply of midwestern democracy: campaigning, speechmaking, demonstrating, and patriotic displays. Matthew Field, a correspondent for the *New Orleans Daily Picayune*, was present in 1843 for the election of train officers outside Independence. "The candidates stood up in a row behind the constituents," he wrote, "and at a given signal they wheeled about and marched off, while the general mass broke after them 'lick-a-ty-split,' every candidate flourishing a sort of tail of his own and the man with the longest tail was elected."[99] These ceremonies were less tests of fitness for trail leadership than communal exercises, connecting strangers both to one another and with the patriarchal social life they had enjoyed at home. The results of the elections and the rules of travel were communicated to the women privately by each head of household.

The visible social life of the camps was overwhelmingly masculine. Women were nearly always back at the family fire or perhaps visiting another woman at hers. But the unattached men in the trains and parties were always congregating in some part of the camp for games of cards or storytelling, or rowdier pastimes like ball games, races, and perhaps fights.[100] These male groupings were a magnet for the married men as well. This was most like the public life at the village crossroads back home.

The male camaraderie of country life, in fact, was exaggerated by the dangers and excitements of the trail. "Men were drawn together on the plains as in every day walks of life," William Thompson remembered, "only the bonds were closer and far more enduring. The very dangers through which they passed together rendered the ties more lasting."[101]

This chance for an exaggerated and extended occasion of masculine good times lured men to the trail. Truly one of the great attractions of the trip was the notion of spending the entire spring and summer "in the rough" with the boys, away from the routines of farm work. Trail work was hard, to be sure, but farm drudgery held none of this romantic allure. The idea of an overland emigration struck romantic chords deep within the male breast. One midwestern visitor reported that men "spoke of 'Old Kentuck' and 'Old Virginny' in a tone that sounded like deep emotion," and Indiana farmers "related with glowing eyes" tales of how their fathers had emigrated from the valleys of Appalachia.[102] William Oliver told of how the men at an inn along the National Road in Manhattan, Indiana, listened almost reverently as a gnarled old frontiersman recounted his adventures, supposedly at the side of Daniel Boone, hunting "Injuns."[103] On the trail men could live out collective fantasies that some had experienced in the early days of the midwestern frontier but most had only dreamed of on their staid and settled farms. Here on the trail was an opportunity to bring to life that male self-image. The project of Oregon and California settlement itself included a male vision of life in a time and place where men played a man's role with long rifle and hunting knife as well as plough and cradle.

Hunting has continually recurred as a theme in these pages because of the importance it assumed for emigrant men. It was in this context of male fantasy and the measurement of masculine identity against the standard of earlier, heroic generations of men that hunting took on its meaning. At home the rifle had retained its symbolic if not practical place as the key instrument of male activity. As such, the rifle was the object around which men organized their conception of the trip. By insisting that their rifles would again become the means of securing nourishment for their families, men allowed their own projections to set the form and the content of the journey. Matthew Field captured something of this with a description of the emigrants passing through Westport, men to the front, "rifles on their shoulders, . . . looking as if they were already watching around the corners of the streets for game."[104] Hunting, of course, supplied very little of the actual nourishment for the overland travelers, and experienced observers, from the beginning, advised against wasting valuable time on the hunt. But the men nonetheless insisted on approaching the trip as at

least partly a hunting expedition. Masculine dreams were spun
from visions and images embedded deep within men's character but understood in the simplicity of childhood verse:

> Rise up my dearest dear
> And present to me your hand,
> And we'll march you in succession
> To some far and distant land,
> To some far and distant land,
> To some far and distant land;
> And we'll march you in succession
> To some far off distant land.
> There the boys will plow and hoe,
> And the girls will spin and sew;
> We'll travel through the cane-break,
> And shoot the buffalo.[105]

Hunting was essential to the male way of perceiving what they
were about, just as basic as the division of labor. Men believed
the trail experience could be a fulfillment of all they had been
trained to do and raised to hope for.

In some ways, then, the trip across the plains fulfilled male
dreams of camaraderie, action, and achievement. For women
the experience was perceived in quite another way. First, there
was no relief from the daily drudgery of women's work. To be
fair, the work so familiar at home was the same on the trail, only
more difficult and more frustrating—as any mother who has
tried roadside camping with a family of children can testify.
The burden of work, however, took second place to the disrup-
tion the emigration brought to women's social and cultural
lives. Women constructed a social life on the trail, but in their
diaries and recollections they demonstrated a deep regret at
their inability to sustain close and deep attachments with other
women. Men by habit participated in a cultural life that
abounded in outward forms of sociability, and they found it
relatively easy to adapt to life on the trail. Women, whose
cultural needs were traditionally met in closer quarters, with an
intensity that could survive periods of isolation, found the

superficial relations of the trail inadequate; for them, the trip
was a lonely experience.

The failure of the more organized trains was a bitter disappointment to women who had benefited from the number of
families—and women—the trains brought together. Women
traveling alone with their husbands and children, in the catch-
as-catch-can manner of the trail, always had to be on the look-
out for female company. Watching for women became a central
preoccupation: July 18, 1853, a group of packers passed by, "no
women but twenty men in the camp"; July 19, "twenty one men,
well armed, but no ladies." Each day the survey was made.[106]
When two parties with womenfolk happened into each other's
company, the women often pressured their men to travel together. Rebecca Ketcham was anxious to join forces with one
party "for they have four ladies in the company, and I think it
would be pleasant for us all. There is one young lady who rides
on horseback. If we could ride together I think it would be
pleasant for both."[107] Long rides and long talks together would
have made Rebecca happier.

But since men usually saw little reason to slow or quicken
their own pace to match that of strangers, more often women
had to be content with the fleeting contact they made with other
women along their way. "I visited a lady today at a train which
had halted not far from ours," Margaret Frink wrote, "an
unusual incident on this journey."[108] Mrs. Frink had a particularly rough time since she traveled with the nearly all-male Gold
Rushers, but her perceptions were typical for women in all
years. "You can't imagine," Mrs. Benjamin Ferris wrote, "how
relieved I am to find I am not the only female of the party. . . .
Mrs P. is an exceedingly quiet appearing lady, and has an infant
only four weeks old. I am determined to like her. . . ." Mrs.
Ferris, a fashionable lady from New York, commented on the
fragile feminine contacts: "We are as much acquainted in five
minutes as though we had known each other all our lives. The
formalities of the drawing-room are here out of place—it is 'How
do you do?' with a hearty shake of the hand, *sans ceremonie*."[109]

Brief contacts were not always all women had. If several
women found themselves traveling together, or if a family
party included a number of female kin, they would visit to-

gether as they traveled along, perhaps walking in a group "talking over our home life back in 'the states,' telling of the loved ones left behind, voicing our hopes for the future in the far west and even whispering a little friendly gossip of emigrant life."[110] Occasionally the women of a party would form a group for a little excursion. "This morning was bright and beautiful. Fedelia, Susan and myself [sisters-in-law] started before the teams that we might enjoy its fullness and the beauty of the scene."[111] Groups of women would visit while they did their washing or tended to their toilet. And women continued to attend to the little conveyances of friendship whenever they could: "Sally Homm came to see me, and tucked my dress and commenced to shorten Jessie clothes."[112]

Perhaps women's most important relations with each other were expressed in the sisterhood of the sickbed. Women took it upon themselves to act in nurturant and nursing roles for the sick and injured about them, most especially for stricken women. "Tonight we visited an ajoining camp to see a lady and her little daughter who had been turned over in a carriage today while coming down a steep mountain-side," Frances Sawyer noted.[113] Many a woman had her spirits lifted by the gentle hands of a formerly unknown nurse who came in from a nearby camp to sit up with the afflicted. At one point along the road Esther Lyman was so ill "I fully expected to die. Joseph was almost distracted at the thought, and I think my grave would have been on the plains, if I had not had a comfortable place to ride in and one of the best of sisters to care for me."[114] The quality of mutual feminine concern is well shown in an entry from Lucy Ide's diary. A woman in a party of strangers died one night.

> We advised them to hitch up their teams and come over to us and we would do all we could for them. They did so. She had no lady friend with her, but her friends did all they could and seemed almost heart broken. The little child was only eight months old, but the men cared for it as nicely as a woman. . . . Lucinda and Mrs. H. Hunter washed and dressed the corpse. She was a nice looking lady, very poor and looked as though she had been sick a long time. I went

to her trunks and got out her clothes; she had everything
very nice—had suit after suit of underclothing, and one suit
beautifully made and laid by itself I thought, especially just
for this occasion, it so impressed me that I took it. We put it
on her, and the men went to town and purchased a coffin,
in which she was gently placed. You can scarcely imagine
how sad we felt, as we lay camped by the river bank, with
this strange lady lying dead, dressed for burial in a covered
wagon, a few steps away. Lucinda, Lena and Nellie Eager
sat up by the wagon (occasionally wetting her face) all
night.[115]

At such times women took charge, and men took directions. In
the many mentions both women and men made of sickness and
injury along the trail, women played the active roles, men the
passive.

This was even more the case with childbirth, when men were
absolutely incapacitated and women in fine fettle. Woman's
work continued on the trail, and childbirth was no exception to
the rule. Of the 122 families reconstructed for this study, 16
wives bore children on the trail; this is slightly higher than the
general birthrate for the mid-nineteenth century and suggests
that neither pregnancy nor expected delivery somewhere out
on the road was perceived as a barrier to women's travel.[116] But
at delivery women wanted women to assist: what woman was
prepared and willing to be alone, with just her husband? If
there was no sister in camp, men desperately rode ahead or
back looking for a surrogate midwife or doctor. These situations were common, and stories such as this one, told by Merritt
Kellogg, typical. A man came galloping into the Kellogg camp
late one night.

He said that his company was ten miles ahead and that with
them was a young woman who was about to be confined.
He said that she was the only woman in the company. Her
husband was a young man and they had not been married
quite a year. All of the men, ten in all, in their company,
were with one exception, single men. The one exception
was a rough sort of fellow. He said he had come back in
search of a woman to help the young woman in her trou-

ble. [The tale] touched my wife's heart and she said, "I am
lame, and ought not to go, but that woman needs help."
She then slipped on a pair of my trousers under her dress,
then mounted the mule man-fashion, and galloped away
with the man. . . .

The baby was born and both mother and child were
doing well [when they arrived the next morning]. My wife
cared for them both through the night and then turned
in to her bed in our wagon and we hitched up an drove
on. . . . All the pay my wife received was the thanks of
the couple, who, like ourselves were travelling without
money. She also had the satisfaction that a person feels in
doing for others as they would like others to do for them
under similar circumstances.[117]

At these dramatic times women's relationships with one another impressed even on themselves male documentation of
trail life. With childbirth suddenly upon them, men, too, understood the importance of women's relationships with women.
But for women there was no forgetting at any time; the need
was only more desperate at delivery. Women were haunted by
the fear that the trauma of leaving home would be repeated in
the loss of whatever feminine company they had been able to
find along the way.

When Charlotte Stearns Pengra began her trip in 1853 with
her father's party, the Stearns clan, she was prepared to enjoy
the trip in the company of her sister and two sisters-in-law.[118]
On April twenty-eighth while the party was camped, Mrs.
Pengra, with several women from other parties, rode back a few
miles to attend a woman suffering from something Mrs. Pengra
labeled the "camp colic." "I thought her case almost helpless,"
she wrote in her diary, "but after applying numerous remedies
we suceeded in relieving her." Upon her return Charlotte
found that the party had separated (for reasons unstated) and
was to reunite in Council Bluffs. For the next few days Charlotte and Bynon Pengra, with their children and Mr. Pengra's
brother, traveled alone, trying to link up with their kin. "I feel
lonely and almost disheartened," she wrote. When they reached
Council Bluffs, found none of their family waiting, and realized

they must have passed them somewhere among the Iowa hills,
she wrote, "Feel very tired and lonely—our folks not having
come up." Two days later, Wednesday the eleventh of May,
with every day spent waiting a dangerous delay, Mr. Pengra
made up his mind to move his wagon to the Missouri ferry.

> All was hurry and bustle this morning till about noon
> preparing to start for the river, washing the waggon and
> packing, cooking, ironing and doctoring one of our steers
> feet kept us all busy—till we started then I felt that indeed I
> had left all my friends save my husband and his brother to
> journey over the dreaded Plains, without one female ac-
> quaintance for a companion,—of course I wept and grieved
> about it but to no purpose. . . . I dropt a farewell line and
> directed it to David [her brother], also a short letter to Wm
> [a family friend]—and left them at the [post] office as we
> passed through the city.

Crossing on the ferry she met "a Mrs Fordham from Rock
Island, a lady that I have seen before on this journey, received
an invitation to join them." Here was a chance for company!
But that evening she wrote despondently, "Are not encamped
with them tonight . . . , have no company near so—feel rather
lonely." The Stearns clan arrived in Council Bluffs the next
day, and Charlotte's sister found the letter waiting. In her diary
Velina wrote:

> Sister's letter was written Wednesday. They have gone on.
> Her letter shows what anguish of spirit she felt at times
> being separated from us just as she entered the most
> dangerous part of the journey. Dear Sister, shall we ever
> meet again in this world, or is our separation for time? Oh,
> may God protect you through the way and bring you to the
> desired haven![119]

The sisters would not see each other again until they both
arrived in Oregon.

For Mrs. Pengra the demands of the trail continued, working
all evening and into the night, traveling hard during the days.
Through May and June the Pengras traveled with the Fordhams and another family, the Allisons. Charlotte struck up a

friendship with Mrs. Allison: "I have found her a sister Adventist." During the period Charlotte's entries in her diary are studded with references to her small affairs with these women. For instance, on May 20, "word came to the camp that a lady encamped some two miles back was sick and needed aid. Accordingly Mrs Allison and I hunted up our husbands got them to saddle two horses and started—had a pleasant ride, found the lady quite comfortable in bed in a waggon with a little daughter—perhaps an hour old. Gave it a name (Sarah Emily Bondfield) wished her success and rode back—reached our camp about dark, well pleased with our expedition." Despite the overwhelming work load, these occasions of feminine society kept Charlotte reasonably well disposed.

She had to know in advance, however, that the Allisons and Fordhams were bound for California. When they reached the parting of the ways after South Pass, early in July, the parties separated, leaving Charlotte to travel on in the company of her husband, brother-in-law, three single men, and her children. For the rest of the journey Mrs. Pengra recorded seeing and talking with only one woman, and from that parting in early July her diary entries turned dour and upset. The dominant theme became her work and her exhaustion: "Tired enough for the rest that night comes to give"; "Very tired"; "As usual am very tired"; "Am very tired." Finally, on August ninth she came down with an undiagnosed fever and flux which confined her to the wagon for a week. Perhaps what bothered her most she recorded on July seventh: "Feel very lonely having no female companion."[120]

The loneliness, isolation and dread of loss that women felt frequently brought to mind friends they had left behind. "How often I have thought of my dear friend Mary E. Ballard," Harriet Cummings confided. "How earnestly do I pray that she may be happy and that she may never know sorrow and care. How I would like to see her and hers."[121] "This is a beautiful morning," Esther McMillan Hanna wrote. "I think of home and the dear ones there; each day I am getting farther from them."[122] Agnes Stewart, desperately missing her lifelong friend Martha, wondered "whether it is my nature to love so well, or because I have no one else to love, I do not know. But one thing I do know; I miss you more than I can find words to express."[123]

This catalogue of women's laments could be continued for pages, so vocal were women about their disrupted relationships. It is the contrast with men, however, that is most striking. In their diaries most family men accompanied by their wives were virtually silent about the loneliness or isolation they must have felt. But then men were by no means short on company; there were always other men on the road. More importantly, men were on familiar ground, easily able to communicate with strangers through the silent languages of male competitions and solidarities, if not casual conversation. Women, on the other hand, were living out a male-constructed enterprise with little control over its social terms. What feminine relations they could construct existed only at male pleasure. The anguish women expressed was a measure of the importance that same-sex relations held for them, and of how much they needed their own autonomous context for living out those relationships.

6

The World of the Family

Despite the vitality of such frontier themes as violence and rowdyism, Indians and mountain men, freedom and the open life, the dominating social motif of the nineteenth-century West was the homestead: a highly self-sufficient farm, autonomously owned, operated, and sustained by a husband, wife, and children. Indeed, the only assured way of attaining permanent social position in the Midwest was through marriage and family making; the separate worlds of men and women existed within this context. In Arthur Calhoun's words, on the frontier "the psychology of domesticity was supreme."[1] Not only did most men and women marry and raise families, they believed this to be their highest calling. Yet given the strict sexual division of labor, the rigid sex roles, and the existence of separate social and cultural worlds for the sexes, the connection of men and women in marriage was of necessity conflictual.

Outside the household mixed-sex gatherings were few: men and women sitting down to a meal at tables spread under the hot skies of Independence Day; men and women dancing together to the fiddler's tune after logrollings, cornhuskings, or harvests. At almost all other times the principle of sexual separation prevailed. At a July Fourth feast on the trail, John Minto remembered the tables being set for dinner four times, "the oldest men—according to the prevailing custom—being served first."[2] On the other hand, William Oliver noted that women at a family feast rushed through their dinners so they could prepare the next course for service to husbands and fathers, who were granted a leisurely meal.[3]

After a working bee, when field and kitchen work were completed, dances were the exception; more often women congregated to gossip in the kitchen while men hung about the front door drinking until it was time to go home.[4] Almost every community had its dances, however. " 'Turkey in the Straw,' 'Arkansas Traveler,' or 'Money Musk' would cause the feet to shuffle and partners for a quadrille would follow circle all, grand tail back, everybvody dance, right hand to partner, grand right and left."[5] On the trail near Fort Bridger in 1847, Loren Hastings wrote that "at night having a fiddle & fiddler, we went up with our wives to Ft. & danced until 2 o'clock. I showed Bridger's wife & other squaws how to dance U.S. dances. There was some wild romance in this."[6] Weddings were the social occasion when the sexes mingled most thoroughly. Dancing and merrymaking went on late into the night. "I have an invitation to a wedding next Thursday," Charles Clarke, a Sangamon County farmer wrote home to his New England parents. "We shall probably stay all night as is the custom in this country."[7] Sometimes the partying and dancing continued the next day at the "infare" thrown by the groom's parents.[8]

When there was a party and dance, married folk as well as the young joined in the dancing. But these mixed-sex occasions were dominated by young people and took on the heavy atmosphere of courtship. Married couples would often retire early in the evening, leaving the floor to the belles and beaux. Accounts of dances on the trail, for example, nearly always emphasized the youthfulness of the dancers. While the married adults anxiously met to decide on a plan for the two-day crossing of the waterless Nevada desert, nineteen-year-old Mary Burrell, her fiancé Wesley Tonner, and other young people from nearby parties staged a "concert" and held a dance on the desert's edge.[9] Young Jacob Harlan remembered that "every night we young folks had a dance on the green prairie," and seventeen-year-old Susan Parrish danced with the young drovers of her train to "Money Musk," "Turkey in the Straw," and "Zip Coon." Compared to their worried parents, Susan remembered that she and her friends "were a happy, carefree lot of young people unmindful of dangers and hardships. . . . There was plenty of frolic and where there are young people together there is always love making."[10]

By "love making" Susan Parrish meant something very different from the casual intimacy that now prevails among the young; rather, lovemaking referred to the kind of relations young men and women established as a part of the process of courtship. Dances and other cross-sex social gatherings were rare chances to establish courtship relations. Nearly six out of every ten emigrant wives married before their twentieth birthdays, and by their twenty-fifth year only one in ten women remained unmarried. Men, who had to prepare themselves to support a wife and family, typically spent some of their youthful years traveling, surveying their prospects, and perhaps starting a farm before marriage. Hence there was a gap between marriage ages for men and women of about five years, but nearly six of ten men were married by twenty-five, eight of ten by thirty.[11] Despite this steady procession to the altar, however, social opportunities for young men and women to meet, get acquainted, and have a good time together were limited by the work they were expected to perform, the isolation of their farms, and the clear boundaries separating the sexual worlds. There was, then, a sense of serious intent in the courtship of the young, for limited social contacts were expected to pay off in marriage at a relatively early age.

Courtship was a search for a proper life mate, someone with whom to set up housekeeping and homesteading. The great bulk of courtship lore and superstition concerned not whether one would be truly loved, but whether one would be married at all, and to whom. Tea leaves, new moons, the stars, and wells were thought to contain signs of these future events. Finishing a quilt and removing it from the frame, young women tossed a cat into the center and bounced it; the cat always moved toward the girl who was to marry next.[12] In Adams County, Illinois, about 1850, two sisters set up a conjure to discover the identity of their future mates. The reflection of a glass of water in a mirror, looked at over the shoulder through a hand-held looking glass, could divine the future.

> One of the sisters said she saw a man riding on a white mule up to the house. The other sister took the glass and screamed and said she saw a coffin, and fainted. It broke up the party that night. And it was not six months until she died. Two years after that the other girl was standing on the front porch and she saw a man riding up the lane on a

white mule to buy some cattle from her father. She
laughed and said "that is the man on the white mule I saw
at the Halow'en party." Time went on and she did marry
the man on the white mule.[13]

Such tales, drawn from local experience, were legion. The
appeal to fates beyond human control had the effect of calming
anxieties about marriage. But why, in a world where after all
literally everyone married, would men and women worry so
about whether or not *they* would find mates?[14] Anxiety over
marriage prospects may well have been a result of the cultural
and social separation of men and women. Courtship and marriage meant a change in behavior that everyone desired and
hoped for; yet few could have predicted, on the basis of their
own experience, what marriage might require of them. The
nagging fear of young people must have been that social relations would go on as they had, men with men, women with
women, that a woman would live an old maid, or a man an old
bachelor, with (as one male emigrant said) "all the eccentricity
usually belonging to that sweet class of fellows."[15] No one
wanted to be eccentric; everyone wished for propriety.

People were anxious to marry, but what of the quality of
feelings between men and women? What of romance? Sexual
attraction we can assume to be a given of human experience.
And assumption must suffice, for aside from the knowledge
that husbands and wives nearly always slept together on the
trail, these historical sources allow not even a glimpse at sexual-
ity; this was one of those human concerns too dangerous to
commit to paper. But what about what Edward Shorter, in his
study of the modern family, calls "the capacity for spontaneity
and empathy in an erotic relationship"; what about marriage as
"a vehicle of self-exploration and self-development"? Shorter
believes that romantic love has been a part of the American
experience since the seventeenth century.[16] But the division of
the sexes surely mitigated against romance; the evidence so far
suggests that this kind of mutual self-exploration must have
been largely unobtainable in the context of midwestern society.
Indeed, nearly all the evidence one can marshal concerning the

relations of midwestern men and women suggests that the
notion of companionate marriage was foreign to the thoughts
and feelings of ordinary farm folks.

The cultural remnants of ordinary people on this question
are few and require a good deal of interpretation. To be fair,
the overland diaries, in which the emigrants spoke for themselves, were written under the most inauspicious of circumstances; for all the romance of the trip itself, there was little
time for intense interpersonal involvements between men and
women on the trail. People were just too busy for that. The
diaries do reveal some interesting details. Many women, for
example, addressed their husbands by their surnames in their
writings: Mr. Hanna, Mr. Dunlap, Mr. Frink, or Mr. Sawyer.[17]
And for their part, husbands rarely mentioned their wives in
anything like a personal manner. Add to this William Oliver's
observation that husbands invariably called their wives, regardless of age, "old woman," and a decidedly unromantic view
of sexual social relations begins to take form.[18]

Unfortunately this evidence does not add up to much.
Folkloric materials offer another way of reconstructing popular
feeling, and in one area of folk expression—traditional
balladry—midwestern people took up romance as an important
theme. An analysis of popular midwestern ballads helps to
recreate the sensibility associated with sexual relations.

The rural farm folks of Indiana, Illinois, Iowa, and Missouri
shared a folksong tradition linking them to the British ballads
of the sixteenth and seventeenth centuries; these ballads, or
"ballats" as they were called along the Ohio, were imported to
the Ohio Valley in the early nineteenth century by Scotch-Irish
settlers from Pennsylvania and the upland South, and from
there spread throughout the Midwest.[19] In 1850, British ballads
filled an important place in the song bag of midwesterners;
indeed, among the songs collected and dated as popular during
the antebellum years, British ballads outnumbered native songs
by two to one.[20]

Native American song took up the question of relations between the sexes only rarely. Traveling bards or local male
songsters avoided sexual topics in deference to nineteenth-
century mixed-sex conventionality, much preferring to com-

pose songs of disasters, occupations, or comic fillips. In marked
contrast to native songs, British ballads in midwestern culture
focused on affairs of the heart. They sang of real people with
real passions and conflicts, but who inhabited a realm of
princes, princesses, knights, devils, and fairies, lending to the
songs an air of timelessness. Perhaps, as one scholar suggests,
British ballads simply "said it all," and native pieces had to make
specific and local statements to become popular.[21] The traditional songs, however, were at the same time franker in their
treatment of sex, physical love, and offbeat relationships. Although American versions invariably watered down the earthy
language and allusions, the sexual content was never obliter-
ated, only disguised.[22] In fact, censorship seemed to discrimi-
nate *in favor* of the English love ballads, for although in England ballad topics ranged from medieval minstrelry, magic, and
historical events to sexual relations, only the last topic enjoyed a
continuing tradition in North America. These ballads, plus a
small number of native love songs, made romance a leading
theme of the midwestern folksong repertoire.[23]

These songs of romance expressed a distinctive and uniform
perspective on the problems of the relations between the sexes.
By no means were they celebrations of romance; rather, they
were cynical about the possibilities for romance, love, and even
marriage, yet sympathetic to the difficult task people faced in
reconciling gender differences. There were no easy answers,
the songs reminded.

Most striking was the ballads' contrasting treatment of men
and women. Women were the more active of the two; indeed,
they were nearly always the central characters. Like "Lily Munroe," who disguised her sex and fought with the army in order
to rejoin her enlisted lover, these women were nothing if not
plucky.

> My waist, I know, is slender,
> My fingers they are small.
> But it would not make me tremble
> To see ten thousand fall.[24]

Men played the hero's part in many British ballads, but almost
none of these achieved folk popularity in North America.[25] In

the romantic ballads of the midwest, men took a backseat to
women, but the flow of the dramatic action was often determined by the flaws in the male character.

Men in the ballads were a constant disappointment to
women. Women's needs for sentiment, passion, and sensuality
combined with constancy were nearly always betrayed by masculine incapacity. Male passions, when aroused, were almost
solely of the flesh, and not to be trusted. Through the songs
women called out a warning to their sisters:

> Come all you fair and tender ladies
> Be careful how you court your men.
> They're like a star in a summer's morning.
> First appear and then they're gone.
>
> They'll tell to you some loving story,
> They'll tell to you some far-flung lie.
> And then they'll go and court another,
> And for that other one pass you by.[26]

Women who succumbed to the male lure of passion met a
common fate: pregnancy, certain disgrace, and final punishment at the hands of their lovers. The songs begin,

> I'll tell you a story about Omie Wise
> And how she was deluded by John Lewis's lies,

and end in a formulaic but telling manner.

> "O pity your infant and spare me my life,
> And let me go rejected and not be your wife."
> But he kicked her and cuffed her, until she couldn't
>   stand,
> And then he drowned little Omie below the mill
>   dam.[27]

Perhaps the most popular and lasting treatment of this theme
was the traditional ballad, "The Daemon Lover," known in the
United States as "The House Carpenter." In its original British
version the devil, disguised as a returning lover, tempted a
woman to abandon her husband and children and go with him
across the sea in romantic reverie. The midwestern variant

made the lover human, but he continued to play the tempter's role. The heroine has a brief moment of romantic glory as she prepared to leave with her lover.

> She went and dressed in her very best
> As everyone could see;
> She glittered and glistened and proudly she walked
> To the streets on the banks of the sea.

But the moment was painful, for every listener knew doom was approaching.

> They hadn't been sailing but about three weeks,
> I'm sure it was not four,
> Till this young lady began to weep,
> And her weeping never ceased any more.[28]

She cries not for her husband, the abandoned house carpenter, but for the children she has lost forever. As the ballad ends the fated lovers sink deep into the salt sea. Romantic love, the song reminded, was a sore temptation to women with passionate needs, yet it was a temptation that would end in disaster—loss of honor, home, and family.

Folksong took a stand against romance. Romantic love, in the words of folksong scholar Bertrand Bronson, "is in these songs an illness from which no one recovers."[29] This does not mean that romantic feelings did not exist, or that people had no need for intense sexual involvements; the evidence does suggest, however, that people interpreted such feelings with caution and hesitated to act in impulsive ways with members of the opposite sex. By these verses, boys and girls grown to men and women in separate sexual worlds were offered few romantic illusions about the possibilities of cross-sexual understanding and mutuality.

Forsaking romance, and marriage as well, was an option presented by the desperate woman's lament, "I Never Will Marry."

> I never will marry
> Nor be no man's wife.
> I intend to be single
> All the days of my life.

The alternative was rarely tested, however, for the woman of the song invariably ended her days quickly with a fatal plunge into "the water so deep."[30] Real women must have found as little consolation in such mock tragedies as in the dreaded possibility of living as old maids. The conflict was sidestepped with a touch of realism and humor in songs like "Grandma's Advice," sung along the Wabash. Grandma typically warns the young woman "of all false young men to beware."

> "And now my dear daughter, pray don't you believe,
> For men will fib and constantly deceive;
> They will cruely deceive you before you are aware
> Then away goes poor old grandma's care."

After following her grandmother's advice and rejecting several suitors, however, the young woman has a change of heart.

> The next to come courting was young Farmer Grove,
> With whom I exchanged most bountiful love;
> Of sweet truthful love one should not be afraid.
> For it's better to be married than to die an old maid.

> And now I'm convinced there must be some mistake,
> When I think what a fuss these old folks make;
> For if all young ladies of young men had been afraid,
> Why grandma herself would have died an old maid![31]

But midwestern song did not hesitate to point out the sadness of the hearth. Songs of lament over unhappy marriages were very common.

> When I was single, I went dressed so fine,
> Now I am married, go ragged all the time.
> CHORUS: Lord, how I wish I was a single girl again.

> Dishes to wash and spring to go to,
> Now I am married I've everything to do.

> Two little children, lyin' in the bed,
> Both of them so hungry, Lord, they can't hold up their
>   heads.

> Wash um and dress um and send um to school,
> Long comes that drunkard and calls them a fool.

> When I was single, marryin' was my crave,
> Now I am married, I'm troubled to my grave.[32]

Women, left with little outlet for their needs except through the drudgery of marriage, were often portrayed as revengeful harpies; married men, on the other hand, generally played weak and docile roles. In "Our Goodman" a drunken husband returns home from his masculine haunts to find another man's horse, hat, sword, etc., where his should be. His wife irritably complains that his eyes are deceiving him, that these objects are really cows, churns, milk dashers, etc. Finally he calls,

> "Come here my little wifey,
> Explain this thing to me.
> How come a head layin' on a pillow
> Where my head ought to be?"
>
> "You blind fool, you crazy fool
> Can't you never see?
> It's nothing but a cabbage head,
> You drunk as you can be."
>
> I've traveled this world over,
> Ten thousand miles or more,
> But a mustache on a cabbage head
> I never saw before.[33]

His wife's transparent lies demean his intelligence, but the husband's drunkenness enables him to play out a fool's role. As the last stanza shows, he sees through her deception but does nothing. Dominated by his resentful wife he acquiesces in his cuckolding.

In another old ballad, the familiar "taming of the shrew" theme is carried out, the husband fully vindicating his masculinity by beating his recalcitrant wife,[34] but such decisive husbandly action was uncommon in song.[35] More typically, as in "The Farmer's Curst Wife," the husband is victim to his wife's hatred. In the song the farmer bargains with the devil to take his bitch of a wife away, but she is as uncontrollable in hell as at home, and the devil returns her.

> She found the old man lyin' late in his bed,
> Oh, daddy, be gay;
> She found the old man lyin' late in his bed,
> She picked up the butter stick and paddled his head.

The poor husband is essentially passive throughout the tale and ends by having the tables turned on him, damned now by his wife's new hell-trained skills at torture. Although the song concludes with the masculine warning,

> That goes to show what a woman can do,
> She's worse than the devil and she's worse than you,[36]

the victor of the piece is indomitable woman. There was no masculine ballad tradition that came close to rivaling the dominating female perspective in these ballads.[37]

After a lifetime of listening, observing, and collecting, Allen Lomax concludes that these songs were "women's songs, attached to the household and fireside. The men, left to themselves, sang humorous or bawdy songs . . . , or composed songs about work or deeds of violence." The songs of "love and death," as Rusk calls them, were "vehicles for fantasies, wishes, and norms of behavior which correspond (with considerable precision, I believe) to the emotional needs of pioneer women in America. In fact the universally popular ballads represented the deepest emotional preoccupations of women who lived within the patriarchal family system."[38]

This feminine perspective is seen most clearly in two of the most popular of midwestern songs, "The False Lover" (known traditionally as "Lady Isabell and the Elf Knight") and "Barbara Allen." The women of these ballads are strong, and while they are not able to overcome their fate (in folk perspective no one really ever does), they make a model showing. In the first, Pretty Polly is seduced by an evil lover (a Bluebeard character) who rides her to a riverside rendezvous.

> "Alight, alight my pretty Polly,
> Alight, alight," said he.
> "For six pretty maids I have drowned here,
> And you the seventh shall be."

Feigning modesty, she asks that he turn while she removes her gold-studded dress for his plunder, and with his back to her, she charges and catapults the unsuspecting gentleman to his death. She returns home, virginity intact, and wiser about the tragic fate of romantic lovers.[39]

In "Barbara Allen" a remorseless Barbara refuses her affections to the heartsick sweet William, and he dies for want of her love. This was probably the single most popular song of the nineteenth century,[40] and clearly it conveyed some message to antebellum midwesterners. Beneath the surface of its deceptively simple narrative line ran powerful emotional currents. A woman bringing a man to his knees, even to his deathbed, was a rare image of feminine power in a society where women had very little. Barbara dies upon William's death, of course, for her act of hardheartedness could not be publicly condoned; but we may guess that it was the collective if private fantasy of feminine power that propelled the ballad to high popularity among women. In these songs women took revenge on men for the painful loss of romantic hope.

Of course there was courtship in the Midwest nonetheless. After dances, church meetings, or any other conceivable mixed-sex activity, young men would line the walk outside the door to ask a young woman, "May I carry you home?" When the relationship had progressed to the stage where the suitor had paid a call on the young woman's family, the couple was said to be "sparkin'." These courtships were very short, and by our standards quite formal.[41] But our standards are inappropriate. Couples wed and settled down to marriages that by nearly all appearances had little to do with romance. A jingle from central Illinois pulls us close to the folk consensus of marriage:

> First month, honey month,
> Next month like pie;
> Third month, you dirty bitch,
> Get out and work like I.[42]

In place of what we expect—an ideal of compatability and mutuality—was the notion that the couple was the center of a

set of economic and social relationships, the homestead, which
was the foundation of the republic. The homestead is perhaps
one of the hoariest of nineteenth-century concepts, figuring in
many studies on nineteenth-century ideology; yet it has not
been fully appreciated, I think, that the concept of the homestead was intrinsically dependent on the participation of both
men and women. It was an ironically bisexual concept for the
masculine West.

In popular opinion a good marriage was a bargain struck
between two strong-willed characters for an equitable and ad-
vantageous division of labor. In the traditional ballad "The
Cambric Shirt" (known also as "The Elfin Knight"), this vision
was presented with romantic overtones:

> [Man] "Go tell her to make me a cambric shirt,
> Rozy-marrow and time;
> Without one stitch of a seamster's work,
> And then she can be a true lover of mine."

> [Woman] "Go tell him to clear me an acre of land,
> Rozy-marrow and time;
> Between the salt sea and the sea sand,
> And then he can be a true lover of mine."

She continues by requesting that he plow it, reap it, thresh it,
and then ends,

> "Go tell the young man when he gets his work done,
> Rozy-marrow and time;
> To come to my house and his shirt will be done,
> And then he can be a true lover of mine."[43]

Typically, however, this view of marriage was devoid of the
romantic shadings of that old ballad, as in "The Young Man
Who Wouldn't Hoe His Corn," carried by New England
pioneers to the Ohio, from where it spread throughout the
corn belt.

> There was a young man who wouldn't hoe his corn;
> He was the laziest man that ever was born.
> He planted it in the month of June.
> And in July it was laid by.

> He went to the fence and he peeped through,
> Saying, "Oh dear me, what shall I do?"
> The careless weeds had grown so high
> They caused this young man for to sigh.
>
> He courted a girl, her name was Sue;
> She was a fair girl both kind and true.
> He told to her his troubles sore,
> But she sent the young man from her door.
>
> Say she, "Do you come here me for to wed,
> When you can't raise your own cornbread?
> Single I am, and single I'll remain,
> For a lazy man I won't maintain."[44]

The song proclaimed a self-evident truth: that the homestead was built on the interdependence of male and female work. A woman, especially, had much to fear from marriage with a lazy or improvident partner, for her responsibilities for her children were not the kind that could be easily ignored.

Men wanted their part of the bargain too. John Lewis Peyton, traveling in northeastern Illinois in late winter, met a young farmer, Jim Bull, engaged to be married that spring. He had cleared the tract of land adjoining his father's farm and felled the trees for a cabin, awaiting only the thaw to call his neighbors together for a house-raising. Bull's mother informed Peyton that his fiancée, Nancy, "was a strong industrious young woman who would attend to Jim's house and business in the best manner and make him a capital wife. That she could cook, wash, sew, knit, milk, churn, do any and everything required of a Western wife, and didn't want much help either. Jim, at any rate, seemed well-pleased at the prospect of possessing her." The lengthy discussion of the marriage was entirely confined to these practical matters.[45]

The happy marriage, then, was one that promised reciprocity, not love.

> Here stands the loving couple,
> Join heart and hands;
> One wants a wife,
> And the other wants a man.

They will get married,
If they can agree;
So it's march down the river,
To hog and hominy.[46]

Love and romance, surely, were welcome additions to a marriage, but the plain truth, as old wives simply but wisely suggested, was that a man or a woman who could not make a good
fire could not make a good marriage.[47]

Good marriages built strong and stable homesteads, and
homesteads, by common understanding, were the foundation
of the democratic republic. Eighteenth-century physiocratic
agrarianism had become a popular democratic ideology in the age
of Jackson. The slave contradiction, present in the agrarian
thought of Jefferson and Crèvecoeur, was negated in the Midwest by the fee-simple homesteads of free farmers.[48] The
homestead was the core of society. There production took
place, and in true prebourgeois fashion, farmers believed agriculture to be the source of all society's wealth. It was the focus
of reproduction as well, where the cultural traditions and
material achievements of one generation were passed on to the
next. It was the homesteaders who decided on the best course
for the country in the patriarchal equality of free male produc-
ers. The homestead was the integrating image of midwestern
culture, a unit that reduced the human and physical environment to a simple understandable whole.[49]

But the homestead itself, the preeminent image of the mid-
nineteenth century, depended directly upon a more basic social
connection, the marriage of men and women and the construction of families. "The family," Arthur Calhoun has written,
"was the one substantial social institution in a nation that had
discarded hierarchical religion and that had reduced government to the minimum, while business corporations had not yet
attained notable development."[50] The world of the homestead
was the world of the family.

For women there was really no choice other than matrimony.
It is important to remember how dependent rural women were
upon marriage. The public world was closed to respectable
women; alternative careers to that of housewife and mother

were almost inconceivable. And as the songs reiterated, a woman's worst fate was to live out the life of an old maid, confined to the house of her father.

The homestead image suggests, however, that men too were dependent upon the connection with women if they were to participate in the shared political and social vision of American society. In the Far West the overabundance of men and scarcity of women were a continual cause of concern. "We want families," western propagandist William Wadsworth wrote, "because we do see, that as year after year they multiply among us, a decided change for the better is apparent in every phase of society. We want families, because their homes and hearth stones everywhere, are the only true and reliable basis of any nation."[51] Society could not be built on the labor of men alone. Sarah Royce remembered that the unmarried miners of Hangtown (later Placerville), California, in the early 1850s "showed a consciousness of being somewhat the worse, for a long, rough journey in which they had lived semi-barbarous lives, and for their continued separation from the amenities and refinements of home. Even in their intercourse with each other, they often alluded to this feeling, and in the presence of women, then so unusual, most of them showed it in a very marked manner."[52]

Like Mrs. Royce, many women noted that men longed not only for feminine company but for the settled society of the homestead, where men and women worked together. This was the attraction of families for single men on the trail. At the end of her journey in 1849, Luzena Wilson was interrupted at her camp-fire kitchen by a miner who startled her with an offer to pay for her simple cooking: " 'I'll give you five dollars, ma'am for them biscuit.' It seemed like a fortune to me, and I looked at him to see if he meant it. And as I hesitated at such, to me a very remarkable proposition, he repeated his offer to purchase, and said he would give ten dollars for bread made by a woman, and laid a shiney gold piece in my hand."[53] The fetish, however, could not replace the relationship it stood for: the cooperation of men and women in marriage, which was in the popular mind the foundation of the social order.

Single men sometimes described their traveling parties as

families, slipping into the language of the most familiar of
social units to give articulation to their needs for company and
solidarity. "We had traveled so far together that we had become attached almost as one family," Enoch Conyers noted in
his diary when his party painfully separated.[54] These self-
deceptions, like those where half an all-male company dressed
in feminine garb to provide the others with dancing partners,
could not outlast the growing sense that without women true
society was impossible. "Meeting is over—I have returned
home," Wesley Tonner wrote in his notebook. "Home did I
say? Yes, although among strangers I am treated as kindly as if
I had brothers sisters and parents here, but it is not the same."[55]

Despite the attractions and solidarities of male society, nothing could replace the connections of marriage and family, for it
was marriage and family that solemnized life and gave it meaning. What good was a farm without a wife to keep the house and
sons to inherit the land and the tradition? Moreover, the cultural organization of work required the participation of men
and women. The wisest counsel was given by those who understood these truths. "Don't live & die in sight of your father's
house, but take a trip to Oregon!" Tallmadge B. Wood wrote
home after arriving in the Willamette Valley. "But if they
should come to *settle here*, I would advise them to bring a wife
along, as ladies are (like the specie) very scarce."[56] When
twenty-one-year-old William Case asked his father's permission
to emigrate it was granted. "But with his consent was given this
advice," Case remembered: 'Don't go, William, before you are
married; take a wife with you.' " He did.[57]

The law of midwestern states provided official endorsement
of notions of reciprocal marriage. Congress, in the Northwest
Ordinance of 1787, and in the 1816 organization of the Missouri Territory, placed the areas that later became the states of
Indiana, Illinois, Iowa, and Missouri under the protection of
English common law; thus, in the Midwest, as in nearly all other
areas of the United States, common-law definitions of marriage
prevailed until amended by state statutes after mid-century.[58]
Through the common law the conventional roles of husband

and wife were legally enshrined: a husband was obligated to provide a residence and household for his family, and to supply his wife with the means of feeding and clothing herself and her children; a wife was legally obligated to be her husband's helpmeet, to perform household and domestic duties freely and willingly without compensation. Both partners to the marriage contract had the exclusive legal right to the society, companionship, and conjugal affections of their spouse; there was a mutual obligation to love, to care for, and to labor faithfully to advance the interests of one's spouse.

But marriage legally obligated more than reciprocity. Legal marriage, like the marital relation in practice, gave the husband extraordinary power over the life and affairs of his wife. The law was the cultural capstone of the system of male privilege which extended from the uneven division of domestic labor through male control of the public world. Although each couple had ultimately to work out the relations of power and authority within their own marriage, the law represented the limits of the permissible and offered a sanctioned model of female subordination. The law, written by men and enforced by men, was a principal vehicle for furthering the ideological and social dominance of the patriarchy.

All women in nineteenth-century North American society, whether married or single, were without the benefits of the most basic civil rights: women could not vote, could not serve on juries, and in most places could not hold public office, all aspects of their general exclusion from the public world. Single women did enjoy almost equal legal status with men in contractual and property rights, but once married, women lost these rights as well, and very few women, of course, remained single. Married women were no longer responsible citizens but dependents, like children and idiots, relying for protection on the legal status of their husband-guardians. More than convention was operating when women dropped their maiden names and assumed the names of their husbands, since according to common-law doctrine, a man and a woman became a single legal person upon marriage, and, as Blackstone opined for every country lawyer in those hundreds of midwestern villages, that person was the husband.

The legal oppression of married women read like a bill of attainder. Since wives had no legal identity they could make no independent legal arrangements or contracts; they could neither sue nor be sued; they could not make an independent will; any contractual obligations undertaken before their marriages became the responsibility of husbands to fulfill. Wives forfeited to their husbands control and management of any and all real property they might have held before their marriage; husbands retained the rights to that property until their deaths, and indeed, if there were living issue of the marriage, the property previously owned by wives could then even be placed in trust for the children and kept out of women's hands. Husbands gained outright ownership of all the prenuptial personal property and chattels of their wives, and to husbands fell the right to proceed with any suits initiated by their wives and receive the settlements as their own. Husbands owned their wives' labor power; any wages wives received while married were legally owed to their husbands. Finally, since husbands and wives were legally one person, men could under no circumstances be charged with stealing from their wives, which gave men the widest possible leeway in their actions.

Husbands were recognized by law as the heads of their families; to them was delegated the obligation to control and discipline their wives. Hence husbands were permitted to physically punish their spouses within "reasonable limits," which by common law meant wives could be beaten as long as the instrument was no bigger around than the man's thumb. Wives were deprived of redress in the courts for injuries received at their husbands' hands. Husbands could legally confine their wives at home, refuse them visitors, even forcibly separate them from their parents. Divorce was difficult to obtain in most midwestern states;[59] petition had to be made for a special legislative divorce. If there was a divorce, the legal assumption was that the custody of minor children went with the head of the family—the husband. For women, therefore, divorce usually meant giving up their children.[60]

It is little wonder that the nascent women's rights movement took reform of the marriage law as one of its first objectives. Feminists supported the Married Women's Property Acts,

which proposed to amend the law to allow married women to
hold their prenuptial property in their own (married) names
and reform women's contractual rights. Feminists had the powerful support, in most states, of legal reformers, wealthy
families who wished to protect the dower property of their
daughters from unscrupulous suitors, and impoverished farmers who hoped to save some of their estate from creditors by
placing it in their wives' names. In the Midwest these reforms of
the common law were in step with the rest of the nation,
beginning during the 1850s.[61] But the implementation of the
intent of the laws was delayed many years by the determined
rear guard of the exclusively male bench and bar which demonstrated real hostility to the acts.[62] In any event, the general rule
of common law continued to apply to relations between husband and wife, despite the fact that the Married Women's Acts
logically renounced the legal fiction of two in one.

The property and contractual reforms would not have had
much of a bearing upon the lives of most farm women in any
case. Only rarely did any of these women enter a marriage with
more than a modest personal dowry. The importance of the law
lay rather in the considerable official authority it lent to the
exercise of husbands' power. The common law sanctioned the
existing power relations between midwestern men and women;
it was patriarchal law.

It is interesting to look at the decision to emigrate to Oregon
or California in the light of the legal model of husbands' power.
In their diaries and recollections many women discussed the
way in which the decision to move was made. Not one wife
initiated the idea; it was always the husband. Less than a quarter of the women writers recorded agreeing with their restless
husbands; most of them accepted it as a husband-made decision
to which they could only acquiesce. But nearly a third wrote of
their objections and how they moved only reluctantly. When
John Jones informed his wife Mary of his plans, she remembered answering impulsively, "Oh, let us not go! But," she
added, "it made no difference."[63] One woman, writing of her
own reluctance to move to Oregon, was reminded of the time
her father had moved their family from Sangamon County to
Missouri:

I came in one evening to see a look on dear mother's face that I had never seen before. I walked away after the usual greeting and sat silent. After a time her voice strengthened and she said, "what do you think your father has done. . . . He has sold the farm and as soon as school closes we are to move to Missouri." . . . What a shock these words gave me.[64]

In her later years Lucy Deady wrote that her mother had known "nothing of this move until father had decided to go."[65]

The decision to emigrate was the kind where husbands' patriarchal power made the difference: legally, after all, husbands had the right to enforce their own independent choice of domicile for the family; its was fully within a husband's prerogative to move his family without even consulting his wife.

Wives, however, were more than simply victims of their husbands' whims. An active struggle between husband and wife was often the consequence of a husband's declaration of his intention to move. Leaving their parents behind, especially their mothers, was the biggest obstacle to moving in most women's minds. Elias Draper remembered that when he approached his wife about leaving for California she exclaimed, "Oh, how can I leave pa and ma and go 3,000 miles away, perhaps never to see them again!" So Elias went to Sarah's mother to enlist her support.

When I approached the subject to her mother she said, "I wish your brother had never come from California, wanting to take my baby away."

I said, "Mother, there is a parental feeling that binds one's children close to them; but you know as children select their companions for life and happiness, they cannot expect to be supported by their parents, therefore it is our duty to support ourselves."

She then said, "you are right, and I will have to give my consent, with the hope of your return some time, when we can enjoy each other's company again."

When Elias returned with report of this conversation, his wife felt she had no choice but to reply sorrowfully, "Allright; I will follow you wherever you want to go." Draper's argument about giving up that "parental feeling" must have seemed slightly self-serving, however, when his mother-in-law discovered that the couple were to accompany *his* parents, who, it turned out, had initiated the original plans to move.[66]

Wives might, of course, argue against the move. A song popular throughout the Midwest during the 1850s recounted such a domestic struggle.

Since times are so hard, I'll tell you, my wife,
I've a mind for to shake off this trouble and strife,
And to California my journey pursue
To double my fortunes as other men do;
    For here we may labor each day in the field
    And the winters consume all that summers doth
      yield.

Dear husband, I've noticed with sorrowful heart
You've too long neglected your plow and your cart;
Your horses, sheep, cattle disorderly run,
And your new Sunday waistcoat goes everyday on.
    Now stick to your farming; you'll suffer no loss,
    For the stone that keeps rolling can gather no
      moss.

Dear wife, let us go, and don't let us wait.
I long to be doing, I long to be great,
And you some great lady, and who knows but I
Some great Governor before we do die.
    For here we may labor each day in the field.
    And the winters consume all that summers doth
      yield.

Dear husband, remember your land is to clear,
It will cost you the labor of many a year.
Your horses, sheep and cattle will all be to buy,
And before you have got them you are ready to die.
    So stick to your farming; you'll suffer no loss,
    For the stone that keeps rolling can gather no
      moss.[67]

With appeals such as these the wife of the song succeeded in
dissuading her husband from moving, just as many wives,
perhaps the majority with feverish husbands, must have done.

Men, however, marched to tunes that elicited powerful re-
ponses that were hard for even the most reasonable of women
to overcome. Hamlin Garland wrote that three generations of
midwestern men set their goals in terms of songs like,

> Cheer up, brothers, as we go
> O'er the mountains, westward ho,
> Where herds of deer and buffalo
> Furnish the fare.
>
> CHORUS: Then o'er the hills in legions, boys
> Fair freedom's star
> Points to the sunset regions, boys
> Ha, ha, ha-ha!
>
> When we've wood and prairie land,
> Won by our toil,
> We'll reign like kings in fairy land,
> Lords of the soil![68]

The sensible criticism of the realistic wife could be completely
overwhelmed by the powerful images of songs that had led men
and women across the Alleghenies and now beckoned their
sons and daughters across the plains:

> Come all you young men, who have a mind for to
>   range,
> Into the western country, your station for to change;
> For seeking some new pleasure we'll all together go
> And we'll settle on the banks of the pleasant Ohio.
>
> Come all you fair maidens wherever you may be,
> Come, join in with us, and rewarded you shall be;
> Girls, if you'll card, knit and spin, we'll plough, reap
>   and sow,
> And we'll settle on the banks of the pleasant Ohio.
> Girls, if you'll card, knit and spin, we'll plough, reap
>   and sow,
> And we'll fold you in our arms while the stormy wind
>   doth blow.[69]

If women were reluctant to accompany their men, however, they were equally unwilling to let them go alone. For a woman with no independent livelihood, being left at home was not a very pleasant prospect. The threat of some husbands to go alone was enough to change women's minds. After several weeks of being held back in his plans to emigrate by his wife's refusal to consider going, Basil Parker remembered telling Matilda that "if it was too much for her to undertake, I would arrange for her to stay while I was gone. At this she said that if I went, she would go with me, and thus the matter was settled."[70] When Gay Hayden came down with the gold fever in early 1850, he announced to his wife Mary Jane that he was leaving her behind. "I was nearly heart-broken at the thought of the separation," she remembered, but she wisely adopted an aggressive defense:

> I said "we were married to live together (he saying "yes") and I am willing to go with you to any part of *God's Foot Stool* where you think you can do best, and under these circumstances you have no right to go where I cannot, and if you do you need never return for I shall look upon you as dead." . . . So it was settled that *we* should go the next year to the California gold fields.[71]

Luzena Wilson found herself backed into the same corner, and for all her distaste for the trip she considered that she had been correct in pushing to go, for if she had not, "I think I should still be in my log cabin in Missouri," waiting for her husband to return from the mines.[72]

We have no way of knowing, of course, how many wives were successful in either getting their restless husbands to take them along or in leashing them. But whatever power wives brought to bear was clearly defensive and responsive. Men held the customary authority to make these decisions, and they did so. Perhaps only when husbands proposed leaving alone, threatening the family unity upon which their authority was based, did wives most successfully challenge their dominance in worldly affairs. It is clear, at any rate, that many emigrating women had been given little if any opportunity to participate in the decision to emigrate. Enos Ellmaker described the process by which most couples probably decided to go: "After my fine [Iowa] farm had received so much improvements yet I was not satisfied with the country; *I finally got the consent of my wife to sell and move* to the far-distant Oregon."[73] Their passive role necessarily meant that many women were reluctant participants in the crossing. "From Mrs Morrison's own lips I learned," wrote John Minto, "that the journey for which she was bending all her energies in preparation, was not in her judgement a wise business movement; but 'Wilson wished to go,' and that settled the question with her."[74]

Women worked valiantly to preserve their domestic environment in transit, for if women had a power it was dependent upon their ability to meet their own, their husband's, and their children's domestic needs. It was in homemaking that women acquired their status, and homemaking, consequently, took up their time on the trail.[75] For their task women demanded more equipment than men alone thought necessary. Sarah Royce remembered that family wagons "were easily distinguished by the greater number of conveniences, and household articles they carried."[76] Some families came outfitted out of all proportion to the load limitations. Hugh Campbell remembered that their family traveled in a spring wagon built extrawide to accommodate a built-in stove, beds, and a rocking chair for his mother.[77] The famous family wagon of the ill-fated Reed family—the Prairie Palace Car—also boasted a stove and even had a stovepipe sprouting from the canvas cover.

Most women made do with much less and yet were able, in the early stages at least, to create an air of homeyness about their camps. Sarah Royce noted the domestic articles of women—culinary equipment, food, boxes of clothing, tubs for washing—"disposed about the outside of the wagon in a home-like way," not simply strewn here and there as in the nearby male camps. "And where bushes, trees or logs formed partial enclosures, a kitchen or sitting room quite easily suggested itself to the feminine heart, yearning for home."[78] Tents became living rooms where women held, as best they could, to the amenities they tried to teach at home. Ed Bryant was received by Nancy Thornton in her tent "as she would have done in her parlor at home."[79] In these settings it was sometimes possible to pretend that home really did abide with the heart. "Mrs Fox and her daughter are with us and everything is so still and quiet we can almost imagine ourselves at home again. We took out our Daguerrotypes and tried to live over again some of the happy days of 'Auld Lang Syne.' " "In the evening the young ladies came over to our house and we had a concert with both guitars. Indeed it seemed almost like a pleasant evening at home. We could none of us realize that we were almost at the summit of the Rocky Mountains."[80]

By this stage of the trip, ascending the foothills of the Rockies, most women had been badly frustrated in their domestic work and needed no reminding of where they were. Along the Platte, the easiest leg of the journey, the water supply was muddy and crowded with "wigglers"; "this unsanitary condition," Charles True remembered, "was difficult for mother, with her life-long habits of scrupulous cleanliness and neatness to reconcile."[81] The animal and human excrement that littered the trail were a constant injury to women's habits. When the captain of their train selected an evening campsite filthy from earlier travelers, normally passive Lavinia Porter threatened her husband; "If you do not drive me to a cleaner place to camp and sleep tonight I will take my blankets and go alone." They moved on, and "the other women looked on my daring unsubordination with wondering eyes, and envious of my cleanly quarters, at last plucked up courage to follow my example, and with much profanity [on the part of the men] the camp was moved."[82] But some conditions could not easily be overcome.

> Our tents stand in what we should style a barnyard at home and I am sure if I were there I should as soon think of setting a table there as in such a place. The stench is sometimes almost unendurable, it arises from a ravene that is resorted to for special purposes by all the Emigration, but such things we must put up with.[83]

As the emigrants moved up the grade approaching the Rockies, it became obvious that the overloaded wagons had to be lightened, and gradually they discarded materials not essential

for survival. Domestic goods, of course, were most easily excluded from the essential category, much to the dismay of the
women. "We came across a heavy old fashioned cook stove
which some emigrant had hauled all those weary miles of
mountain and desert, only to discard it at last," wrote Lavinia
Porter. "No doubt some poor forlorn woman was now compelled to do her cooking by the primitive camp fire, perhaps
much against her will."[84] True recalled that by the time his
party reached the Great Basin all his mother's camping conveniences had been discarded, greatly adding to her labors and
filling her days with anxiety.[85] This anxiety was not only an
effect of added work. Books, furniture, knickknacks, china,
daguerreotypes, guitars—the very articles that most helped to
establish a domestic feel about the camps were the first things to
be discarded. Lightening the wagons, however necessary, was
interpreted by women as a process operating against their
interests. In one party a woman "exclaimed over an escritoire of
rare workmanship" she had found along the trail "and pitied
the poor woman who had to part with it."[86]

The loss of a sense of home—the inability to "keep house" on
the trail—was perhaps the hardest loss to bear, the thing that
drove women closest to desperation. In their diary entries,
women wished fervently for a return to the familiar routines of
home and farm life. Those routines objectively required more
than a fair share from women, but they were comforting in
their conventionality and, perhaps more important, comforting
in the way they reserved a unique position for women. "If I
were in the states now I would be sitting in a comfortable house
besides a fire; but our house now is in the open air," Esther
Hanna wrote.[87] Louisa Frizzell, a strong and determined
woman, nonetheless echoed her younger and more delicate
sister: "I feel tired and weary, O the luxury of a house, a house!
. . . I would have given all my interest in California, to have
been seated around my own fireside."[88] Velina Williams added
her lament: "Oh, for a little home to call my own!"[89] The trip
was so long, so extended, that women began to feel that the
physical foundations of domesticity—their homes—had slipped
irretrievably from them, that they were moving into a wild and
savage land where, perhaps, they would discover that homes
were nonexistent and women frightfully oppressed.

Women, then, clung to the things that belonged to them in the homestead marriage: clearly segregated work, a physical sphere for their activity, important work in reproducing the next generation and rearing healthy and happy young farmers and farm wives. They showed little inclination to trade these roles for the more socially active work that necessity demanded from them on the trail; rather, they attempted to preserve at least the semblance of their traditional roles. Feminine farm roles had little to do with the fetishized domesticity that was a part of the womanly cult flowering in the East, for in most ways these pioneer wives and mothers were the very antithesis of that antiseptic and anesthetized version of femininity. These were working women who accepted, with their husbands, a view of marriage that was oppressive to women in practice but promised meaningful work and the rewards of achievement at tasks distinctively feminine and separate from men. For all the tensions and inadequacies of marriage, when placed under extraordinary stress women's vision could extend only far enough to wish themselves back on their well-ordered homesteads.

Denied the chance to participate in the decision to move, essentially because of the patriarchal bias of marital decision making, failing to accept as their own their husbands' reasons for undertaking the move, women went not because they wanted to but because social expectations left them no choice. Understandably then, many women secretly blamed their husbands for their hardships on the trail. Lucy Rutledge Cook recorded in her letters home that her mother-in-law had vocally but privately complained to her, "Oh, I wish we never had started. . . . She looks so sorrowful and dejected," Lucy worried; "I think if Pa had not passengers to take through she would urge him to return; not that he would be so inclined, for returning is hopeless." The elder Mrs. Cook declared that "no argument used to induce her to leave there seems to have any weight now" and placed the blame for the move on those who had persuaded her against her better judgment—her husband and sons. A few days later Lucy herself was echoing her mother-in-law: "Oh, how I wish we never had started for the Golden Land," but she kept her own laments private too, secreted in her letters home.[90]

A few nights into Indian territory the Hecox–Aram party was joined at their camp one evening by a small group of Indian men who sat up around their fire all night, drinking, dancing, and loudly boasting of war exploits. Margaret Hecox retreated with her four children to the cold, damp wagon where she spent the night "hugging my baby to my bosom, with three badly scared little girls crouched at my feet." A single question reverberated in her head: "What had possessed my husband, anyway, that he should have thought of bringing us away out through this God-forsaken country?"[91] At about the same stage of their journey, Lucy Ide wrote in her diary, "Well, well, this is not so romantic; thoughts will stray back (in spite of all our attempts to the contrary) to the comfortable homes we left and the question arises in my mind—is this a good move—but echo answers not a word."[92]

Women reluctantly agreed to the emigration because they were dependent upon their families for society and companionship and upon their husbands for livelihood and support. Husbands and families were crucial to women's identities; the options for women left behind were lonely ones at best and could be socially and psychologically disastrous. But women were not dragged screaming to the wagons; in this sense no one forced them to go. There were a few examples of resistance; occasionally anxiety or bewilderment erupted into open revolt against going forward.

> This morning our company moved on, except one family. The woman got mad and wouldn't go or let the children go. He had the cattle hitched on for three hours and coaxed her to go, but she wouldn't stir. I told my husband the circumstances and he and Adam Polk and Mr Kimball went and each one took a young one and crammed them into the wagon, and the husband drove off and left her sitting. She got up, took the back track and traveled out of sight. Cut across, overtook her husband. Meantime he sent his boy back to camp after a horse that he had left and when she came up her husband says "Did you meet John?" "Yes," was the reply, "and I picked up a stone and knocked out his brains." Her husband went back to ascertain the

truth, and when he was gone she set one of his wagons on fire, which was loaded with store goods. The cover burnt off and some valuable articles. He saw the flames and came running and put it out, and then mustered spunk enough to give her a good flogging.[93]

Short of violent resistance, it was always possible that circumstances would force a family to reconsider and turn back. Mary Ellen Todd's family traveled in 1852, when cholera was a scourge along the trails. "There was great discouragement among the emigrants . . . , and everyday there were some who were going back. . . . Women cried, begging their menfolk to take them back. It is no wonder that stout hearts began to waver. Consequently, after many heated discussions and more tears," the reluctant men finally consented to return. Mary Ellen remembered that the men "did the hooking up of their oxen in a spiritless sort of way. Yet some of the girls and women were laughing."[94] It would have been no surprise if some women had complained to their husbands as well as to their diaries. The carping woman was a standard image of overland folklore.

> The ladies have the hardest that emigrate by land,
> For when they cook with buffalo wood they often burn
>   a hand;
> And when they jaw their husbands 'round, get mad
>   and spill the tea.
> Wish to the Lord they'd be taken down with a turn of
>   the di-a-ree.[95]

Open resistance, constant complaining: these reactions would certainly have fit the disorder of women's powerlessness. But such stereotypical behavior rarely has an active existence; few women, if any, secretly plotted to sabotage the trip, and the wag who composed that verse about feminine emigrants was probably reflecting male fears of wifely resentment more than the abundance of shrews on the trail. Life is always richer and more complex than such reductionist images suggest. Women's leaving was determined by their social dependency, to be sure, and there was ample room for women to build and feel massive resentments; but their leaving was activated by the things women believed and expected of themselves. Their own social and personal values demanded that they be loving and obedient wives, faithful and ever-present mothers. They struggled with their men about the foolishness of going, but only until threatened with the loss of their wifely status; then they capitulated and packed the trunks. Past this point resistance was hopeless, as Lucy Cook recognized, more important, it would be destructive.

If we are to trust and respect their revelations in their diaries and recollections, the greatest struggle of women on the trail was the struggle to endure the hardship and suffering without becoming bitter and resentful, without becoming the carping wife, without burdening their marital relationship with the bad feelings that burned inside them. If we are to judge them not by our standards but their own, we will not resurrect and applaud every little act of womanly resistance and mean feminine spirit but examine and attempt to understand the powers of endurance that permitted them to act out the role of good wife through the whole hated experience. The women's materials give us a penetrating look at the feminine psychology of social dependency.

"Some there were, no doubt, who would have turned back," Sarah Royce later wrote, in a description which applies well to women, "but they were involved either in family or business relations with others more resolute—or more rash—and, seeing the uselessness of resistance they took up their part of the daily toil, in most cases, without complaining."[96] Indeed, as we have seen, women not only took up their part, but over the long haul they assumed more than their 50 percent, often substituting for men, driving wagons and stock in addition to doing their own wifely work. Wholehearted work may have been a way of overcoming the inward resistance many women felt to working at all for unwanted goals.

Fears and doubts too fearful to be spoken aloud to men were whispered between mothers and daughters, sisters, or traveling female acquaintances. Most women diarists used their daily entries as an opportunity to express their feelings silently. Lavinia Porter recounted in the most melancholy terms her "sad parting" from her sister on the plains of eastern Kansas but added, "Such sorrows are to be endured not described." Endurance was the dominant emotional theme of Lavinia's overland account. "As the days wore on the irksome monotony of the journey began to pall upon me, and I spent many unhappy hours which I tried to conceal within my own breast, sometimes confiding to my journal my woes and disappointments, but managed to keep up a cheerful exterior before my husband and brother." Her resolve was to be "the courageous and valiant frontierswoman," but this outward appearance took a heavy inward toll.

> I would make a brave effort to be cheerful and patient until the camp work was done. Then starting out ahead of the team and my men folks, when I thought I had gone beyond hearing distance, I would throw myself down on the unfriendly desert and give way like a child to sobs and tears, wishing myself back home with my friends and chiding myself for consenting to take this wild goose chase.[97]

Thirty miles out of St. Joseph, Esther Hanna began her trail diary: "I think of home and the dear ones there; each day I am getting farther from them. I feel a sadness steal over me at times when I think that I shall see them no more on earth, but it is all for the best. It is better that my affections should be more turned from earth. Oh, that I could set them upon 'things heavenly and divine!' " Her thoughts continued in a melancholy direction, however, and several days later she added this resolve: "Will try to be calm and submissive." But despite the injunctions of religious scruples and willpower, the sadness continued to "steal over" her. "I have been thinking of home and dear absent friends but must not think too much!" All her resolve was helpless against the power of unhappiness. "I cannot restrain my tears from flowing fast and free." In the dry hills of Wyoming she wrote: "This day has been insupportable! Oh, the dust and excessive heat is scarcely to be endured! I try to be brave but in times like these my spirit falters." In eastern Oregon she wrote, "We expected to endure hardships and we must endure them like good soldiers. May the Lord give us the

strength to do so!"[98] Clearly Esther considered it her duty to
accept the trip as fate, thought it wrong that her spirit put up
resistance, and agonized as much over the difficulty of enduring as over the things to be endured.

This theme of endurance was perhaps the most common
feature of the woman's diaries; strikingly similar words and
phrases were repeated over and over again in the diaries of all
but the most unreasonably cheerful. "I am getting a little tired
of this wearisome trip and am very anxious to get through, but
I intend to take it very patiently as it comes," Frances Sawyer
wrote.[99] When her husband switched their wagon from one
train to another, and Mary Powers was forced to leave friends
she had made along the trail, she wrote home to her mother
that "I could not repress my sad feelings."[100] "Oh, I feel so
lonesome today," Agnes Stewart confided. "Sometimes I can
govern myself, but not always, but I hold in pretty well considering all things."[101] The partnership of marriage was a partnership of mutual duty and responsibility, not a partnership of
feelings. The feelings that Mary and Agnes repressed and
governed were out of place in their family relationships. These
"woman's feelings" had to be kept in "woman's sphere," out of
harm's way.

But the struggle to "hold in" was not easy; it was the most
difficult of all the trail's trials, yet for women the most fundamental. To dwell on life's hardships, when they were so often
not within the power of a woman to change, could drive one to
melancholy, depression, even self-destruction. It was, perhaps,
self-protection, most of all, that dictated their silent course.
Musing on the loneliness and dreariness of her journey, even as
the family traveled the last few miles, Maria Parsons Belshaw
caught herself slipping into a pit of depression: "But I must not
let my mind run in this channel long or my happiness is
gone."[102] She revealed a fragile emotional state. "Passive ac-
quiescence," Gordon Allport writes, "is sometimes the only way
in which seriously threatened minority groups can survive.
Rebellion and aggression would certainly be met by fierce punishment, and the individual himself might succumb to mental
illness induced by constant anxiety and anger."[103]

Disquiet, anxiety, melancholy, and anger were repressed and

hidden from husbands, brothers, and fathers, those most responsible for such feelings. I have previously drawn the inference that woman-to-woman relations encouraged articulation and expression. In their relationships with their menfolk, however, the dynamics of family psychology compelled women to adopt the contradictory emotional mode of inexpression and seeming passivity. Lavinia Porter ran ahead to hide her tears, and Agnes Stewart and Mary Powers struggled to "hold in" and "repress" their sadness, not wanting to reveal themselves to the men about them. The second day out of Council Bluffs, Catherine Haun had an attack of homesickness, but she composed herself. "Then wiping away my tears, lest they betray me to my husband, I prepared to continue my trip. I have often thought that had I confided in him he would have certainly turned back for he, as well as the other men of the party, was disheartened and was struggling not to betray it."[104] Here she protected her husband from his own uncertainty and helped to uphold his manhood; but might she not also have been protecting herself against the later eventuality that she would be blamed as the *sole* cause of their joint failure of will?

There was, as well, a self-motivation to this enduring mode. Especially in the context of the man's world of the trail, it would have been strange had the standards of perseverance which men successfully demonstrated not been, in part, inwardly accepted by women as well. Women might well have despised their own doubts and fears and worked to overcome them, in spite of the detachment they felt from the emigration. Thus did Rebecca Ketcham characterize her anxieties as "wicked fears" and resolve to "try to be patient."[105] Like Rebecca and Esther Hanna, many women somehow felt that repression of feelings and patient endurance would reap a heavenly reward; they looked on the trail as a kind of cross for women to bear. Maria Belshaw comforted herself, "Thy will be done O God not mine, that I may receive a crown of righteousness at thy right hand."[106] And Sarah Royce, after successfully "holding in" during the first of many late-night bouts of homesickness, wrote later that "in the morning there was a mildly exultant feeling which comes from having kept silent through a cowardly fit, and finding the fit gone off."[107]

For men the trip West was an active test of competition, strength, and manliness. It meant measuring themselves against the already romanticized images of their heroic pioneer fathers and grandfathers traversing the Wilderness Road and the Cumberland Gap. For women the trip West was a test of their inner strength. They did their part and more; they were comforting wives and attentive mothers, to the many single men of the trail as well as their husbands. They did all this, because of, not in spite of, their not wanting to leave home in the first place.

The psychology of social dependency, with its costs and rewards, was the result of the systematic oppression of women, of which their marital relations were the key link. Their induction onto the trail, not as full and willing participants but more as reluctant draftees, was the cause not of rebellion and resistance, although there were occasional examples of those, but of self-denial, a kind of active passivity and endurance. The trail experience was, of course, an extreme case; daily life was more amiable to women, with smaller subjugations. But considering the weight of these small evidences of powerlessness over years of marriage, the lives of women had to be largely lives of endurance. On the trail women called up resources of courage and will which were stockpiled for just such emergencies.

7

Conclusion: Men and Women in the Rural American West

From one perspective all marriages can be viewed as practical relationships for performing the domestic labor of society. The relationships of these midwestern men and women, however, had this practical function at their centers: they were partnerships in production, processing, and consumption. The economic relations of family members to one another held families together and rooted them in the social order.

Until the Civil War the working lives of most midwesterners were shaped by two preeminent facts: first, the relative isolation of their homesteads from markets and their households from neighbors; and second, the dependence of farm labor on hand-tool technology. These two factors meant that most production was for use and that most families were oriented to internal economic processes. A revolution in midwestern agriculture began in the years just preceding the Civil War, was greatly accelerated by wartime demand, and was consolidated by massive movements of people and capital during the post-bellum period. But in the meantime most midwestern families lived on a level where the economics of subsistence, not the demands of the market, set the structure of relations among men, women, and children.

In this context the familial division of labor by sex was the basic social division of labor as well; the overall differences between men's and women's work were greater than the differences among the work of all midwestern men. Women worked in domestic space but in addition performed from a third to a half of the productive work of the farm. Farm wives were responsible for the dairy (milk, butter, and cheese), the henhouse (eggs and roasters), the garden (all the fresh vegeta-

179

bles for table and many of those preserved for cold months), and in the earlier years for a textile crop of cotton or flax. Until mid-century, midwestern women spun those fibers into yarn, wove the yarn into cloth, and cut the cloth for home-sewn family clothing. Beginning in the fifties homespun was gradually replaced by store-bought calico and gingham, but clothes were still tailored at home by skillful feminine hands. Men controlled the surrounding homestead, produced an essential corn crop for consumption and as large a marketable grain crop as possible, raised a herd of hogs and some sheep, tended the farm stock, cleared and plowed the land, built, repaired, and decided when to leave it all for a new location.

Corresponding with these economic realities and work relationships, people viewed marriage as the central relationship of a happy homestead. The culture decreed women to be helping wives and loving mothers, men productive farmers and protective husbands and fathers. The reciprocity of the homestead portrayed the kind of marriage to which men and women aspired: a dutiful and responsible partnership of labor, from which grew feelings of connection and affection.

But there was little sense of marriage as life's grand companionship. Indeed, there seems to have been little appreciation of companionate values. Men and women tended to see romance as a dangerous basis for a stable relationship; passion they judged obstructive to the practical tasks of building a solid marriage. And for both men and women, the strongest and most significant social connections, that is, those connections linking them with social units larger than the family, were accomplished not by couples, but by same-sex groupings: in male gatherings from working bees to local elections, and in female communications at quiltings or around the delivery bed.

Nonetheless, the family was the most critical social unit for men and women alike. Without marriages there could be no homesteads, no family to cook and sew for, no family to raise a house for. The first step in coming to terms with adult identity was facing marriage and the family. Those who failed in marriage failed in life.

Having paid our kudos to family values, however, we must immediately recognize the inequity of men's and women's situation in marriage. The spaces of the sexes were not only separate but intrinsically unequal. Men enjoyed the means for wide social communication; it was their responsibility to use that means in their capacity as heads of household in a patriarchal society ostensibly governed by heads of household. Women, on the other hand, as one woman's song lamented, were

> always controlled, they're always confined.
> Controlled by their family until they are wives,
> Then slaves to their husbands the rest of their lives.[1]

Women played no public roles but remained in their domestic spaces, in a mild kind of rural American purdah.

The relative inequality of the sexes in their social relations was the foundation of patriarchy, of masculine power and prerogatives. Even under conditions of the simplest agricultural economy, even under conditions of pure subsistence, the division of labor which confined women to the household implied an unequal division of power and authority. In all agricultural societies, women are more or less excluded from the public world. "The overall status of women in agriculture or peasant society is one of institutionalized dependency, subordination and political immaturity."[2] In its unequal division of power between men and women, then, the Midwest was typical of settled agricultural societies.

To be sure, farm women's ills were exacerbated by the growth of the market, for under commercial pressures gender divisions were widened, men's economic activity was further divorced from the household, and family economic unity shattered; for farm women there was, in consequence, a further devaluation of their already questionable status. But let there be no mistake, male privilege was an aspect of the cultural heritage of the land, expanded, not created, by the growth of capitalist market forces.[3] Lacking in public roles, women were dependent upon men, while men enjoyed considerable responsibility and latitude in their social relations. The presence of children placed the imprimatur of biology on the arrangement and provided male privilege with a natural cover: women were viewed as inherently responsible for domestic society, while men were free to work or wander.

The gender cultures of man to man and woman to woman must be interpreted in the light of these family matters. Woman-to-woman contacts stressed empathy and support, for farm women perceived their life stations as hard ones to be endured, but endured best with the sympathy of sisters. Abigail Scott Duniway remembered her mother, Ann Scott, whispering painfully at the birth of yet another daughter (her ninth child, her twelfth delivery): "Poor baby! She'll be a woman someday! Poor baby! A woman's lot is so hard!"[4] Needing support but lacking social contacts, women clung to their feminine kin and neighbors. Lacking time to socialize, women developed the power of language; they communicated a feminine lore rich with sayings and aphorisms which conveyed the power of feminine support in the loneliest of isolated hours.

There was, as well, an ideal of women's behavior and belief which corresponded with women's social situation. Women were to be sensitive to manners, morals, and the feelings of others. Western women's actual social roles as mothers, wives, and sisters were sufficient to justify the cultural production of these models. Eastern ideologies of femininity certainly filtered into the West, but they simply reinforced the existing traditional roles.[5]

Men's contacts with one another were more communal, open, and exaggerated. Men's character types corresponded: they were rough, aggressive, and egotistic. Occasions of male solidarity included celebratory spectacles of masculine power. Men's relations with one another, however, were double-faced: behind the hail-fellow engagement lurked a competitive spirit that proffered a willingness and desire to succeed, even at the expense of others. Moreover, through the mechanism of the market men conceived a way to realize their longed-for success. The competitive spirit of frontier masculinity was only a railroad and a reaper away from the competitive economy of small capitalist farmers.

Masculine culture fostered the growth of another kind of spirit. Men took as their models the Indian-fighting frontiersmen they imagined their fathers and grandfathers to have been. They longed for a similar test of their own masculinity. Thus they were driven to experiences such as the overland emigration, for on the trail they would be following, as it were, the blazes of previous masculine generations.

In the emigration to the Far West we see some of these factors working in consort—and in conflict. Oregon was a place to take families, because Oregon was a place for homesteading. California, of course, offered gold and prompted a mass male movement otherwise seen only during wars or revolutions. But the miners went as sojourners, not as emigrants; the mining population was transient, and in nonmining areas a more normal sex ratio recurred within ten years of the rush.[6] California, too, was largely a place men went with families—or wished they had.

Men took their families to claim new, richer farmlands, to raise cash crops, and to exploit new markets (the mines, the Orient, or the ports of the world). These were men with dreams of success, but most were not yet successful. They left the isolated Midwest, as their forebears had left the Atlantic, just before their former homes were entangled by commercial connections. But these emigrant men also took their families because they were in part living out a continuing male adventure of life on the wild fringes of society, an adventure entirely masculine. In short, for men, the overland emigration was an archetypal nineteenth-century event, for it was conceived in the spirit of progress, publicly designated to fulfill economic goals, yet infused and overlaid with male projections and identifications.

Most women, for their part, only reluctantly participated in these male fantasies. They went because of the terms of obedience which marriage had imposed and which they had accepted. Their presence and work, however, made the emigration a family matter, and unattached men applied for the privilege of accompanying every family. Women on the trail were a source of great strength to the parties.

Some have suggested that women's working roles on the trail and, in general, women's productive roles on their frontier farms contributed to a relative equality between sexes. "Generally speaking," Caroline Bird writes, "frontier conditions . . . have motivated men and women to similar or androgynous goals."[7] "When Eastern ladies were fainting at a coarse word or vulgar sight," Page Smith offers, "their Western sisters fought off Indians, ran cattle, made homes and raised children in the wilderness. It was in the West, in consequence, that women had the greatest status."[8] Both Smith and Bird have borrowed their views from Arthur Calhoun, with whose opinions, in matters of American family history, one has always to contend.

> The frontier helped to liberalize the American family. . . . Women stood by their husbands' side and fought for life and little ones against human and other foes. Ladies whose husbands lost everything threw aside ease and luxury and fared boldly into the far West where they endured without complaint toils, danger, sickness and loneliness. Reciprocity in the marriage relation was the logical consequence where woman bore a man's share in the struggle for existence.[9]

This was hardly the assessment of contemporaries. Emigrant women, in their own evaluation, came much closer to the spirit of the frontier aphorism; "This country is all right for men and dogs, but it's hell on women and horses."[10] Perhaps not everyone joined in that consensus, but male and female opinion on the question of the status of women conjoined in a curious but revealing manner. John Ludlum McConnel, in his book of frontier description and proscription, described the frontier wife from the masculine perspective:

> There is no coyness, no blushing, no pretense of fright or nervousness—if you will, no romance—for which the husband has reason to be thankful! The wife knows what her duties are and resolutely goes about performing them. She never dreamed, nor twaddled, about "love in a cottage," or "the sweet communion of congenial souls" (who never eat anything): and she is, therefore, not disappointed on discovering that life is actually a serious thing. She never whines about "making her husband happy"—but sets firmly and sensibly about making him *comfortable*. She cooks his dinner, nurses his children, shares his hardships, and encourages his industry. She never complains of not

having too much work to do, she does not desert her home
to make endless visits—she borrows no misfortunes, has
no imaginary ailings. Milliners and mantua-makers she
ignores—"shopping" she never heard of—scandal she
never invents or listens to. She never wishes for fine car-
riages, professes no inability to walk five hundred yards,
and does not think it a "vulgar accomplishment" to know
how to make butter. She has no groundless anxieties, she is
not nervous about her children taking cold: a doctor is a
visionary potentate to her—a drug-shop is a depot of
abominations. She never forgets whose wife she is,—there
is no "sweet confidante" without whom she "can not
live"—she never writes endless letters about nothing. She
is, in short, a faithful, honest wife: and, in "due time" the
husband must make *more* "three-legged stools"—for the
"tow-heads" have now covered them all![11]

Women, when given the chance to speak up for themselves,
could describe the same situation from a very different angle.
Abigail Scott Duniway, herself an Oregon emigrant of 1853,
spoke for farm women when she said a frontier farmer's wife
"has to be lady, nurse, laundress, seamstress, cook and dairy-
woman by turns, and . . . attends to all these duties unaided,
save by the occasional assistance of an indulgent husband who
has cares enough of his own."[12] Compare her version of the
frontier woman:

It was a hospitable neighborhood composed chiefly of
bachelors, who found comfort in mobilizing at meal time at
the homes of the few married men of the township, and
seemed especially fond of congregating at the hospitable
cabin home of my good husband, who was never quite so
much in his glory as when entertaining men at his fireside,
while I, if not washing, scrubbing, churning, or nursing the
baby, was preparing their meals in our lean-to kitchen. To
bear two children in two and a half years from my marriage day, to make thousands of pounds of butter every
year for market, not including what was used in our free
hotel at home; to sew and cook, and wash and iron; to bake
and clean and stew and fry; to be, in short, a general

pioneer drudge, with never a penny of my own, was not a pleasant business. . . . My recreation during those monotonous years was wearing out my wedding clothes, or making over for my cherished babies the bridal outfit. . . .

My good husband was not idle; he was making a farm in the timber and keeping a lot of hired men, for whom I cooked and washed and mended, as part of the duties of a pioneer wife and devoted mother.

As I look back over those weary years, the most lingering of my many regrets is the fact that I was often compelled to neglect my little children, while spending my time in the kitchen, or at the churn or wash tub, doing heavy work for the hale and hearty men—work for which I was poorly fitted, chiefly because my faithful mother had worn both me and herself to a frizzle with just such drudgery before I was born.

When Mr. Duniway decided to mortgage their homestead to raise cash for improvements, Abigail remembered:

It dawned on me suddenly as I was picking a duck that it would ruin us financially if those notes were signed. I tried hard to be silent, being a nonentity in law, but my hands trembled, my heart beat hard, and I laid the pinioned duck on its back and repaired to the living room to investigate. My husband had already signed two notes, and was in the act of signing the third, when I leaned over his shoulder and said, tremulously: "My dear, are you quite certain about what you are doing?" The other fellow looked daggers at me, but said nothing, and my husband answered, as he signed the last note, "Mama, you needn't worry; you'll always be protected and provided for!" I wanted to say: "I guess I'll always earn all the protection I get," but I remembered that I was nothing but a woman; so I bit my lips to keep silent and rushed back to my work, where for several minutes, I fear that duck flesh suffered, for I didn't pluck the feathers tenderly.[13]

There is, in these sexually different perspectives, a reflection of a single reality: the domestic confinement and hard toil of

women. Where McConnel and Duniway differed was in their
respective estimations of the worth to women in being kept
barefoot and pregnant. Some modern observers have noted
western women's importance to production and jumped to the
conclusion that in consequence their rewards were greater and
their equality with men more complete.[14] But in fact the frontier extended the impact that agricultural settings have historically had on relations between the sexes: with men controlling
the access to society and controlling the products that were
potentially exchangeable on the market, they controlled the
acquisition of power and status as well; women, confined to the
domestic space, left without social power, were dependent for
status upon their relations with their husbands.[15]

The winds of change were blowing in other quarters. In the
cities and the industrial countrysides of the East there were
growing opportunities for women's employment outside the
home—an entry into the public world. Practical equality of the
sexes was, and is yet, to be achieved in the social production of
the modern world just then being born. The move West called
upon people not to change but to transfer old sexual roles to a
new but altogether familiar environment.

Appendix I:
Tables

Table AI.1. Previous Residence of Emigrant Families

State	N	%
Missouri	27	23.5
Illinois	26	22.6
Iowa	18	15.7
Indiana	14	12.2
Michigan	6	5.2
Arkansas	5	4.4
Wisconsin	5	4.4
Other states (9)	14	12.2
Subtotal	115	100.2
Not known	7	
Total	122	

Table AI.2. Occupations of Emigrant Male Heads of Household

Occupation	N	%
Farmer	54	60.7
Professional[a]	11	12.4
Craftsman	9	10.1
Small merchant	8	9.0
Minister	7	7.9
Subtotal	89	100.1
Not known	33	
Total	122	

[a]Includes physician, lawyer, editor, and schoolteacher.

Table AI.3. Emigrants' Place of Origin and Place of Birth

Region	Origin		Birth	
	N	%	N	%
Midwest	98	86.0	7	9.9
South	7	6.1	11	15.5
Ohio River	5	4.4	19	26.8
Mid-Atlantic	4	3.5	19	26.8
New England	—	—	8	11.3
Out of U.S.	—	—	7	9.9
Totals	114	100.0	71	100.2

Table AI.4. Families by Stages in Family Cycle:
Emigrants and North Carolina, 1934

Stages	Emigrants		N. Carolina[a]	
	N	%	N	%
Newlywed families (no children)	16	13.7	43	2.6
Young families (all children under 15)	59	50.9	819	49.6
Mid-stage families (with children over 15)	40	34.5	775	46.9
Mature families (no children)	1	0.9	16	1.0
Totals	116	100.0	1653	100.0

[a] Source: Nelson, *Rural Sociology*, pp. 310–11.

Table AI.5. Characteristics of Emigrant Families by Stages

Stages	Means		
	Years married	No. of children	No. of adult moves of husband
Newlywed	0.8	0.0	0.4
Young	8.0	3.0	1.4
Midstage	21.1	4.8	2.2
All families	10.8	3.0	1.5
All with children	8.6	3.8	1.7

Table AI.6. Ages of Emigrant Husband
and Wife by Family Stages

Stages	Wife's age			
	Mean	Median	Range[a]	Values
Newlywed	21.3	21.0	1	20–22
Young	27.8	28.0	3	25–31
Mid-stage	41.4	39.5	4.5	34–44
	Husband's age			
	Mean	Median	Range[a]	Values
Newlywed	24.7	25	3.5	21.5–28
Young	34.3	34	6.5	27.5–40
Mid-stage	46.4	45	6.5	37.5–51

[a]Semi-interquartile range.

Table AI.7. Economic Ranking of Emigrant Families by Male Occupation

Occupation	Poor	Middling	High	Totals
Farmer	19	6	3	28
Professional	1	6	2	9
Craftsman	—	2	—	2
Small merchants	—	4	3	7
Minister	1	—	—	1
Subtotals	21	18	8	47
Not known				75
Total				122

Table AI.8. Inventory of Essential Outfit, Costs, and Weights: Emigrant Party of Four

Area	Item	Amount	Unit cost ($)	Cost ($)	Weight (lbs.)
Transport	wagon	1	90.00	90.00	600
	oxen	4 yoke	50.00/yoke	200.00	120
	gear		100.00	100.00	400
Food	flour	600 lbs.	2.00/100 lbs.	12.00	60
	biscuit	120 lbs.	3.00/100 lbs.	3.60	4
	bacon	400 lbs.	5.00/100 lbs.	20.00	100
	coffee	60 lbs.	7.00/100 lbs.	4.20	200
	tea	4 lbs.	50.00/100 lbs.	2.00	200
	sugar	100 lbs.	10.00/100 lbs.	10.00	120
	lard	200 lbs.	6.00/100 lbs.	12.00	40
	beans	200 lbs.	8.00/100 lbs.	16.00	8
	dried fruit	120 lbs.	24.00/100 lbs.	28.80	8
	salt	40 lbs.	4.00/100 lbs.	1.60	25
	pepper	8 lbs.	4.00/100 lbs.	.32	
	saleratus	8 lbs.	4.00/100 lbs.	.32	
	whiskey	1 keg	5.00/keg	5.00	

Goods				
rifle	1	30.00	30.00	10
pistols	2	15.00	30.00	10
powder	5 lbs.	.25/lb.	1.25	5
lead	15 lbs.	.04/lb.	.60	15
shot	10 lbs.	.10/lb.	1.00	10
matches			1.00	1
cooking utensils			20.00	25
candles and soap	65 lbs.	from home	from home	65
bedding	60 lbs.	from home	from home	60
sewing kit	10 lbs.	from home	from home	10
essential tools			from home	20
clothing			from home	100
Totals			$589.69	2,216

Source: Compiled from guidebooks listed in bibliography.

Table AI.9. Emigrant Families in Wagon Trains by Years

	1843–1845		1846–1851		1852–1855		1856–1868		Totals	
	N	%	N	%	N	%	N	%	N	%
In trains	16	88.9	14	48.3	18	32.1	9	47.4	57	46.7
Without trains	2	11.1	15	51.7	38	67.9	10	52.6	65	53.3
Totals	18	100.0	29	100.0	56	100.0	19	100.0	122	100.0

Table AI.10. Types of Emigrant Parties by Years

Party Type	1843–1845		1846–1851		1852–1855		1856–1868		Totals	
	N	%	N	%	N	%	N	%	N	%
Conjugal	7	43.8	12	40.0	12	27.2	5	27.8	36	30.5
Voluntary	2	12.5	10	26.7	13	53.7	5	27.8	30	25.4
Kinship	7	43.8	8	33.3	29	24.1	8	44.4	52	44.1
Totals	16	100.1	30	100.0	54	100.0	18	100.0	118	100.0

Table AI.11. Sex and Age Composition of Overland Emigration by Years

	% Total emigration				% Adult emigration						Number	
	A men	B women	C children	D total	E married ♀ & ♂	F single ♂	G total	H hired ♂ in fam.	I total in fam.	J total N	K est. N for yr.	L % total of est.
1843[a]	28.9	12.5	58.7	100.1	60.4	39.6	100.0	26.1	86.5	1,000	1,000	100
1844[b]	38.3	14.9	46.9	100.1	56.0	44.0	100.0	24.1	80.1	747	2,000	38
1846[c]	40.6	20.3	39.1	100.0	50.9	49.1	100.0	28.7	79.6	320	1,000	32
1850[d]	92.9	5.7	1.4	100.0	11.6	88.4	100.0	5.0	16.6	42,536	55,000	77
1852[e]	72.8	11.5	15.8	100.1	27.3	72.7	100.0	11.7	39.0	11,236	50,000	20
1853[f]	65.1	14.8	20.1	100.0	37.1	63.0	100.1	15.9	53.0	15,219	20,000	76
Total (excl. 1850)	65.8	13.5	20.7	100.0	34.1	66.0	100.1	14.6	48.7	28,522	74,000	39
1853 Ore.	47.4	21.6	30.9	99.9	62.6	37.4	100.0	27.0	89.6	3,507	4,600	76
1853 Calif.	70.4	12.7	16.9	100.0	30.6	69.4	100.0	13.1	43.7	11,712	15,400	76

Explanation of columns: E , assuming all women married, then 2B/A + B = E; F, assuming all women married, then A − B/A + B = F; H, assuming .86 single men/family, then .86B/A + B = H; I, E + H = I; J, number upon which percentages are based; K, estimates provided by Mattes, *Great Platte River Road*, p. 23. [a]Mattes, *Great Platte River Road*, p. 13; [b]Minto, "Recollections"; Clyman, *Journals*, p. 317; [c]Bancroft, *History of Oregon*, 1:556; [d]Watkins, *Publications*, p. 230; [e]Watkins, *Publications*, p. 349; [f]Watkins, *Publications*, p. 252.

Table AI.12. Estimated Number of Children on Overland Trail

Year	N
1843	587
1844	938
1846	391
1850	770
1852	7,900
1853	4,020

Source: Table AI.11, columns C, K.

Table AI.13. Age-Specific Fertility for Emigrant Women

Age reached	N	F	F'	%
20	75	0.5	0.7	10.4
25	50	1.5	1.9	31.3
30	41	3.0	3.9	62.5
35	29	4.5	5.8	93.6
40	13	4.6	5.9	95.8
45	6	4.7	6.1	97.9
50	4	4.8	6.2	100.0

Explanation: F = mean number of children reaching age 5 per number of married women reaching a given age; F' = F adjusted for infant mortality, assuming 780/100 infants survived to enumeration at age 5 (see chapter 2, note 71); % = percentage of childbearing completed.

Table AI.14. Twenty-Nine-Month Cycle of Childbirth

Pregnancy
- 1 J conception
- F
- M
- A
- M
- J
- J
- A
- S
- O birth;

Nursing (amenorrhea)
- N lactation begins
- D
- 2 J
- F
- M
- A
- M
- J
- J
- A
- S
- O
- N menstruation
- D
- 3 J ovulation
- F
- M
- A
- M

Pregnancy
- J conception
- J
- A
- S
- O
- N
- 4 D
- J
- F
- M birth

29-month cycle

pregnancy	9 mos.
postpartum amenorrhea	13
anovulatory cycles	2
ovulatory cyles to conception	5
	29 mos.

SOURCE: Adapted from R. G. Potter, "Birth Intervals: Structure and Change," *Population Studies* 17 (1963): 155–66.

Appendix II:
Notes on Method

There are several short discussions of method interspersed throughout the text, but to preserve the narrative I chose to place some of the lengthier discussions here.

Selection of Materials

For this study of men and women on the overland trail it was necessary to separate documents of family life from the mass of available overland trail materials. I used several criteria: included were materials written by emigrants of the 1840s through the 1860s who planned to settle at their journey's end, and who traveled in association with women as well as men. Obviously excluded were the accounts of men who traveled in completely masculine company; diaries and recollections of unattached men compose the largest group of diaries and were the most difficult to weed out. Because the Gold Rush years were so completely male, the family criteria determined that there would be little discussion of emigration in the years 1849–51. For a study of families, I was interested mainly in the personal documents of married men and women or others— children, unmarried kin, or hired hands—who traveled as members of families.

Unfortunately there was no way to determine, by simply examining the title or the author of a particular account, the family status of the writer. Because 1849, 1850, and 1851 were almost exclusively male years and few men traveled with their families, I decided early in the research to exclude documents from those years. Out of the nearly 800 identified diaries and recollections, this exclusion ruled out almost 200. For the rest it was necessary to read into each of the available documents (sometimes nearly to the end) before I uncovered the writer's family and traveling status. After a long process of reading and discarding among over 450 documents, I assembled a mass of

Table AII.1. Emigrant Family Documents by Type

	Diaries	Letters	Recollections	Total
Men	22	8	52	82
Women	28	4	55	87
Totals	50	12	107	169

primary evidence which included 169 diaries and recollections of family members.[1] In addition I utilized the diaries and recollections of 115 single men who traveled with or in proximity to emigrating families, for additional descriptive material.

It is fair to raise the question as to how well these families represent the family emigration as a whole. Unfortunately, aside from the emigrant accounts there are no readily available and systematic sources of information about the composition or character of the emigration population that can be used for independent checks of validity. An intensive study of Oregon and California settlers, perhaps utilizing land-claim records, could provide a base against which one could assess the typicality of emigrant writers, but I judged this project too ambitious for the present study.

Drawing Out Behavioral and Cultural Information

I used the diaries, letters, and recollections to collect information about the behavior and beliefs of emigrant men and women in their day-to-day lives in their homes and on the trail. To begin, I carefully noted on a previously prepared and standardized sheet all genealogical, residential, occupational, and other personal historical information, as well as the traveling arrangements (party size, train size, and so on) that writers discussed in their narratives. Using these data, supplemented by that culled from a great number of family histories, genealogies, and diverse Oregon, California, and midwestern materials, I was able to reconstitute the genealogies and traveling parties of 122 emigrant families.[2] The reconstitutions, often lacking in one or two pieces of vital information but largely complete, provided me with the resources to draw conclusions about family demography, party and train composition, and the occupations, geographic origins, and previous mobility of emigrants.

Secondly, for the study of the division of labor, I compiled an inclusive catalog of daily-life activities on the trail.[3] This list was unbiased as to sex; either men or women could potentially perform each task. I was greatly assisted in compiling this catalog by the suggestions of P. G. Herbst, "The Measurement of Family Relationships," who writes that "the reliability of measurements obtained is directly related to the degree to which an unbiased random distribution of areas of behavior within the family can be obtained."[4] I tried to compile a complete list by carefully building up the catalog through checks and rechecks against the diaries during a preliminary period of reading.

In evaluating this behavioral inventory, as in other areas of data evaluation, I allowed the diary information to take the leading role. My judgments of the division of labor were in each instance based on firm indications obtained by the behavioral survey of the diaries. Recollections provided valuable and often colorful material to flesh out the indications from the diaries. In those instances where the recollections provided independent indications of activity not corroborated by the diaries, I have tried to be careful to note the derivation of the information in the body or notes of the text.

Notations of behavior on a check sheet did not replace collection of materials on note cards. However, I utilized a standardized set of subject headings for the collection of notes in order to ensure that I asked the same questions of each document.[5] These subject headings covered both behavioral and cultural information, a method that enabled me to locate passages and statements in the diaries and recollections passed over in earlier readings without the rigor of standardized questions.

Finally, in order to place the materials on trail life in context, I used midwestern travel accounts, recollections, and secondary studies of farm life in order to develop a structural description of midwestern society and culture. I found that my diary study helped to direct my reading of midwestern life, especially in researching aspects of the division of labor.

Studying the Diaries as Whole Documents: Content Analysis

In addition to plundering behavioral and cultural information from the materials, I also wanted to consider and study the
diaries as whole documents, in the expectation that if women
and men shared different cultural orientations, they could well
have written different kinds of journals. But the observable
differences between the diaries of men and women are subtle.
In order to test the thematic concerns of the diarists in a
systematic way I used a content-analysis method.

In the study of cultural materials one is ultimately looking for
the distinctive features of a particular culture. The various
parts of a culture are interrelated and unified by a set of
principles; it is these cultural regularities—values—that can
most distinguish the culture of a people. Systematic anthropology has taken up this study of values following the work of
Clyde Kluckhohn and particularly the Five Cultures project of
Harvard University in the 1950s and sixties. This work, conve-
niently summarized for historians by Berkhofer,[6] cannot be
used directly in historical analysis because of the inapplicability
of its methodology to historical materials. However, Ralph K.
White has proposed a content-analysis method of assessing
values that is applicable to historical, first-person narratives.
Essentially, White suggests testing written materials with a pre-
determined list of values. Using the sentence as the unit of
measure, he proposes noting each time the writer makes a
statement that implies the employment of a given value.[7]

Table AII.2. Tabulated Results of Content Analysis:
Percentage Distribution of Measured Thematic Content by Sex[a]

Category	Men	Women
Practical	28	24
Physiological	26	27
Aesthetic[b]	21	23
Amiable[c]	6	15
Aggressive[d]	15	7
Other	4	4
Total	100	100

[a] See Table AII.3, "Values Categories"; [b] value category = "Beauty"; [c] value categories = "Friendship," "Affection," and "Happy children"; [d] value categories = "Aggression" and "Dominance."

Table AII.3. Value Categories

1. *Physiological*

   Rest
   Health
   Safety
   Comfort
   Activity

2. *Social*

   Sexual love
   Family companionship
   Family affection
   Happy children
   Family home
   Friendship
   Community
   Pleasant personality
   Conformity
   Manners
   Modesty
   Generosity
   Tolerance
   Group unity
   National greatness

3. *Egotistical*

   Independence
   Achievement
   Recognition
   Self-regard
   Dominance
   Aggression
   Emotional security
   Happiness
   Strength
   Determination
   Intelligence
   Appearance
   Temperance
   Competence

4. *Playful*

   New experience
   Excitement
   Beauty
   Humor
   Self-expression

5. *Practical*

   Economic value
   Ownership
   Work

6. *Moral*

   Morality
   Truthfulness
   Justice
   Obedience
   Purity
   Religion

7. *Miscellaneous*

   Carefulness
   Culture
   Cleanliness
   Adjustment
   Knowledge

Although White's method has found little use among historians,[8] it offers a manner of moving beyond intuitive judgment and indicating the main concerns of the author of the narrative. Historians' interest is apt to be caught by the well-articulated statement; weaving these into a narrative is supposed to replicate the main concerns of the historical writer or writers. If there are no quotable quotes, however, this method fails, and in any event the approach always owes most to the particular and perhaps momentary sensibility of the individual historian. A method of building an incremental judgment about the central concerns of a narrative historical document is clearly preferable. Using the White method of value analysis is one such way.

The list of fifty-three values that I employed (see table AII.3) was compiled from White's study and two others.[9] The list is by no means intended as a model of human values in their complexity and interconnection. It was merely an attempt to reconstruct a *deliberately mechanistic* measure for use in evaluating historical narrative material.

After subjecting twenty-two men's and twenty-eight women's diaries to a somewhat simplified version of White's value analysis, I tabulated the results and made a ranking of values for each diary, based on frequency of occurrence. I then further tabulated the five most frequently occurring values for each diary and ranked them on two grand lists, one each for men and women, and compared the results. The final tabulation appears in table AII.2; discussion of results is in the introduction and chapter 6.

Comparing table AII.3 with table AII.2, it is readily apparent that the majority of value notations occurred in a small number of the categories. It is important, however, that the measure (in this case the value categories) be varied enough to allow for a wide range of results. In the case of the diaries, I expected the results from the content analysis to confirm my impressionistic evaluation after a preliminary reading. In fact, the results not only forced me to reevaluate my thinking, but pointed out important areas of emigrant concern (for example, the male preoccupation with hunting) which I otherwise would have missed, and which became crucial interpretative aspects of the entire study.

Notes

PREFACE

1. Johnny Faragher and Christine Stansell, "Women and Their Families on the Overland Trail to California and Oregon, 1842–1867," *Feminist Studies* 2 (1975): 150–66.

INTRODUCTION

1. Barbara Welter, "The Cult of True Womanhood: 1820–1860," *American Quarterly* 18 (1966): 151–74; Carroll Smith-Rosenberg, "The Female World of Love and Ritual: Relations between Women in Nineteenth-Century America," *Signs* 1 (1975): 1–29; Katherine Kish Sklar, *Catharine Beecher: A Study in American Domesticity* (New Haven: Yale University Press, 1973); Peter Gabriel Filene, *Him/Her/Self: Sex Roles in Modern America* (New York: Harcourt Brace Jovanovich, 1974).

2. This notion is central to the whole body of functionalist sociology of the family. For a major work of history in this tradition, see Edward Shorter, *The Making of the Modern Family* (New York: Basic Books, 1975).

3. In this study the term *patriarchy* will refer to "a set of social relations which has a material base and in which there are hierarchical relations between men, and solidarity among them, which enable them to control women." Heidi Hartmann, "Capitalism, Patriarchy and Job Segregation by Sex," *Signs* 1, no. 3, pt. 2 (1976): p. 138.

4. For an extended discussion of this point, see Robert F. Berkhofer, *A Behavioral Approach to Historical Analysis* (New York: Free Press, 1969).

5. See Eugene D. Genovese, "American Slaves and Their History," in *In Red and Black: Marxian Explorations in Southern and Afro-American History* (New York: Pantheon Books, 1971), pp. 102–28, esp. p. 102; David M. Potter, "American Women and American Character," in Don E. Fehrenbacher, ed., *History and American Society: Essays of David M. Potter* (New York: Oxford University Press, 1973), p. 303; Carl N. Degler, *Is There a History of Women?* (Cambridge: Clarendon Press, 1975), p. 9; Joan Kelly-Gadol, "The Social Relations of the Sexes: Methodological Implications of Women's History," *Signs* 1 (1976): 809–23, but esp. 812–17.

6. Smith-Rosenberg, "The Female World of Love and Ritual," is an ambitious attempt to come to terms with women as historical subjects and actors but one which founders on the two errors discussed here. Smith-Rosenberg examines exclusively feminine sources—principally diaries and letters—and on that basis concludes that the female world was one "in which men made but a shadowy appearance" (p. 2). The central problem here is the conceptual distinction between thought and behavior. Smith-Rosenberg lets her readers

mistakenly assume that these writings accurately depict women's actual movements and relations, that the "world" of women's diaries and letters was, in fact, the World. Of course, it was not. What she really shows is that in their writings women *allowed* men to appear in only shadowy ways. In itself this says nothing about women's actual behavior. Those women were not only sisters but daughters of fathers, wives of husbands, and mothers of sons as well; they spent a good deal of their active and emotional lives relating to men and to the world of men, as well as to women and their world. By failing accurately to place women and their writings in the reconstructed context of women's actual movements, work, responsibilities, roles, and relations—nearly all of which were historically shaped by sexual relations between women *and* men—Smith-Rosenberg ends by painting a romantic and sentimental portrait of woman-to-woman relations. Accepting the validity of her evidence, the comparison between the actual behavior of women and their writings may indicate that there was a deep ambivalence, a split between women's culture and women's social position, that helps us to illuminate the social contradictions infusing the sexual struggle. It seems to me that this latter kind of investigation ought to be the substance of men's and women's social history.

7. Mary Elizabeth Warner, "Wagon Train to California," p. 4 (syntax slightly rearranged). For complete references of emigrant accounts, see bibliography.

8. Merrill Mattes, *The Great Platte River Road: The Covered Wagon Mainline via Fort Kearny to Fort Laramie* (Lincoln: Nebraska State Historical Society, 1969), provides an excellent scholarly guide to the emigrant accounts, but the text is poorly organized and lacks focus. David M. Potter, "Introduction," in *The Trail to California: The Overland Journal of Vincent Geiger and Wakeman Bryarly* (New Haven: Yale University Press, 1962), pp. 1–73, and Dale Morgan, "Introduction," in *Overland in 1846: Diaries and Letters of the California-Oregon Trail* (Georgetown, Calif.: Talisman Press, 1963), are both good scholarly introductions. John D. Unruh, "The Plains Across: The Overland Emigrants and the Trans-Mississippi West, 1840–1860" (Ph.D. diss., University of Kansas, 1975), is a major scholarly work on the trail, exhaustively researched, with several stimulating sections (and an excellent chapter on emigrant–Indian relations), but with a dry as dust approach that characterizes too much of Overland Trail history. Still, Unruh's is now the authoritative work. For other minor works of scholarship, see the bibliography. For a major review of all the literature on the trail, see Unruh, "The Plains Across," chap. 1 and notes, pp. 593–605.

The most interesting studies are popularly written. David Lavender, *Westward Vision: The Story of the Oregon Trail* (New York: McGraw Hill, 1963), is good on the 1820s, 1830s, and early 1840s. George R. Stewart, *The California Trail: An Epic with Many Heroes* (New York: McGraw Hill, 1962), is excellent for the main years of emigration. Stewart has also written *Ordeal By Hunger: The Story of the Donner Party* (New York: Henry Holt, 1936); together with Bernard DeVoto, *The Year of Decision, 1846* (Boston: Little, Brown, 1943), these provide a deep, yet intimate look at the emigrants of 1846. Perhaps the best single account from the viewpoint of women as well as men is A. B. Guthrie, Jr., *The Way West* (New York: William Sloan Associates, 1949), a well-received novel based on a profound grasp of the primary sources.

9. *Missouri Gazette*, May 15, 1813; quoted in Gregory M. Franzwa, *The Overland Trail Revisited* (St. Louis: Patrice Press, 1972), p. 3.

10. *The Oregonian and Indian's Advocate*, January 1839; quoted in Clifford Merrill Drury, ed., *The First White Women Over the Rockies*, 3 vols. (Glendale, Calif.: Arthur H. Clark, 1963–66), 3: 315–16. For documents of the important 1836 and 1838 emigrations of missionary women, see Drury, *First White Women*, and *The Diaries and Letters of Henry H. Spaulding and Asa B. Smith* (Glendale, Calif.: Arthur H. Clark, 1958), also edited by Drury.

11. *Daily Missouri Republican*, February 27, 1849; quoted in Unruh, "The Plains Across," p. 99.

12. There are many books which describe the overland route, but I have found these to be the best: Franzwa, *The Overland Trail Revisited*, a travel guide with a lively written historical introduction; Irene Paden, *The Wake of the Prairie Schooner* (New York: Macmillan, 1943), delightfully and knowledgeably written; Ingvard Henry Eide, *Oregon Trail* (Chicago: Rand McNally, 1973), a beautiful combination of excerpts from emigrant diaries accompanied by Eide's photography of the route; Thomas H. Hunt, *Ghost Trails to California* (Palo Alto: American West Publishing Company, 1974), which duplicates Eide's effort for the Humboldt route, with striking color photographs and detailed maps. For detailed description of the many alternate routes and cutoffs, see studies cited in Unruh, "The Plains Across," p. 597, n. 29.

13. Mattes, *Great Platte River Road*, is devoted to the Missouri River–Fort Laramie section of the route.

14. LeRoy Hafen and Francis Marion Young, *Fort Laramie and The Pagent of the West, 1834–1890* (Glendale, Calif.: Arthur H. Clark, 1938).

15. Frank C. Robertson, *Fort Hall: Gateway to Oregon Country* (New York: Hastings House, 1963).

16. Mattes, *Great Platte River Road*, p. 23, reviewing each year, estimates 350,000; Unruh, "The Plains Across," pp. 173–74, with more apparent precision, estimates 53,000 Oregon and 200,000 California emigrants between 1840 and 1860.

17. See Mattes, *Great Platte River Road*, for the most comprehensive bibliography in print. I was able to utilize exhaustively the abundant Overland Trail materials of the Western Americana collections of the Beinecke Rare Book and Manuscript Library and Sterling Memorial Library, Yale University, supplemented by less extensive use of other important collections at the Henry E. Huntington Library, San Marino, California; the Bancroft Library, University of California, Berkeley; the Newberry Library, Chicago; the California State Library, Sacramento; and the Kansas State Historical Society, Topeka. For a discussion of the principles of selection for the family materials, as well as an inventory of the diaries, letters, and recollections by sex and method of reconstitution, see appendix II and table A.II.1.

18. Arthur Ponsonby, *English Diaries*, 2d ed. (London: Methuen, 1923), p. 11.

19. For a full discussion of the method and a tabulation of the results of the content analysis, see appendix II and table A II.2.

20. Helen Carpenter, "A Trip Across the Plains," pp. 27–28; George Belshaw, "Letters," pp. 222–23.

21. William Kahler, "Diary, 1852," n.p.

22. Thomas Cramer, "Diary of a Journey from Kansas to California," p. 2.

23. Mrs. E. A. Hadley, "Diary," p. 2. A similar concern with economics can be found in almost any woman's diary; see, for example, Mrs. Cecelia Emily McMillen Adams, "Crossing the Plains in 1852"; Maria Parsons Belshaw, "Diary"; Mrs. Elizabeth Dixon Smith Geer, "Diary"; Sarah A. Wisner, "A Trip across the Plains."

24. Henry Allyn, "Journal of 1853," p. 379.

25. Ponsonby, *English Diaries*, p. 17.

26. P. V. Crawford, "Journal of a Trip Across the Plains," p. 151.

CHAPTER 1

1. Francis Parkman, *The Oregon Trail* (New York: New American Library Signet Classics, 1950), p. 419. See table AI.1.

2. Of the adult male work force of these four states, 85.9 percent were in agricultural occupations, 82.3 percent in the north-central census districts (including these four states plus Ohio, Michigan, and Wisconsin). This compares with 67.9 percent in the mid-Atlantic district and 61.6 in New England. Richard Easterlin, "Inter-regional Differences in Per Capita Income, Population and Total Income, 1840–1950," in National Bureau of Economic Research, *Trends in the American Economy in the Nineteenth Century*, Studies in Income and Wealth, vol. 24 (Princeton: Princeton University Press, 1960), pp. 97–98.

3. See table AI.2. Of the 25 Oregon male heads of household who contributed either a diary or a recollection to this study, 22 appear in the federal population schedules for the 1850 census, and 18 of these, or 82 percent, also appear in the agricultural schedules as farm operators. Of the nonfarmer emigrants, 7 out of 10 had taken up farms in Oregon. See Oregon State Archives, *Pioneer Families of the Oregon Territory, 1850*, Bulletin no. 3, Publication no. 17 (Eugene, Ore., 1951). Although I have not collected systematic postemigration data for the rest of the heads of household in this study, these findings correspond with the data I have randomly accumulated.

4. Clarence H. Danhof, *Change in Agriculture: The Northern United States, 1820–1870* (Cambridge, Mass.: Harvard University Press, 1969), p. 150.

5. The Sharp family left three documents: Cornelia A. Sharp, "Diary: Crossing the Plains from Missouri to Oregon in 1852"; Joseph A. Sharp, "Crossing the Plains"; and James M. Sharp, *Brief Account of the Experiences of James Meikle Sharp*. James Sharp's account is the most complete in background detail.

6. Phoebe Goodell Judson, *A Pioneer's Search for an Ideal Home*, p. 9. By the 1840s the preemption principle was fully established. Any squatter on unclaimed land could, when the land was surveyed and came up for auction, exercise the first right to buy at a minimum price, usually $2 an acre. In Oregon the Donation Land Act of 1850 provided for grants of 320 acres to single men, 640 to married men; provisions extended until 1855. In California the complexities of Mexican titles left much attractive land vulnerable to squatters.

7. Camilla Thomson Donnell, "The Oregon Pilgrimage," p. 8.

8. Francis Parkman, "The Overland Trail Journal," vol. 2 of *The Journals of Francis Parkman*, ed. Mason Wade (New York: Harper, 1947), p. 442.

9. See, for example, Margaret M. Hecox, *California Caravan: The 1846 Overland Trail Memoir of Margaret M. Hecox*, and Nancy A. Hunt, "By Ox-Team to California."

10. The willingness to move and change has long been noted as a characteristic of North American—as opposed to European peasant—farmers. Paul Gates, representing the consensus of opinion in agricultural history, takes this factor to be the essential component in characterizing American farmers. "American farmers regarded their land as the means of quickly making a fortune through the rising land values which the progress of the community and their own individual improvement would give it. Meanwhile they mined the land by cropping it continuously to its most promising staple. They did not look upon it as a lifetime investment, a precious possession whose resources were to be carefully husbanded, whose soil they could enrich and would ultimately pass on to their children more valuable and more productive than when they acquired it." Gates thus emphasizes the element of change in the structure of farming. Paul W. Gates, *The Farmer's Age: Agriculture, 1815–1860* (New York: Holt, Rinehart, and Winston, 1960), pp. 399–400. Clearly, a study of migration would support this emphasis. As will become clear in chapter 2, however, I think a more complicated change/tradition structure describes farming more adequately. For a suggestive use of this mixed structure, see James Henretta, *The Evolution of American Society, 1700–1815: An Interdisciplinary Analysis* (Lexington, Mass: D. C. Heath, 1973).

11. Ray Allen Billington, *Westward Expansion: A History of the American Frontier*, 3d ed. (New York: Macmillan, 1967), p. 5. See Table AI.3.

12. Out of the 122 reconstituted families, I was able to complete mobility histories for 58 male heads of household and 21 women. These histories were drawn from diaries and journals, supplemented by family histories, genealogies, local histories, and other sources. I considered a history completed when I could locate an individual residentially for each year up to the year of emigration. By movement I mean such movement as would be noted in the sources; generally I have not counted moves within a county.

13. This model is not meant to include all types of family structure but merely to provide a general model. I find the concepts of life cycle and family types ably summarized in Lowry Nelson, *Rural Sociology* (New York: American Book Company, 1948), pp. 307–12.

14. See table AI.4. North Carolina, circa 1930, is, of course, a good distance from the Midwest, circa 1850. The two do have the advantage of probably sharing a basic rural social composition. See Nelson, *Rural Sociology*, pp. 310–11.

15. There were elderly couples on the trail, usually grandparents in kin parties, but I have found only one journal of an older married person—John Udell, *John Udell's Journal.* Because the Udells were the only family in the last stage, I will confine myself to the first three family types in the discussion to follow. In North Carolina, elderly couples were residing with grown children (Nelson, *Rural Sociology*, p. 310); hence, by accident, both mature categories appear the same in table AI.4.

16. See table AI.5.

17. This typology has not been simply imposed on the data but has a validity based on the clustering of age-values. Since I have grouped the families into three sequential stages, it is to be expected that the median ages of the husband and wife would increase in each successive stage. More significantly, the ages of the wives are not distributed randomly within each age range but tend to cluster around the median for each stage. Thus the semi-interquartile range (defined as half the difference of the range of values for the mid 50 percent of the cases of a stage) is less than the difference between the medians for two stages in all cases but one. In other words, this is a positive indication that people did not emigrate at just any time but at particular points in the family life cycle. (See table AI.6.)

The median and the quartile deviation are preferable as measures here because they are uninfluenced by extreme, atypical values, unlike the mean and standard deviation. Roderick Floud, *An Introduction to Quantitative Methods for Historians* (Princeton: Princeton University Press, 1975), recommends this approach in demographic work. Because men tend to marry and remarry at a greater variety of ages than women, the age of the wife is a better index to the family life cycle. For a similar assessment, see Crandall A. Shifflett, "The Household Composition of Rural Black Families: Louisa County Virginia, 1880," *Journal of Interdisciplinary History* 6 (1975): 235–60.

18. In 1850 per capita wealth in the north-central census districts was $249, in the mid-Atlantic district, $358, in New England, $417; calculated from tables in Joseph C. G. Kennedy, *Preliminary Report of the Eighth Census, 1860* (Washington, D.C.: Government Printing Office, 1862), pp. 130, 195. Per capita annual income was similarly distributed: $47 in the north central districts, $77 in the mid-Atlantic, $83 in New England; Easterlin, "Interregional Differences," pp. 97–98.

19. See table AI.7.

20. Peter H. Burnett, "Letters," p. 421. Burnett had considerable knowledge on this point; he made the move from Tennessee to Missouri in 1817, and after two moves within Missouri returned to Tennessee in 1826, finally moving back to Missouri again in 1830.

21. Clarence Danhof, "Farm Making Costs and the Safety Valve," *Journal of Political Economy* 44 (1941): 317–59.

22. Danhof, *Change in Agriculture*, pp. 114–15. Merrill E. Jarchow, *The Earth Brought Forth: A History of Minnesota Agriculture to 1865* (St. Paul: Minnesota Historical Society, 1949), p. 6, cites the Minnesota commissioner of statistics' estimate (1860) of $795 to start a farm; William Oliver, *Eight Months in Illinois*, pp. 240–46, suggested a range of $500 to $1,000, depending on the availability of labor; Robert E. Ankli, "Farm-Making Costs in the 1850s," *Agricultural History* 48 (1974): 51–74, reviewing recent work with census data, revises Danhof's estimate of $1,000 down to $500.

23. Benjamin F. Bonney, *Across the Plains by Prairie Schooner*, p. 1.

24. See table AI.8.

25. R. Carlyle Buley, *The Old Northwest: Pioneer Period, 1815–1840* (Indianapolis: Indiana Historical Society, 1950), 1:153.

26. "If you want to come you must start by the first of April with six or seven yoke of oxen to the wagon and as much as one or two hundred dollars in cash." Lafayette Spencer to William Spencer, Oregon Territory, December 27, 1852, in Lafayette Spencer, "Journal of the Oregon Trail," *Annals of Iowa* 8 (1908): 309.

27. Elisha Brooks, *Pioneer Mother of California*, p. 5.

28. Ezra Meeker, *Covered Wagon Centennial and Ox Team Days*; Lavinia Honeyman Porter, *By Ox Team to California: A Narrative of Crossing the Plains in 1860.*

29. "Advice to Prospective Emigrants to Oregon," *Iowa Capitol Reporter*, March 25, 1843, reprinted in *Oregon Historical Quarterly* 15 (1914): 297; Joel Palmer, *Journal of Travels*, in Early Western Travels, 1748–1846, ed. R. G. Thwaites (Cleveland: Arthur H. Clark, 1906), 30:258, 259, 262. See also Burnett, "Letters," p. 417, and Joseph E. Ware, *The Emigrants' Guide to California* (Princeton: Princeton University Press, 1932), p. 5. Overton Johnson and William Winter, on the other hand, recognized the need but feared the added weight and suggested that the wise farmer-traveler send his tools by ship around the Horn; *Route across the Rocky Mountains* (Princeton: Princeton University Press, 1932), p. 182. By the late 1850s, when the availability of tools on the coast had brought down the price, guidebooks advised leaving tools behind; see Randolph B. Marcy, *The Prairie Traveler: A Hand-Book for Overland Expeditions* (London: Tribune, 1863), p. 13.

30. There was a significant difference here between farmers and others. A full 45 percent of men with occupations other than farmer traveled to the Missouri crossings by boat or train, but only 17 percent of the farmers.

31. At the beginning of the 1847 season there were over a hundred retail establishments catering to the emigrant trade in Independence. George W. Buchanan, "Oregon and California" (a circular written for the *Western Expositor*), *Oregon Historical Quarterly* 11 (1910): 310–11.

32. Louis Hunter, *Steamboats on the Western Rivers* (Cambridge, Mass: Harvard University Press, 1949), pp. 48–49, 488. For railroad connections with the Missouri, see Robert E. Riegel, "Trans-Mississippi Railroads during the Fifties," *Mississippi Valley Historical Review* 10 (1923): 165–68. For a lengthier discussion of the jumping-off points, see Mattes, *Great Platte River Road*, chap. 4, and Unruh, "The Plains Across," chap. 5.

33. See table AI.9.

34. Stanley Vestal, *The Old Sante Fe Trail* (Boston: Houghton Mifflin, 1939), pp. 55–75, passim; David Lavender, *Westward Vision: The Story of the Oregon Trail* (New York: McGraw-Hill, 1963), chap. 12.

35. See George Wilkes, *A History of Oregon* (New York: n.p., 1945), 2:70; Edward E. Parrish, "Crossing the Plains," p. 95; Joel Palmer, *Journal of Travels*, p. 42; and Samuel Tetherow, *Captain Sol Tetherow, Wagon Master*, p. 23.

36. In general this picture fits nearly all the organized trains from 1843 through 1848. See Harrison C. Dale, "The Organization of the Oregon Emigrating Companies," *Oregon Historical Quarterly* 16 (1915): 205–27.

37. Mary E. Ackley, *Crossing the Plains and the Early Days in California*, p. 19.

38. Randall H. Hewitt, *Across the Plains and over the Divide*, p. 102.

39. John Minto, "Reminiscences," p. 133.

40. See, for example, Burnett, "Letters," p. 407; Tetherow, *Captain Sol Tetherow;* George L. Curry, Letter of May 1, 1846, in Dale Morgan, ed., *Overland in 1846: Diaries and Letters of the California-Oregon Trail* (Georgetown, Calif.: Talisman Press, 1963), pp. 520–23.

41. "Oregon Meeting," reprinted from the *Ohio Statesman*, April 26, 1843, *Oregon Historical Quarterly* 3 (1902): 392.

42. J. Henry Carleton, *The Prairie Logbooks*, ed. Louis Pelzer (Chicago: Caxton Club, 1943), p. 182.

43. Ibid., p. 233.

44. Tetherow, *Captain Sol Tetherow*, p. 8.

45. Parkman, *The Oregon Trail*, p. 50.

46. Vestal, *Old Sante Fe Trail*, pp. 57–75, passim; Everett N. Dick, *Vanguards of the Frontier* (New York: D. Appleton-Century, 1941), pp. 187–204; Bernard DeVoto, *Across the Wide Missouri* (Boston: Little, Brown, 1947), p. 34.

47. See, for example, James W. Nesmith, "Diary of the Emigration," pp. 339–40.

48. For a good discussion of these points in more detail, see David J. Langum, "Pioneer Justice on the Overland Trails," *Wyoming Historical Quarterly* 5 (1974): 421–39.

49. Edward Jay Allen, "Oregon Trail," n.p.

50. Henry Allyn, "Journal of 1853," p. 381.

51. Noah Brooks, "The Plains Across," p. 807.

52. See, for example, Mrs. Velina A. Williams, "Diary of a Trip across the Plains in 1853," p. 196; Sarah Royce, *A Frontier Lady; Recollections of the Gold Rush and Early California*, p. 21; Mrs. Lee Whipple-Haslam, *Early Days in California: Scenes and Events of the '50s As I Remember Them*, p. 10; and Hewitt, *Across the Plains*, pp. 130–31. See also Unruh, "The Plains Across," pp. 197–214.

53. Peter H. Burnett, *Recollections and Opinions of an Old Pioneer*. This conclusion is based on my own reading and cannot be documented precisely.

54. My own conclusions on these points are corroborated by Jean Webster, "The Myth of Pioneer Hardship on the Oregon Trail," *Reed College Bulletin* 24 (January 1946): 27–46. For discussion of emigrants and Indians, see Robert

L. Munkres, "The Plains Indian Threat on the Oregon Trail before 1860," *Annals of Wyoming* 40 (1968): 193–221, and Unruh, "The Plains Across," chap. 7, where emigrant-Indian cooperation is stressed.

55. I have reconstructed the traveling arrangements as a part of reconstituting 122 emigrant families. Because a few of these families traveled together, the 122 families constituted 118 parties. See table AI.10.

56. Joseph Aram, "Reminiscences"; Hecox, *California Caravan; The History of Jo Daviess County, Illinois* (Chicago: H. F. Kett, 1878), pp. 550, 575–76, 610.

57. Roxanna C. Foster, "The Third Trip across the Continent"; Mary Burrell, "Mary Burrell's Book"; *The History of Will County, Illinois* (Chicago: William LeBaron, Jr., 1878), p. 858.

58. Hewitt, *Across the Plains*; Mrs. Francis H. Sawyer, "Overland to California."

59. George Belshaw, "Journey from Indiana to Oregon"; Maria Parsons Belshaw, "Diary"; T. H. Ball, *Lake County Indiana* (Chicago: J. W. Goodspeed, 1873), pp. 101, 147–48, 319–20; T. H. Ball, ed., *Lake County, Indiana, 1884* (Crown Point, Ind.: Lake County Star, 1884), p. 400.

60. William Barlow, "Reminiscences of 70 Years." In three-generational families norms of residential association are at issue: does the second-generation married couple associate mainly with the parents of the husband (patrilocal) or the wife (matrilocal)? Among these 27 extended family parties there were 17 instances of patrilocal, 19 matrilocal, and 5 bilocal associations. Here parental associations would seem to have been a preferential rather than a customary matter.

61. Jesse Applegate, "A Day with the Cow Column in 1843"; Jesse A. Applegate, *Recollections of My Boyhood* (Rosebud, Ore.: Review Publishing Company, 1914).

62. Celinda E. Hines, "Diary of Celinda E. Hines." The party was later joined by the Judsons; see Judson, *Pioneer's Search*.

63. Mrs. Mary Jane Long, *A True Story: Crossing the Plains in the Year of 1852 with Ox Teams.*

64. Stuart and Caleb Richey, "Letters." James Akin, Jr., *Journal*, is the record of Eliza Richey Akin's son.

65. Hunt, "By Ox-Team."

66. We have three records of the Stearns emigration: Orson A. Stearns, "Appendix [to Mrs. Williams' Diary: Recollections]"; Charlotte Emily Pengra, *Diary of Mrs. Bynon J. Pengra*; and Velina A. Williams, "Diary." Parties of this size were as large as small trains.

67. See table AI.11.

68. Rebecca Ketcham, "From Ithaca to Clatsop Plains."

69. Thomas Holt, in his journal record of efforts to assist the stranded 1846 emigrants on the southern (Applegate) route to Oregon, described nearly all the emigrants he encountered as members of families. Indeed, when he distributed rations, he divided it among "the families." Thomas Holt, "Journal," in Morgan, *Overland in 1846*, 1:317.

70. For a discussion of the register, see Julia Cooley Altrocchi, *The Old California Trail* (Caldwell, Idaho: Caxton Printers, 1945), p. 18. Cumulative

figures reported in Albert Watkins, ed., *Publications of the Nebraska State Historical Society*, vol. 20 (Lincoln, 1922), pp. 230, 239, 252. LeRoy Hafen and Francis Young, *Fort Laramie*, p. 164, claim that 80 percent of the passing emigrants signed up.

71. See table AI.12.

72. *Missouri Daily Republican*, April 15, 1852, quoted in Watkins, *Publications*, p. 238.

73. Jack D. Eblen has shown the difference between the social and sexual composition of mining and farming populations in his demographic survey, "An Analysis of Nineteenth Century Frontier Populations," *Demography* 2 (1965): 405.

74. Eblen, "Frontier Populations," p. 412, also found that adult women were nearly all married. There were of course some single women on the trail; for mentions see C. B. Glasscock, *Lucky Baldwin*; Theodore Edgar Potter, *Autobiography*; and William H. Knight, "An Emigrant's Trip." But the numbers of single women were so small as not to seriously affect the assumption I make here.

75. See table AI.11, columns E and F.

76. Ibid. The Oregon and California statistics are given in the *Missouri Daily Republican*, November 4, 1853, quoted in Watkins, *Publications*, p. 252.

77. There were .86 hired men per family. Assuming again that most women were married and traveling with families, we can consider .86 times the percentage of women to be an approximation of the percentage of single men traveling in families; see table AI.11, column H. Overall, then, it is likely that about 11.6 percent of the emigration were single men in families, or 20.2 percent of all single men.

78. For the years 1843–48 and 1852–66, excluding the Gold Rush years to avoid biasing the sample in favor of all-male parties.

79. Adding the hired male and married percentages (table AI.11, column I) gives an idea of the percentage of emigrants moving within the family system.

80. Farm laborers constituted a minimum of 25 percent of the midwestern work force in 1860; calculated from statistics in *Eighth Census of the United States, 1860: Population*, pp. 662–63. All authorities agree that hired hands were underenumerated in the census, the main evidence for these conclusions. The published census reports do not distinguish between farm workers and farmers until 1860, and even then the latter category includes sharecroppers, tenants, and renters as well as proprietors. The manuscript population schedules, indexed by county, could be employed to develop a more accurate picture, as Curti demonstrates; see Merle Curti, *The Making of an American Community* (Stanford: Stanford University Press, 1959), pp. 449–58. For an extended treatment of agricultural workers, see David Schob, *Hired Hands and Plowboys: Farm Labor in the Midwest, 1815–1860* (Urbana: University of Illinois Press, 1975), especially pp. 250–72. See also Gates, *Farmer's Age*, pp. 196–99, 272–75, and Curti, *American Community*, pp. 140 ff., 146, 459. See chap. 2 for a discussion of the shift to commercialism.

81. Schob, *Hired Hands*, pp. 228–30.

82. Burrell, "Mary Burrell's Book"; Margaret Hall Walker, *The Hall Family Crossing the Plains*. The best background on the Donner–Reed party is George R. Stewart, *Ordeal by Hunger: The Story of the Donner Party* (New York: Henry Holt, 1936), especially chap. 2. The Donner literature is enormous, but one can be content with Stewart supplemented by C. F. McGlashan, *History of the Donner Party. A Tragedy of the Sierras* (Truckee, Calif.: Crowley & McGlashan, 1879). The advertisement is reprinted in Morgan, ed., *Overland in 1846*, 2:491.

83. Minto, "Recollections," pp. 125, 127, 159. See also John Minto, "Biography of Robert Wilson Morrison," *Transactions of the Oregon Pioneer Association* (1894): 53–57. On worker-family contracts generally, see Schob, *Hired Hands*, pp. 209–33.

84. Virginia Wilcox Ivins, *Pen Pictures of Early Western Days*, p. 121.

85. Mrs. John T. Gowdy, *Crossing the Plains: Personal Recollections of the Journey to Oregon in 1852*, p. 1. Cf. Schob's comments on farm family–worker relations: "Farm hands in pre–Civil War America were usually considered members of the family, or at least treated on a fairly equal basis." Schob, *Hired Hands*, p. 228.

86. Jessy Quinn Thornton, *Oregon and California in 1848*. For Stanton's story in detail, see Stewart, *Ordeal by Hunger*, pp. 22–23, 55, 77–86, 113, 116, 120–25.

CHAPTER 2

1. A central aspect of peasant systems is the essential immobility of the landed producer. See A. V. Chayanov, *The Theory of Peasant Economy* (Homewood, Ill.: American Economic Association, 1966), p. 51. Kenneth A. Lockridge has compared seventeenth-century Puritan towns with peasant systems in *A New England Town, The First Hundred Years: Dedham, Massachusetts, 1636–1736* (New York: W. W. Norton, 1970), p. 19.

2. Henretta, *Evolution of American Society*.

3. This is necessarily a highly schematic characterization. It corresponds with my reading of the literature on the changes that took place as North American farming was integrated into the capitalist market system. The best studies include Percy W. Bidwell and John I. Falconer, *History of Agriculture in the Northern United States, 1620–1860* (Washington, D.C.: Carnegie Institute, 1925); Gates, *Farmer's Age*; Danhof, *Change in Agriculture*.

4. Buley, *Old Northwest*, 1:202. See also James E. Davis, *Frontier America, 1800–1840: A Comparative Demographic Analysis of the Settlement Process* (Glendale, Calif.: Arthur H. Clark, 1977), pp. 20, 138, and chap. 7. John Fraser Hart, "The Middle West," *Annals of the Association of American Geographers* 62 (1972): 258–62, is an excellent introduction to the region, its history, economy, and culture.

5. Buley, *Old Northwest*, 1:202.

6. Avery Craven, "The Advance of Civilization into the Middle West in the Period of Settlement," in Dixon Ryan Fox, ed., *Sources of Culture in the Middle West* (New York: D. Appleton-Century, 1934), pp. 39–71, comments on the

growth of cultural institutions. For a critique of the idea of pure self-sufficiency, see Rodney C. Loehr, "Self-Sufficiency on the Farm," *Agricultural History* 26 (1952): 37–41. Loehr makes the perfectly reasonable point that no one was ever really self-sufficient, but he fails to see the utility of using the concept to clarify the differences between primarily home-consumption farming and specialized, commercial agricultural production. The distinction is important here because between these two systems are great differences in the organization and effects of the labor process. Loehr was criticizing a variant of antiquarian social history which he dismissed as romantic. But the study of daily life must be rehabilitated. The labor process—work itself, the object of that work, and its instruments—must be at the center of social history.

7. Sam Bowers Hilliard, *Hog Meat and Hoecake: Food Supply in the Old South, 1840–1860* (Carbondale: Southern Illinois University Press, 1972), pp. 13–14; Ted Gronert, *Sugar Creek Saga: A History and Development of Montgomery County [Indiana]* (Crawfordsville, Ind.: Wabash College, 1958), pp. 15–16.

8. Hilliard, *Hog Meat*, p. 14; Benjamin P. Thomas, *Lincoln's New Salem*, rev. ed. (New York: Knopf, 1954), p. 37. For a theoretical orientation to subsistence farming in a capitalist environment, see Boguslaw Galeski, *Basic Concepts of Rural Sociology* (Manchester: University of Manchester Press, 1972), pp. 37–38.

9. Douglass C. North notes that western farmers entered the commercial system in waves of expansion: 1816–19, 1832–39, 1849–57. If his "West" is divided into a series of regions corresponding to settlement patterns, however, it becomes clear that the Midwest I am discussing here underwent a surge of growth that propelled it decisively into the market economy only during the last wave, 1849–57; "Agriculture in Regional Economic Growth," in Stanley Coben and Forest G. Hill, eds., *American Economic History: Essays in Interpretation* (Philadelphia: J. B. Lippincott, 1966), pp. 258–66. For supporting evidence from a variety of perspectives, see the following: Danhof, *Change in Agriculture*, p. 8; Bidwell and Falconer, *History of Agriculture*, pp. 165–66; Gates, *Farmer's Age*, pp. 185–86; Paul W. Gates, *Agriculture and the Civil War* (New York: Knopf, 1965), p. 222; Earle D. Ross, *Iowa Agriculture: An Historical Survey* (Iowa City: State Historical Society of Iowa, 1951), pp. 26–50; Jarchow, *The Earth Brought Forth*; Evadene A. Burris, "Keeping House on the Minnesota Frontier," *Minnesota History* 14 (1933): 263–82; George F. Lemmer, "Farm Machinery in Ante-Bellum Missouri," *Missouri Historical Review* 40 (1946); 467–80, passim, but especially p. 473; Huburt Schmidt, "Farming in Illinois a Century Ago as Illustrated in Bond County," *Journal of the Illinois State Historical Society* 31 (1938): 138–59 passim; Gronert, *Sugar Creek Saga*, pp. 15–16. Paul David concludes that the crucial factor in the adoption of the reaper was the "altered market environment" in the fifties; see his "The Mechanization of Reaping in the Ante-Bellum Midwest," in Henry Rosovsky, ed., *Industrialization in Two Systems* (New York: John Wiley & Sons, 1966), pp. 3–39, especially p. 27.

10. Gates, *Civil War*, p. 130. For similar conclusions, see Bidwell and

Falconer, pp. 263–64; Schmidt, "Farming in Illinois," p. 145; Richard Bardolph, "Illinois Agriculture in Transition, 1820–1870," *Journal of the Illinois State Historical Society* 41 (1948): 249–50; Robert E. Ankli, "Agricultural Growth in Antebellum Illinois," ibid. 63 (1970): 387–98, especially p. 388.

For additional perspectives on this self-sufficiency economy, see Michael Merrill, "Cash Is Good to Eat: Self-sufficiency and Exchange in the Rural Economy of the United States," *Radical History Review* 3 (1976): 42–71.

11. See Wayne D. Rassmussen, "The Impact of Technological Change on American Agriculture, 1862–1962," *Journal of Economic History* 22 (1962): 578–91, especially pp. 580–81; Rassmussen, "The Civil War: A Catalyst of Agricultural Revolution," *Agricultural History* 39 (1965): 187–95. The best reference for improvements in farm technology is Leo Rogin, *The Introduction of Farm Machinery . . . during the Nineteenth Century* (Berkeley: University of California Press, 1931). For individual studies of adoption, see Lemmer, "Farm Machinery"; Schmidt, "Farming in Illinois"; Buley, *Old Northwest*, 1:180; and Bidwell and Falconer, *History of Agriculture*, p. 299. McCormick's sales out of his Chicago plant did not exceed 1,000 per year until 1855, when he sold 2,000. The next year sales climbed to 4,000; by 1865 McCormick was selling over 7,000 reapers annually. See Herbert A. Keller, "The Reaper as a Factor in the Development of the Agriculture of Illinois, 1834–1865," *Transactions of the Illinois State Historical Society* (1927): 110.

12. Gates, *Civil War*, p. 234. In a study of Champaign County, Illinois, Robert Severson found that farm mortgages were rare before 1854, that is, before the coming of the railroad: "Pre-1854 Champaign County is best described as an area of subsistence agriculture." Robert Severson et al., "Mortgage Borrowing As a Frontier Developed: A Study of Mortgages in Champaign County, Illinois, 1836–1895," *Journal of Economic History* 26 (1966): 153.

13. Rodney C. Loehr, "Minnesota Farmers' Diaries," *Minnesota History* 18 (1966): 291.

14. Hand power continued as the prime productive force through the nineteenth century. As Carl Hamilton, writing of the end of the century, remembered;

> Farming was that kind of business. Each hill of corn was important to the point of stopping the whole procedure of horse-drawn cultivation to uncover it—by hand. When harvest came the ears on those stalks would be picked, one at a time—by hand. Taken into the crib, it might even be scooped off the wagon—by hand. Eventually it would be shelled. Much of it would be pushed into the sheller—by hand. It would be elevated, in the shelled state, into a wagon. And then if it was being used for feed it would be scooped into the feed wagon or truck—by hand. Cobs would pile up on one side of the sheller. They would be scooped into a wagon, taken either to the cob house or shoved into a basement window—by hand. Eventually a pail at a time they would end up in the kitchen cookstove.

Finally the ashes would be carried out—by hand. The energy cycle was complete.

Hamilton, *In No Time at All* (Ames: Iowa State University Press, 1975), p. 72.

15. Ross, *Iowa Agriculture*, p. 21. In addition, overland emigrants carried hammer, wrench, and handsaw for quick repairs of wagons and running gear. One might add a multipurpose knife and a whetstone to the list of essentials. For illustrations and discussions of tools, see Oneita Fisher, "Life in a Log Home," *Annals of Iowa* 37 (1965): 561–73.

16. Loehr, "Diaries," p. 289; William Oliver, *Eight Months in Illinois* (Chicago: W. M. Hill, 1924; original ed. 1843), p. 97.

17. Buley, *Old Northwest*, 1:178.

18. Estimated from man-hour discussion in Buley, *Old Northwest*, 1:182. For figures on improved acres, see J. D. B. DeBow, *Statistical View of the United States . . . Compendium of the Seventh Census* (Washington, D.C.: U.S. Census Office, 1854), p. 169.

19. Oliver, *Eight Months*, pp. 85–86.

20. Bidwell and Falconer, *History of Agriculture*, pp. 166–70.

21. Buley, *Old Northwest*, 1:214.

22. Schmidt, "Farming in Illinois," p. 149; Oliver, *Eight Months*, pp. 77–78; William Brown, *America: A Four Years' Residence* (Leeds: privately printed, 1849), pp. 33–34.

23. As Chayanov points out, because of this connection between level of consumption and available labor, there was an incentive to high fertility and, at certain times in the family life cycle, the addition of economically active kin to the household; *Theory of Peasant Economy*.

24. William Ferguson, quoted in Harvey L. Carter, "Indiana in Transition, 1850–1860," *Agricultural History* 20 (1946): 108.

25. The following section is based on numerous sources, but see especially Logan Esarey, *The Indiana Home* (Crawfordsville, Ind.: R. E. Banta, 1943); Loehr, "Diaries"; Eric Sloane, *Seasons of America Past* (New York: Wilfred Funk, 1958); Henry C. Taylor, *Tarpleywick: A Century of Iowa Farming* (Ames: Iowa State University Press, 1970); and Hamilton, *In No Time*.

26. Kerosene lamps came into wide use during the early 1860s; Burris, "Keeping House," pp. 265–67.

27. W. O. Rice, "The Pioneer Dialect of Southern Illinois," *Dialect Notes* 2 (1902): 233.

28. "Animistic" is used here in its general sense—the belief in spirits—and is not meant to imply more specific forms like ancestor worship, object worship, and so on.

29. Frank R. Kramer, *Voices in the Valley: Mythmaking and Folk Belief in the Shaping of the Middle West* (Madison: University of Wisconsin Press, 1964), p. 107. In this essay, filled with insights, Kramer's analysis depends upon a distinction drawn between southern ("animistic") folklore and Yankee ("logical") thought. Kramer would have us believe that every Yankee was a peddler,

every southerner, a primitive. I grant that Kramer is to be allowed some license in his mythopoeic reconstruction, but his contrasts stretch historical truth too far. The folk collection he uses, Daniel L. Thomas and Lucy B. Thomas, *Kentucky Superstitions* (Princeton: Princeton University Press, 1920), is built on logical structures, rules of contrast, and analogy which recur in collections from "Yankee" areas of Illinois and Iowa. See, for example, Earl J. Stout, *Folklore from Iowa*, American Folk-Lore Society, *Memoirs*, vol. 29 (New York, 1936); Harry M. Hyatt, *Folk-Lore from Adams County, Illinois*, 2d rev. ed. (New York: Alma Egan Hyatt Foundation, 1965). One does not need to abandon the notion that regional origins were important to agree with Thomas Clark that "fundamentally there was little difference, North or South, in the actual structures of the communities"; Thomas D. Clark, *Frontier America* (New York: Charles Scribner's Sons, 1959), p. 302. The difference that Kramer has found but misidentified is not one of origins but of new modes of thought introduced by new, commercial styles of life. The Yankee peddler was the advance guard of a new society, not a New England invasion.

30. Oliver, *Eight Months*, p. 71.

31. Kramer, *Voices in the Valley*, p. 70. For a further discussion of midwestern superstition, see chap. 5.

32. William Cooper Howells, *Recollections of Life in Ohio from 1813–1840* (Cincinnati: Robert Clarke, 1895), p. 157.

33. I distinguish between the terms *sex* and *gender* by limiting sex to the biological status of a person, either male or female; gender is the culturally assigned status of a person in regard to what is deemed masculine or feminine behavior or belief. Gender roles, then, consist of attributes, beliefs, and behaviors appropriate for masculine men and feminine women. See Resca M. Vaughter, "Review Essay: Psychology," *Signs* 2 (1976): 122 n.

34. Michael P. Banton, *Roles: An Introduction to the Study of Social Relations* (London: Tavistock Publications, 1965), p. 71.

35. Banton, *Roles*, p. 19. Is there any longer any need to cite references for the assertion that biology is *not* destiny? See Eleanor Emmons Maccoby, ed., *The Development of Sex Differences* (Stanford: Stanford University Press, 1965), and Maccoby and Carol Nagy Jacklin, *The Psychology of Sex Differences* (Stanford: Stanford University Press, 1974), for both text and bibliography. Simone de Beauvoir, *The Second Sex* (New York: Random House, Vintage Books, 1974), remains the best general discussion after several years of remarkable feminist writings.

36. Harriet Holter, *Sex Roles and Social Structure* (Oslo: Universitetsforlaget, 1970), p. 55; Letha Scanzoni and John Scanzoni, *Men, Women and Change: A Sociology of Marriage and Family* (New York: McGraw-Hill, 1976), p. 16; Thomas C. Cochran, "The Historian's Use of Social Role," in Louis Gottschalk, ed., *Generalization in the Writing of History* (Chicago: University of Chicago Press, 1963), p. 103.

37. Sociologists and social psychologists usually employ the concept of role to refer to the abstract roles or norms—the script, as it were—said to structure

behavior. Thus T. H. Newcomb, cited in Banton, *Roles*, p. 27, distinguishes between roles, as abstract social norms, and role behavior, as activity in response to norms. Although the distinction between belief and behavior—culture and society—is useful and one that I have employed throughout this work, the distinction between "role" and "role behavior" extends this analytical device beyond method to overconceptualized conclusions. In reality, as with all human phenomena, there is only the nexus of attitude and behavior.

The best work on gender roles continues to be done in anthropology, where field observation of behavior determines the focus; this tradition runs from Margaret Mead, *Male and Female: A Study of the Sexes in a Changing World* (New York: William Morrow, 1949), to Ernestine Friedl, *Women and Men: An Anthropologist's View* (New York: Holt, Rinehart, and Winston, 1975). For an excellent symposium of recent work, see Reyna R. Reiter, ed., *Toward an Anthropology of Women* (New York: Monthly Review Press, 1975).

38. Cochran, "Social Role," p. 104. See also Robert Berkhofer, *A Behavioral Approach to Historical Analysis* (New York: Free Press, 1969), p. 91; Shirley S. Angrist, "The Study of Sex Roles," *Journal of Social Issues* 25 (1969): 222.

39. While this may suffice as a structural logic, it would not do as a causal assumption. Historically, the definition of masculinity and femininity itself has often acted as a fetter on (or less frequently, a stimulus to) what men and women could do, and thus culture has become the active force in the formation and change of the division of labor. I proceed here on the assumption that to begin by examining the organization of sex-specific behavior provides a reasonable context for the evaluation of evidence about attitudes and feelings. By following this methodological convention, however, I do not wish to imply judgments about a specific genesis and development of the sexual division of labor to 1850, or judgments concerning the historical play of cultural and behavioral forces in the development of relations between the sexes in the century since. These are matters calling not for assumptions but for specific historical investigation.

For a historical and structural discussion of the origins of men's and women's work, I have found the following most helpful and influential: M. Kay Martin and Barbara Voorhies, *Female of the Species* (New York: Columbia University Press, 1975); Kathleen Gough, "The Origins of the Family," Gayle Rubin, "The Traffic in Women: Notes on the 'Political Economy' of Sex," and Karen Sacks, "Engels Revisited: Women, the Organization of Production, and Private Property," all in Reiter, ed., *Toward an Anthropology of Women*; and Judith K. Brown, "A Note on the Division of Labor by Sex," *American Anthropologist* 72 (1970): 1073–78. Heidi Hartmann, "Capitalism, Patriarchy, and Job Segregation by Sex," *Signs* 1, no. 3, pt. 2 (1976): 137–69, is an excellent review and evaluation of the literature.

40. General sources for the following discussion of men's and women's work are Taylor, *Tarpleywick*, Sloane, *Seasons of America*, and Esarey, *Indiana Home*.

41. Calculated from figures in Buley, *Old Northwest*, 1:182.

42. Men were responsible for cleaning the privy. Most farms had out-houses used by women and children but disdained by men as effeminate. Ibid., 1:223.

43. Ibid., 1:153, 319.

44. Ibid., 1:217–18; Marjorie Caroline Taylor, "Domestic Arts and Crafts in Illinois (1800–1860)," *Journal of the Illinois State Historical Society* 33 (1940): 294. Jo Ann Carrigan, "Nineteenth Century Rural Self-sufficiency," *Arkansas Historical Quarterly* 21 (1962): 132–45, reprints from an antebellum manu-script many kitchen, garden, wash-day, and medicinal formulas and recipes, most from women's experience.

45. Oliver, *Eight Months*, pp. 109–10; Hamilton, *In No Time*, p. 163.

46. M. G. Wadsworth, in *History of Sangamon County, Illinois* (Chicago: Inter-State Publishing Company, 1881), p. 176; Everett N. Dick, *The Dixie Frontier* (New York: Knopf, 1948), p. 104; Buley, *Old Northwest*, 1:216–17.

47. For American variations of this traditional English chant, see Chuck Perdue, "Come Butter Come: A Collection of Churning Chants from Georgia," *Foxfire* 3 (1966): 20–24, 65–72.

48. Buley, *Old Northwest*, 1:392.

49. Loehr, "Diaries," p. 296; Taylor, *Tarpleywick*, p. 15.

50. Howells, *Recollections*, pp. 156–57.

51. For this discussion of diet I have relied on Buley, *Old Northwest*, 1:218–21; Evadene A. Burris, "Frontier Food," *Minnesota History* 14 (1933): 378–92; Burris, "Keeping House"; Edward Everett Dale, "The Food of the Frontier," *Journal of the Illinois State Historical Society* 40 (1947): 38–61; Hamilton, *In No Time*, pp. 143–45.

52. Taylor, "Domestic Arts," p. 287; Charles Beneulyn Johnson, *Illinois in the Fifties* (Champaign, Ill.: Flanigan-Pearson, 1918), pp. 18 ff; Ocie Lybarger, "Every Day Life on the Southern Illinois Frontier" (Master's thesis, Southern Illinois University, 1951), pp. 47 ff.

53. Samuel Willard, "Personal Reminiscences of Life in Illinois, 1830–1850," *Transactions of the Illinois State Historical Society* 11 (1906): 80; Evadene A. Burris, "Furnishing the Frontier Home," *Minnesota History* 15 (1934): 192; Richard Lyle Power, *Planting Corn Belt Culture* (Indianapolis: Indiana Histori-cal Society, 1953), pp. 109–10; Charles Beneulyn Johnson, "Everyday Life in Illinois near the Middle of the Nineteenth Century," *Transactions of the Illinois State Historical Society* 13 (1914): 51.

54. Buley, *Old Northwest*, 1:233–34; Hamilton, *In No Time*, p. 146.

55. Taylor, *Tarpleywick*, pp. 9, 13. For general studies, see Rolla Milton Tryon, *Household Manufactures in the United States, 1640–1860* (Chicago: Uni-versity of Chicago Press, 1917); Luther Hooper, "The Loom and Spindle: Past, Present and Future," in Smithsonian Institute, *Annual Report* (Washing-ton, D.C. 1914), pp. 629–78; Taylor, "Domestic Arts"; and Jared Van Wage-nen, Jr., *The Golden Age of Homespun* (Ithaca: Cornell University Press, 1953).

56. Howells, *Recollections*, p. 123.

57. William Oliver, *Eight Months*, pp. 89–90. "Inventories of the property

of estates all through the period mention wheels"; Schmidt, "Farming in Illinois," p. 144.

58. Van Wagenen, *Golden Age of Homespun*, pp. 264–65; Sloane, *Seasons of America*, p. 118.

59. Johnson, *Illinois*, p. 16.

60. Van Wagenen, *Golden Age of Homespun*, pp. 264–65; Sloane, *Seasons of America*, p. 118; Buley, *Old Northwest*, 1:205.

61. The emigrants of 1846 were, according to Parkman, "enveloped in brown homespun, evidently cut and adjusted by the hands of a domestic female tailor"; *Oregon Trail*, p. 50. See also Schmidt, "Farming in Illinois," p. 151; Taylor, *Tarpleywick*, p. 13.

62. Buley, *Old Northwest*, 1:201–10; Margaret Gilbert Mackey and Louise Pickney Sooy, *Early California Costumes, 1769–1847* (Stanford: Stanford University Press, 1932), pp. 101–10.

63. Wiley Britton, *Pioneer Life in Southwestern Missouri* (Kansas City: Smith-Grieves Company, 1929), p. 130.

64. Aunt Jane (of Kentucky), quoted in Elizabeth Wells Robertson, *American Quilts* (New York: Studio Publications, 1948), pp. 59–60.

65. Taylor, "Domestic Arts," p. 303; Patricia Mainardi, "Quilts: The Great American Art," *Radical America* 7 (1973): 39–40; quote in Mainardi, "Quilts," p. 40.

66. Soapmaking, Buley reports, was the last domestic manufacture to pass from the farm household; *Old Northwest*, 1:223. Soapmaking was still a common activity among Kansas farm women in the 1920s; Edgar Schmiedler, *The Industrial Revolution and the Home: A Comparative Study of Family Life in Country, Town, and City* (Washington, D.C., 1927), pp. 4–6.

67. Hamilton, *In No Time*, pp. 35, 37.

68. Schmiedler, *Industrial Revolution and the Home*, p. 6.

69. Vance Randolph, *The Ozarks: An American Survival of Primitive Society* (New York: Vanguard Press, 1931), p. 59.

70. *Compendium of the Eleventh Census; 1890: Part I—Population* (Washington, D.C.: Government Printing Office, 1893), p. 866.

71. Grabill estimates an age-specific infant (0–5) mortality of 220 out of 1,000 live births for the nineteenth century as a whole; W. H. Grabill, C. V. Kiser, and P. K. Whelpton, *The Fertility of American Women* (New York: John Wiley, 1958), p. 379.

72. See table AI.13, which does not measure the effect of terminated pregnancies; thus the following discussion will underestimate the rate of conception among women, and the calculated childbearing cycle should be taken as a maximum number of months.

73. See table AI.14. Mean = 29.0 months (s = 6.3). Standard deviation (s) measures dispersion of the data about the mean; s = 6.3, then, indicates that there is a high probability that any given case will be within 6.3 months of 29.0. For discussion of this measure, see Floud, *Quantitative Methods*, pp. 72–77.

74. S. B. Nerlove, "Women's Workload and Infant Feeding Practices: A Relationship with Demographic Implications," *Ethnology* 13 (1974): 207–14, establishes that in societies where women contribute significantly to the production of subsistence, mothers tend to introduce their babies to supplemental food earlier than mothers in other societies. This insight was the result of a quite logical reversal of standard assumptions: "Consider first how the energies of adult women are used for the acquisition of subsistence and for other economic tasks, and then, once these requirements have been established, to see how child-spacing and child tending are accommodated to the requirements of the woman's task"; Friedl, *Women and Men*, p. 8. This premise has been basic to my study.

75. Buley, *Old Northwest*, 1:310.

76. Lactation does indeed have the effect of prolonging postpartum amenorrhea and delaying ovulation. Lactation beyond a year, however, by which time the infant must be receiving its essential protein from supplemental sources, has little continued effect in delaying the menses. See Nancil L. S. Gonzales, "Lactation and Pregnancy: A Hypothesis," *American Anthropologist* 66 (1964): 873–78, and A. P. Perez, "Timing and Sequence of Resuming Ovulation and Menstruation after Childbirth," *Population Studies* 25 (1971): 491–503. Assuming a year's nursing, the 29.0-month interval between conceptions would be reasonable. If, on the other hand, babies were shifted to solid foods earlier, we would suspect that men and women were practicing a form of self-conscious family limitation, probably abstinence. See Louis Henry, "Some Data on Natural Fertility," *Eugenics Quarterly* 8 (1961): 87, 200–11. The notion that nursing prevents conception was long dismissed by male physicians as an old wives' tale. Only in the last twenty years has this piece of woman's wisdom been confirmed by science. It has, of course, been discussed and successfully practiced by young as well as old wives for centuries.

77. Using the scale employed by Nerlove, "Women's Workload," pp. 208–10. The several variables can be only approximated—the dependence of the midwestern economy on hunting, husbandry, and agriculture, respectively, and the determination of women's participation in the various subsistence activities listed. Scaling at the lowest range for women (that is, giving high relative importance to hunting, or estimating women's participation at low levels) and at the maximum (giving husbandry relative importance; or estimating women's participation at high levels) provides the range of 32 to 46 percent.

78. Dr. W. W. Hall, "Health of Farmer's Families," in *Report of the Commissioner of Agriculture for the Year 1862* (Washington, D.C.: Government Printing Office, 1863), pp. 462–63. All subsequent quotations from ibid., pp. 462–70, passim.

79. The following all document the same situation for farm women in the first quarter of the twentieth century: Randolph, *The Ozarks*, pp. 41–43; Schmiedler, *Industrial Revolution and the Home*; Edward B. Mitchell, "The

American Farm Woman As She Sees Herself," in U. S. Department of Agriculture, *Yearbook of Agriculture, 1914* (Washington, D.C.: Government Printing Office, 1915), pp. 311–18; U. S. Department of Agriculture, "The Needs of Farm Women," Reports nos. 103–106 (Washington, D.C.: Government Printing Office, 1905).

80. Daniel Drake, quoted in Harriet Martineau, *Retrospect of Western Travel* (London: Saunders and Otley, 1838), 3:224.

81. See Randolph, *The Ozarks*, pp. 41–43; Esarey, *Indiana Home*; Taylor, *Tarpleywick*; Sloane, *Seasons of America*.

82. Friedl, *Women and Men*, pp. 8, 135.

83. Of these, only whiskey was a male product. Buley, *Old Northwest*, 1:235; Taylor, *Tarpleywick*, p. 14; Hamilton, *In No Time*, pp. 46, 168.

84. Mitchell, "American Farm Woman," p. 314.

85. Mary Meek Atkeson, *The Woman on the Farm* (New York: Century, 1924), pp. 4–5.

86. "The Wife Who Wouldn't Spin Tow," Vance Randolph, *Ozark Folksongs*, 4 vols. (Columbia: State Historical Society of Missouri, 1946–1950), 1:123–24.

87. "The Scolding Wife," Paul G. Brewster, "Some Folk Songs from Indiana," *Journal of American Folk Lore* 57 (1944): 282–83; Mary O. Eddy, *Ballads and Songs from Ohio* (New York: J. J. Angustin, 1939), p. 214; last verse supplied in another version, "The Dumb Wife Cured," Randolph, *Ozark Folksongs*, 3:119.

88. I am here concerned only with the most obvious problems of the division of labor. For the larger question of the cultural roles of men and women, see chaps. 4–6.

89. Randolph, *The Ozarks*, p. 42.

90. Hamilton, *In No Time*, p. 73.

CHAPTER 3

1. Noah Brooks, "The Plains Across," p. 805; T. Emery Bray, "The Great American Trail [Eliza Vincent's oral history]," pp. 9–11, incorporates this section of Brooks's narrative without acknowledgment.

2. Rebecca Ketcham, "From Ithaca to Clatsop Plains," p. 256.

3. William Thompson, *Reminiscences of a Pioneer*, p. 2.

4. Enos Ellmaker, "Autobiography," p. 9; Thompson, *Reminiscences*, p. 2; Merritt G. Kellogg, *Notes Concerning the Kelloggs*, p. 54.

5. John L. Johnson, "Diary of an Overland Journey," pp. 11–12.

6. Mrs. Margaret Alsip Frink, *Journal of the Adventures of a Party of California Gold Seekers . . .* ; Sarah A. Wisner, "A Trip across the Plains"; Johnson, "Diary," pp. 11–12; Adrietta Applegate Hixon, *On To Oregon! A True Story of a Young Girl's Journey into the West*; Virginia Wilcox Ivins, *Pen Pictures of Early Western Days*, p. 53; William Kahler, "Diary, 1852."

7. Hixon, *On To Oregon!*, p. 8. See also Ivins, *Pen Pictures*, p. 53.

8. Margaret Gilbert Mackey and Louise Pickney Sooy, *Early California*

Costumes, 1769–1847 (Stanford: Stanford University Press, 1932), pp. 101–10; Edward Warwick and Henry C. Pitz, *Early American Costume* (New York: Century, 1929), pp. 291–98. For emigrant discussions, see Lavinia Honeyman Porter, *By Ox Team to California: A Narrative of Crossing the Plains in 1860*, p. 10; E. Allene Dunham, *Across the Plains in a Covered Wagon*, p. 2; Catherine M. Haun, "A Woman's Trip across the Plains," pp. 4–5.

9. James M. Sharp, *Brief Account of the Experiences of James Meikle Sharp*, p. 19; Celinda E. Hines, "Diary of Celinda E. Hines," p. 82.

10. Thompson, *Reminiscences*, p. 3. Most emigrants who discussed clothing testified that it was homespun. Among the more notable and interesting comments, see Peter H. Burnett, *Recollections and Opinions of an Old Pioneer*, p. 11; Martha Louise Hill Gillette, *Overland to Oregon*, p. 23; Juliet F. Olmstead, "Random Sketches," pp. 243–44; Mary A. Jones, "Story of My Life," p. 2. For an exception, see Haun, "A Woman's Trip," pp. 4–5.

11. Edwin Bryant, *What I Saw in California*, p. 50.

12. See Ketcham, "From Ithaca," p. 251; Kahler, "Diary"; and Henry Allyn, "Journal of 1853," p. 377.

13. Jones, "Story of My Life," p. 2.

14. Lucy Rutledge Cooke, *Crossing the Plains in 1852: Narrative of a Trip from Iowa to "The Land of Gold,"* p. 14. See also Randall Hewitt, *Across the Plains and over the Divide*, p. 124; Joaquin Miller, *Overland in a Covered Wagon*, p. 70; Mary L. Rockwood Powers, Letters to Her Mother, p. 2; Eleanor Allen, *Canvas Caravans: Based on the Journals of Esther Belle McMillan Hanna . . .* , p. 25; Porter, *By Ox Team*, p. 12.

15. Ivins, *Pen Pictures*, p. 53. She could make preserves from dried fruit; the other things must have been repacked from food processed the fall before.

16. Dunham, *Across the Plains*, p. 2.

17. Louise M. Rahm, "Diary," n.p.

18. Helen Carpenter, "A Trip across the Plains," pp. 3–4.

19. Caroline Matilda Kirkland, *A New Home; or, Life in the Clearings*, ed. John Nerver (New York: Putnam, 1953), p. 34.

20. Frink, *Journal of the Adventures*, p. 12.

21. Hixon, *On to Oregon*, pp. 7–8.

22. Ivins, *Pen Pictures*, p. 55.

23. Charles Frederick True, *Covered Wagon Pioneers*, p. 25.

24. Frances C. Peabody, "Across the Plains DeLuxe in 1865," p. 72.

25. Brooks, "The Plains Across," p. 807. See also Hewitt, *Across the Plains*, p. 122; Mary Burrell, "Mary Burrell's Book," p. 17.

26. Agnes Stewart, "Journey to Oregon," p. 80.

27. Carpenter, "Trip across the Plains," p. 20.

28. George Belshaw, "Journal from Indiana to Oregon," pp. 21–22 (punctuation added).

29. See, for example, Thomas Cramer, "Diary of a Journey from Kansas to California," p. 8, and Wisner, "Trip across the Plains," p. 21.

30. See, for example, Harriet Sherrill Ward, *Prairie Schooner Lady: The Journal of Harriet Sherrill Ward, 1853*, p. 57; John Udell, *John Udell Journal*, p. 44; and Charlotte Emily Pengra, *Diary of Mrs. Bynon J. Pengra*, p. 8.

31. See, for example, Edward Jay Allen, "Oregon Trail," n.p.

32. Jesse Applegate, "A Day with the Cow Column in 1843," p. 379.

33. Ketcham, "From Ithaca," p. 277.

34. Sarah Royce, *A Frontier Lady: Recollections of the Gold Rush and Early California*, p. 24.

35. George Belshaw, "Journey," p. 20.

36. George Belshaw to Henry Belshaw, "Letters," pp. 222–23.

37. For comments on the detested guard duty, see Ketcham, "From Ithaca," p. 382, and Francis Parkman, *The Oregon Trail* (New York: New American Library, Signet Classics, 1950), p. 64.

38. See, for example, Johnson, "Diary," p. 38.

39. These aspects of leadership are discussed fully in chaps. 4–6.

40. Brooks, "The Plains Across," p. 807; Hewitt, *Across the Plains*, p. 122; Burrell, "Mary Burrell's Book," p. 17.

41. These questions are discussed at length in chapter 6.

42. This was something family men might disregard but single men quickly discovered. "In this section of the country we had found out . . . that supper won't come of itself—so we . . . made a fire, and by its cheering blaze made some 'piping hot' coffee and cooked some ham, which (with our pilot bread) we ate as men who had earned it—and then sat up part of the night cooking rice and dried apples for next day's journey." And again: "Everyman became his own washerwoman." Allen, "Oregon Trail," n.p.

43. Hewitt, *Across the Plains*, p. 36. Perhaps precisely because he was frank in this regard, Hewitt was an unusually acute male observer of women's work.

44. Mrs. Amelia Stewart Knight, "Diary of an Oregon Pioneer of 1853," p. 49.

45. Hewitt, *Across the Plains*, pp. 296–97, 305, 350; Lydia Allen Rudd, "Diary of Overland Journey from St. Joseph, Missouri to Burlington, Oregon, By Way of the Oregon Trail, the Dalles, Oregon City and Salem," n.p.; Andrew S. McClure, *The Diary*, p. 74; Hines, "Diary," pp. 108–9.

46. Carpenter, "Trip across the Plains," p. 28.

47. James Clyman, *James Clyman, Frontiersman*, ed. Charles L. Camp (Portland, Ore.: Champoeg Press, 1960), p. 75.

48. Mrs. Lodisa Frizzell, *Across the Plains to California in 1852*, p. 5.

49. Virginia Reed Murphy, "Across the Plains in the Donner Party (1846)," p. 414. For stories of women learning to cook over a campfire, see Porter, *By Ox Team*, pp. 9–10; Ivins, *Pen Pictures*, pp. 68–69; Haun, "A Woman's Trip," p. 7; and Arrazine Angeline Cooper, "Pioneer Across the Plains," pp. 139–40.

50. A. J. Allen, *Ten Years in Oregon*, p. 148.

51. See, for example, Sarah J. Cummins, *Autobiography and Reminiscences*, p. 30.

52. Allen, *Canvas Caravans*, p. 37.

53. McClure, *Diary*, p. 9.

54. Mrs. Cecelia Emily McMillen Adams, "Crossing the Plains in 1852," pp. 292, 321.

55. Clyman, *James Clyman*, p. 71.

56. Enoch W. Conyers, "Diary," p. 425.

57. Ketcham, "From Ithaca," p. 268.

58. Carpenter, "Trip across the Plains," p. 28; Allen, *Canvas Caravans*, p. 29.

59. James Frazier Reed, "Diary," p. 274. I have found only a few instances of men gathering the chips; see, for example, Hugh Cosgrove, "Reminiscences," p. 261.

60. For renditions emphasizing the queasiness of women, see Samuel Hancock, *Narrative of Samuel Hancock*, pp. 9–10; C. H. Crawford, *Scenes of Earlier Days*, p. 9; Cummins, *Autobiography*, p. 26; and Hixon, *On To Oregon!*, p. 24. These are all recollections. Diary accounts, for example, Conyer, "Diary," p. 441, make no mention of any controversy at all, which tends to discount the notion that women's complaints were at all significant.

61. Mrs. David Eccles, Interview, p. 263. See also Hixon, *On to Oregon!*, pp. 20, 36; Porter, *By Ox Team*, p. 42; Ellmaker, "Autobiography," p. 12.

62. Perhaps the most fascinating detailed day-to-day account of cooking is Pengra, *Diary*. See also Adams, "Crossing the Plains," p. 296; Henry Bradley and Nancy J. Bradley, "Journal," p. 8; Cramer, "Diary," p. 3; and Allyn, "Journal," p. 416.

63. Helen Stewart, *Diary*, p. 4. See also Hines, "Diary," p. 109; Porter, *By Ox Team*, p. 42; and Walter H. McIntosh, *Allen and Rachel: An Overland Honeymoon in 1853*, p. 58.

64. Bryant, *What I Saw in California*, pp. 10–11.

65. James Longmire, "Narrative of a Pioneer," p. 51.

66. Loren B. Hastings, "Diary of . . . a Pioneer," pp. 2, 4; Edward E. Parrish, "Crossing the Plains," p. 101; Mrs. Elizabeth Dixon Smith Geer, "Diary," p. 162.

67. Hewitt, *Across the Plains*, p. 322.

68. George Belshaw, "Journey," p. 32.

69. See, for example, Pengra, *Diary*; Knight, "Diary"; and Hastings, "Diary."

70. Bryant, *What I Saw in California*, p. 32.

71. Ketcham, "From Ithaca," p. 283.

72. Mary L. Rockwood Powers, "The Overland Route: Leaves From the Journal of a California Emigrant," *Amateur Book Collector* 1 (December 1950): 11.

73. Geer, "Diary," p. 167.

74. For a discussion of children on the trail, see Ruth Barnes Moynihan, "Children and Young People on the Overland Trail," *Western Historical Quarterly* 6 (1975): 279–94.

75. Gillette, *Overland to Oregon*, pp. 40–41; Hines, "Diary," pp. 79 ff., passim; Burrell, "Mary Burrell's Book."

76. Carpenter, "Trip across the Plains," pp. 27–28.

77. Sawyer, "Overland," p. 3; Hixon, *On to Oregon!*, p. 17; Ketcham, "From Ithaca," p. 338.

78. Jessy Quinn Thornton, *Oregon and California in 1848*, p. 54.

79. Elias J. Draper, *Autobiography of Elias J. Draper, A Pioneer of California*, p. 18; McIntosh, *Allen and Rachel*, p. 58; Kellogg, *Notes*.

80. See Mary E. Ackley, *Crossing the Plains and Early Days in California*, p. 20; Cooke, *Crossing the Plains*, p. 15; Powers, "The Overland Route," *Amateur Book Collector* 1 (September 1950): 2.

81. "Crossing the Plains" (1855), in Richard A. Dwyer and Richard E. Lingenfelter, *The Songs of the Gold Rush* (Berkeley: University of California Press, 1964), p. 41.

82. John A. Johnson, "Letters to His Wife," n.p.; see letters of April 1, 22, and 29 and May 3 and 10, 1849.

83. Ketcham, "From Ithaca," p. 275.

84. Cooke, *Crossing the Plains*, p. 61.

85. Sawyer, *Overland to California*, p. 3.

86. Albert Jerome Dickson, *Covered Wagon Days*, pp. 63–64. This is a semifictional account based on a diary.

87. Joel Barnett, *A Long Trip in a Prairie Schooner*, p. 105.

88. See Powers, Letters to Her Mother, p. 2.

89. Hixon, *On to Oregon!*, p. 15; Margaret Hall Walker, *The Hall Family Crossing the Plains*, p. 27.

90. See, for example, Jones, "Story of My Life," p. 5, and Pengra, *Diary*, p. 55.

91. See, for example, Lydia Milner Waters, "A Trip across the Plains in 1855," pp. 74–75; Ward, *Prairie Schooner Lady*, p. 24; Pengra, *Diary*, p. 8; Cummins, *Autobiography*, p. 28; Dunham, *Across the Plains*, p. 10; Thompson, *Reminiscences*, p. 9; and Thomas W. Prosch, *David S. Maynard and Catherine T. Maynard: Biographies of Two of the Overland Immigrants of 1850*, p. 18.

92. Burnett, *Recollections*, p. 108.

93. Sawyer, "Overland to California," p. 10. See also Helen Stewart, *Diary*, p. 17; Waters, "A Trip," p. 66; and Mrs. John T. Gowdy, *Crossing the Plains: Personal Recollections of the Journey to Oregon in 1852*, p. 2.

94. Haun, "A Woman's Trip," p. 4.

95. Susan P. Angell, "Sketch of Mrs. Susan P. Angell, A Pioneer of 1852," p. 55.

96. Ward, *Prairie Schooner Lady*, p. 153. See also Nancy A. Hunt, "By Ox-Team to California," p. 12; Murphy, "Across the Plains," p. 413; Susan Thompson Lewis Parrish, "Westward in 1850," p. 2; Hewitt, *Across the Plains*, pp. 98, 143; and Jacob Wright Harlan, *California '46 to '88*, p. 36. Most diarists record only one or two spontaneous evening dances over the whole trip. Burrell, "Mary Burrell's Book," pp. 19, 28, 30, 31, 35, notes five such evenings, but hers is an exception. The notion of nightly social gatherings is a product of the less reliable recollections.

97. Helen Stewart, *Diary*, p. 19; Agnes Stewart, "The Journey to Oregon,"

p. 91; Mrs. Catherine V. Waite, *Adventures in the Far West*, p. 56; Haun, "A Woman's Trip," p. 31; Hastings, "Diary," p. 17; Parkman, *Journals*, 2:447.

98. Haun, "A Woman's Trip," p. 30.

99. Helen Stewart, *Diary*, pp. 6, 10, 12; Mrs. Maria Hargrave Shrode, "Overland By Ox-Train in 1870," p. 18; Allyn, "Journal," p. 430; John Minto, "Reminiscences . . . ," p. 140.

100. Hewitt, *Across the Plains*, p. 98. See also Ward, *Prairie Schooner Lady*, p. 69.

101. John S. Zieber, "Diary," p. 314.

102. Parrish, "Crossing the Plains," p. 91; Minto, "Reminiscences," p. 141.

103. Peter H. Burnett, "Letters," p. 420.

104. Minto, "Reminiscences," p. 148.

105. Adams, "Crossing the Plains," p. 292.

106. Parrish, "Crossing the Plains," p. 93. Minto believed Parrish's estimate to be low because of the great number of wounded cows that escaped to die miles away; Minto, "Reminiscences," p. 150.

107. Burnett, "Letters," p. 420.

108. Belshaw, "Journey," p. 14.

109. Minto, "Reminiscences," p. 149.

110. Phoebe Goodell Judson, *A Pioneer's Search for an Ideal Home*, p. 23.

CHAPTER 4

1. W. O. Rice, "The Pioneer Dialect of Southern Illinois," *Dialect Notes* 2 (1902): 231

2. Harriet Ward, *Prairie Schooner Lady*, pp. 83, 96, 130.

3. E. Allene Dunham, *Across the Plains*, pp. 6–7.

4. Mrs. Elizabeth Lord, *Reminiscences of Eastern Oregon*, p. 48.

5. Alonzo F. Brown, *Autobiography*, pp. 21–22.

6. Peter Burnett, *Recollections and Opinions of an Old Pioneer*, p. 10.

7. Ward, *Prairie Schooner Lady*, p. 39.

8. George Belshaw, "Journey from Indiana to Oregon," pp. 1, 5; "Letters," p. 223.

9. Randall H. Hewitt, *Across the Plains and over the Divide*, p. 333.

10. Margaret M. Hecox, *California Caravan*, pp. 52–53.

11. Mrs. Benjamin G. Ferris, *The Mormons at Home*, pp. 20–21.

12. Andrew S. McClure, *Diary*, p. 87.

13. William Keil, "Letters from . . . Missouri to Oregon," p. 34.

14. Andrew J. Chambers, "Pioneer History," p. 10.

15. Basil G. Parker, *The Life and Adventures of Basil G. Parker*, p. 17.

16. Mrs. Matthew P. Deady, "Crossing the Plains to Oregon in 1846," p. 59.

17. Hecox, *California Caravan*, p. 28.

18. Lavinia Honeyman Porter, *By Ox Team to California*, p. 78.

19. Arrazine Angeline Cooper, "Pioneer across the Plains," pp. 140–41.

20. Agnes Stewart, "The Journey to Oregon," pp. 80, 84.

21. Maria Parsons Belshaw, "Diary," p. 327.

22. Sarah J. Cummins, *Autobiography and Reminiscences*, p. 30.

23. See George R. Stewart, *Ordeal by Hunger: The Story of the Donner Party* (New York: Henry Holt, 1936), p. 17.

24. Porter, *By Ox Team*, p. 30.

25. Stewart, "Journey to Oregon," p. 79.

26. Porter, *By Ox Team*, p. 30.

27. "The Boys Won't Do To Trust," in Vance Randolph, *Ozark Folksongs*, 4 vols. (Columbia: Missouri State Historical Society, 1946–50), 1: 217.

28. Edward Jay Allen, "Oregon Trail," n.p.

29. Mariett Foster Cummings, "Second Trip across the Continent," p. 120.

30. Porter, *By Ox Team*, p. 19. Most men and women, however, seemed to accept pipe smoking among women, especially old "grannies." See, for example, Benjamin F. Bonney, *Across the Plains by Prairie Schooner*, p. 2; George Belshaw, "Letters," p. 219. Generally, the more southern the home of the emigrants, the more likely were the women to use tobacco (Everett N. Dick, *The Dixie Frontier* [New York: Knopf, 1948], pp. 286, 309).

31. J. Orin Oliphant, ed., "Mrs. Lucy A. Ide's Diary 'In a Prairie Schooner, 1878,' " p. 131.

32. Nancy A. Hunt, "By Ox Team to California," p. 10.

33. Helen Marnie Stewart, *The Diary of Helen Marnie Stewart*, pp. 5, 9, 19, 22.

34. Ward, *Prairie Schooner Lady*, p. 52.

35. Rebecca Ketcham, "From Ithaca to Clatsop Plains," p. 267.

36. Maria Parsons Belshaw, "Diary," p. 330.

37. Hewitt, *Across the Plains*, p. 127.

38. Lucy Rutledge Cooke, *Crossing the Plains in 1852*, p. 7.

39. Samuel Dexter Francis, "Journal," p. 91.

40. Elizabeth Keyes, "Across the Plains," p. 73.

41. Nancy J. Bradley and Henry Bradley, "Journal," p. 61.

42. Enoch W. Conyers, "Diary," p. 460; see also p. 467.

43. Mary L. Rockwood Powers, "The Overland Route; Leaves From the Journal of a California Emigrant," *Amateur Book Collector* 1 (November 1950): 6.

44. Edwin Bryant, *What I Saw in California*, p. 49.

45. See pp. 29–30.

46. Mrs. Lee Whipple Haslam, *Early Days in California*, p. 9.

47. Edward Jay Allen, "Oregon Trail," n.p.

48. Katherine Dunlap, "Journal," p.20. Randall Hewitt also thought that "a trip like this overland journey will come nearer to bringing out the good and bad instincts of human beings than anything else which can be named" (*Across the Plains*, p. 202).

49. Mrs. Margaret A. Frink, *Journal of the Adventures of a Party of California Gold-Seekers*, p. 102.

50. John A. Johnson, "Letters to His Wife," n.p.

51. Elkanah Walker, "Diary," in Clifford Merrill Drury, ed., *First White Women over the Rockies*, 3 vols. (Glendale, Calif.: Arthur H. Clark, 1963–66), 3: 260.

52. Henry J. Carleton, *The Prairie Logbooks*, ed. Louis Pelzer (Chicago: Caxton Club, 1943), pp. 181–82.

53. Cooke, *Crossing the Plains*, p. 58.

54. John Minto, "Reminiscences," p. 141.

55. James Longmire, "Narrative of a Pioneer," p. 51.

56. William A. Maxwell, *Crossing the Plains*, p. 22.

57. James Frazier Reed, "Letter of June 16, 1846," pp. 274–76. "Sucker" was the contemporary label for a resident of Illinois.

58. Ward, *Prairie Schooner Lady*, pp. 66–67, 70.

59. Agnes Stewart, "Journey to Oregon," p. 86.

60. Sarah A. Wisner, "A Trip across the Plains," p. 26.

61. John L. Johnson, "Diary of an Overland Journey," pp. 81–82 (punctuation added).

62. See Stewart, *Ordeal by Hunger*, pp. 63–65.

63. Agnes Stewart, "Journey to Oregon," pp. 88, 89.

64. Mary E. Ackley, *Crossing the Plains and Early Days in California*, p. 23.

65. Chambers, "Pioneer History," p. 7.

66. Ward, *Prairie Schooner Lady*, p. 46.

67. Catherine M. Haun, "A Woman's Trip across the Plains," p. 27.

68. Among accounts stressing competition as a value of the ante-bellum age, see Richard Hofstadter, *The Age of Reform* (New York: Random House, Vintage Books, 1955), chap. 3, and Edward Pessen, *Jacksonian America: Society, Personality, and Politics* (Homewood, Ill.: Dorsey Press, 1969), chap. 2 and 4.

69. I have found Mark A. May, Gordon Allport, and Gardner Murphy, *Memorandum on Research in Competition and Cooperation* (New York: Social Science Research Council, 1937), pp. 13–44, helpful in thinking about the psychology of competition. See also Mark A. May and Leonard Doob, *Competition and Cooperation* (New York: Social Science Research Council, 1937).

70. McClure, *Diary*, p. 69.

71. J. M. Shively, *Route and Distances to Oregon and California*, p. 6.

72. Sarah Royce, *A Frontier Lady*, p. 12.

73. See Samuel Tetherow, *Captain Sol Tetherow, Wagon Master,* and Roland Keith Clark and Lowell Tiller, *Terrible Trail: The Meek Cutoff, 1845* (Caldwell, Idaho: Caxton Printers, 1966).

74. See the roster of emigrants in Clark and Tiller, *Terrible Trail*.

75. Samuel Hancock, *Narrative of Samuel Hancock*, pp. 12–13, 32, 9. Cf. also George Belshaw's comments about women, p. 90.

76. Alexis de Tocqueville, *Democracy in America* (Garden City, New York: Doubleday Anchor Books, 1969), p. 603.

77. See the comments of George Herbert Mead quoted in Michael P. Banton, *Roles: An Introduction to the Study of Social Relations* (London: Tavistock Publications, 1965), p. 25.

78. Helen Carpenter, "A Trip across the Plains," p. 20.

79. Ward, *Prairie Schooner Lady*, p. 153.

80. Helen Marnie Stewart, *Diary*, p. 11.

81. *The Second Sex* (New York: Random House, Vintage Books, 1974), pp. xvii–xviii.

82. This is so obvious that we tend to think of costume as a neutral factor. My discussion is inspired, however, by the notion that people dress themselves in accordance with a customary set of signs.

> Costume may serve as a mode of constraint in a very direct sense: women's dress, for example, hinders physical freedom and requires modest demeanour if it is not to be soiled. Young Arabs of the upper classes used once to let the nails of their little fingers grow long; anyone but a man of leisure would have been unable to do this, so it served effectively as an indicator of their wealth.

Banton, *Roles*, pp. 77–78.

83. Ketcham, "From Ithaca," p. 263.

84. Dunham, *Across the Plains*, p. 10.

85. Solomon Kingerly, "Three Letters," p. 86 (text as in original).

86. Cooke, *Crossing the Plains*, p. 24. See also Jane D. Kellogg, "Memories of Jane D. Kellogg," p. 93.

87. Mrs. Frances H. Sawyer, "Overland to California," p. 4.

88. For later years see Marie Nash, "Diary," p. 2, and Cora Wilson Agatz, "A Journey across the Plains in 1866," p. 172. Charles Nelson Gattey, *The Bloomer Girls* (New York: Coward-McCann, 1968), claims that the costume was generally forgotten by 1860.

89. Ward, *Prairie Schooner Lady*, p. 58.

90. Ketcham, "From Ithaca," p. 263.

91. Virginia Wilcox Ivins, *Pen Pictures of Early Western Days*, p. 64.

92. The lack of attention to the topic in the diaries may indicate that the embarrassment was mainly an aspect of recollection, not experience.

93. Frink, *Journal*, pp. 18–19.

94. Luzena Stanley Wilson, *Luzena Stanley Wilson, '49er*, p. 9.

95. Porter, *By Ox Team*, p. 136.

96. Loren B. Hastings, "Diary of Loren B. Hastings," p. 13.

97. Ward, *Prairie Schooner Lady*, p. 168.

98. Agnes Stewart, "Journey to Oregon," p. 80.

99. Ward, *Prairie Schooner Lady*, p. 82.

100. Lydia Milner Waters, "A Trip across the Plains in 1855," p. 77.

101. Adrietta Applegate Hixon, *On to Oregon!*, pp. 21, 8, 45–46.

102. Henry M. Hyatt, *Folk-Lore from Adams County, Illinois*, 2d rev. ed. (New York: Alma Egan Hyatt Foundation, 1965), p. 631.

103. R. Carlyle Buley, *The Old Northwest: Pioneer Period, 1815–1840*, 2 vols. (Indianapolis: Indiana Historical Society, 1950), 1: 363–64.

CHAPTER 5

1. I have followed Carrol Smith-Rosenberg, "The Female World of Love and Ritual: Relations between Women in Nineteenth Century America," *Signs* 1 (1975): 1–29, in using the term "world." The word "culture" does not quite work here, first because we are discussing not attitude and values alone but behavior as well. Occasionally, however, I have employed the term men's or women's culture when I want to discuss an aspect of belief that is a part of either men's or women's world. Second, we quickly run into the semantic jungle of culture: subculture, counterculture, and so on. By the use of the term "worlds" I want to imply a wholly contained view of the world and a way of acting in it, without implying that one world is dominant, the other subordinate. The male world, the female world, and as I hope to show in the next chapter, the world of the family were all necessary elements in making up the world of the Midwest.

For a similar use of the term "worlds," see Mirra Komarovsky, *Blue-Collar Marriage* (New York: Random House, 1962), pp. 32–33 ff.

2. Rebecca Ketcham, "From Ithaca to Clatsop Plains," p. 382.

3. Margaret A. Hecox, *California Caravan*, p. 42.

4. Jesse Applegate, "A Day with the Cow Column in 1843"; Ezra Meeker, *Covered Wagon Centennial and Ox Team Days*; David J. Langum, "Pioneer Justice on the Overland Trails," *Wyoming Historical Quarterly* 5 (1974); 421–39.

5. Harriet Ward, *Prairie Schooner Lady*, p. 57.

6. Randall H. Hewitt, *Across the Plains and over the Divide*, pp. 79–80.

7. Sarah Royce, *A Frontier Lady*, p. 11.

8. Francis Parkman, *The Oregon Trail Journal*, in *The Journals of Francis Parkman*, ed. Mason Wade (New York: Harper, 1947), 2: 429.

9. Benjamin P. Thomas, *Lincoln's New Salem*, rev. ed. (New York: Knopf, 1954), pp. 12–15. Lincoln's association with New Salem in the 1830s has made that village and Menard and Sangamon counties the focus of a considerable mass of published memoirs, recollections, anecdotes, and historical work— thus its usefulness here. I have found Thomas, *New Salem*, along with T. G. Onstot, *Pioneers of Menard and Mason Counties* (Forest City, Ill.: privately printed, 1902), and Carl Sandburg, *Abraham Lincoln: The Prairie Years* (New York: Harcourt Brace, 1927), especially good for their discussion of public social and cultural life.

10. This account of logrolling during the thirties, forties, and fifties is drawn principally from William Oliver, *Eight Months in Illinois* (Chicago: W. M. Hill, 1924; original ed. 1843), p. 73; William Brown, *America: A Four Years' Residence* (Leeds: privately printed, 1849), pp. 28–29; Cliff Frank, "The Indiana Log-Rolling," *Folk-Say: A Regional Miscellany* 1 (1929): 79–85; Logan Esarey, *The Indian Home* (Crawfordsville, Ind.: R. E. Banta, 1943); Everett N. Dick, *The Dixie Frontier* (New York: Knopf, 1948), pp. 126–27; and Ocie Lybarger, "Every Day Life on the Southern Illinois Frontier" (Master's thesis, Southern Illinois University, 1951), p. 52.

11. Charles J. Latrobe, *The Rambler in North America* (London: R. B. Seeley & W. Burnside, 1835), p. 136.

12. Mrs. P. T. Chapman, *A History of Johnson County Illinois* (n.p., 1925), p. 80.

13. *History of Posey County, Indiana* (Chicago: Goodspeed Publishing Company, 1886), p. 293.

14. Oliver, *Eight Months*, p. 74. For more on women at these occasions, see p. 126.

15. Rowan Herndon, quoted in Thomas, *New Salem*, p. 114.

16. Oliver, *Eight Months*, pp. 75–76. See also Dick, *Dixie Frontier*, pp. 127–30.

17. Oliver, *Eight Months*, pp. 236–37.

18. *History of St. Joseph County, Indiana* (Chicago: C. C. Chapman, 1880), p. 373.

19. Thomas, *New Salem*, p. 49.

20. New Salem "was a typical pioneer town," "typical of that of the West in general"; ibid., pp. 25, 135.

21. Ibid., p. 24.

22. Ibid., p. 41. Compare the male life of the traditional European village; see, for example, Rayna R. Reiter, "Men and Women in the South of France: Public and Private Domains," in Reiter, ed., *Toward an Anthropology of Women* (New York: Monthly Review Press, 1974), pp. 252–82.

23. Onstot, *Pioneers*, pp. 132–33.

24. Thomas, *New Salem*, p. 141.

25. Ibid., p. 39. See also Lybarger, "Every Day Life," pp. 119–20.

26. Thomas, *New Salem*, pp. 42–44; Dick, *Dixie Frontier*, pp. 142–44; Thomas D. Clark, *The Rampaging Frontier: Manners and Humors of Pioneer Days in the South and Middle West* (Indianapolis: Bobbs-Merrill, 1939), p. 30; Oliver, *Eight Months*, pp. 120–22.

27. Thomas, *New Salem*, p. 66. See also Benjamin P. Thomas, *Abraham Lincoln: A Biography* (New York: Modern Library, 1968), pp. 26–27.

28. Dick, *Dixie Frontier*, pp. 139, 146, and Clark, *Rampaging Frontier*, pp. 34–37.

29. George W. Wilson, *History of DuBois County* [Indiana] (Jasper, Ind.: privately printed, 1910), p. 123; Thomas, *New Salem*, pp. 42–44, 81.

30. Sandburg, *Lincoln*, p. 154. On muster day, see also Lybarger, "Every Day Life," p. 117 f.

31. Thomas, *New Salem*, p. 71.

32. John Lewis Peyton, *Over the Alleghanies and across the Prairies* (London: Sunkin, Marshall, 1870), p. 299.

33. *History of St. Joseph County, Indiana*, p. 372. See also Lybarger, "Every Day Life," p. 188 f.

34. Thomas, *New Salem*, p. 62; Charles Beneulyn Johnson, *Illinois in the Fifties* (Champaign: Flanigan-Pearson, 1918), p. 142.

35. Onstot, *Pioneers*, p. 134. For a discussion of this aspect of male community life in the New Salem area, see Kunigunde Duncan and D. F. Nickols, *Mentor Graham: The Man Who Taught Lincoln* (Chicago: University of Chicago Press, 1944).

36. Oliver, *Eight Months*, p. 120.

37. Thomas, *New Salem*, p. 40.

38. Certainly a gender- or sex-specific analysis of the etiology of American culture would be well worth the effort. For an excellent start in this direction, albeit from the complementary perspective, see Ann Douglas, *The Feminization of American Culture* (New York: Knopf, 1977).

39. James Haines, "Social Life and Scenes in the Early Settlement of Southern Illinois," *Transactions of the Illinois State Historical Society* 10 (1906); 38. See also Dick, *Dixie Frontier*, p. 147.

40. Oliver, *Eight Months*, pp. 122–23.

41. Onstot, *Pioneers*, pp. 189–91. See also Wilson, *DuBois County*, pp. 117–19; Lybarger, "Every Day Life," p. 115 f.

42. Charles Albert Johnson, *The Frontier Camp Meeting: Religion's Harvest Time* (Dallas: Southern Methodist University Press, 1955), pp. 216, 228, 244 n.; Thomas, *New Salem*, pp. 24, 50–52.

43. Allen Wiley, quoted in Johnson, *Frontier Camp Meeting*, pp. 224–25. For a similar description of camp meetings in the New Salem area, see Duncan and Nichols, *Mentor Graham*, p. 116 f.

44. R. Carlyle Buley, *Old Northwest: Pioneer Period, 1815–1840*, 2 vols (Indianapolis: Indiana Historical Society, 1950), 1: 363–64. Ted Gronert, *Sugar Creek Saga: A History and Development of Montgomery County* [Indiana] (Crawfordsville, Ind.: Wabash College, 1958), pp. 34–43, passim, is good on this sexual segregation.

45. On the passing of the old male style, see Onstot, *Pioneers*, p. 134 f.

46. Sandburg, *Lincoln*, pp. 67–68.

47. See Rayna Green, Introduction to Vance Rancolph, *Pissing in the Snow and Other Ozark Folktales* (Urbana: University of Illinois Press, 1976), pp. ix–xxix, for discussion of bawdy folklore collecting.

48. W. O. Rice, "The Pioneer Dialect of Southern Illinois," *Dialect Notes* 2 (1902); 225–49; O. W. Hanley, "Dialect Words from Southern Indiana," *Dialect Notes* 3 (1906): 113–23; Rollo Walter Brown. "A Word List from Western Indiana," *Dialect Notes* 3 (1912): 570–93; Lybarger, "Every Day Life," appendix.

49. *Spirit of the Times*, November 1, 1856, p. 40; quoted in Vance Randolph and George P. Wilson, *Down in the Holler* (Norman: University of Oklahoma Press, 1953), p. 99.

50. W. O. Rice, "Pioneer Dialect"; Lybarger, "Every Day Life," pp. 24, 161. For interpretation of these midwestern usages I have been guided by the suggestions of Vance Randolph. The nineteenth-century midwestern tongue was very like the Ozark speech Randolph heard and noted in the first quarter of the twentieth century. See Randolph and Wilson, *Down in the Holler*, pp. 114 ff.

51. Green, Introduction to Randolph, *Pissing in the Snow*, xv–xvi, suggests this view of a prudish folk was actually the product of prudish folklore collectors.

52. Oliver, *Eight Months*, p. 185.

53. See pp. 33–34.

54. Henry M. Hyatt, *Folk-Lore from Adams County, Illinois,* 2d rev. ed (New York: Alma Egan Hyatt Foundation, 1965), is a remarkable collection of over sixteen thousand items collected in the 1920s and thirties, much of it from people in their seventies and eighties who recalled childhood experiences of the mid-nineteenth century. Other major collections include Earl J. Stout, *Folklore from Iowa.* American Folk-Lore Society Memoirs, vol. 29 (New York, 1936); Daniel L. Thomas and Lucy B. Thomas, *Kentucky Superstitions* (Princeton: Princeton University Press, 1920); and Vance Randolph, *Ozark Superstitions* (New York: Columbia University Press, 1947). For others see "Folklore in the Midwest: An Annotated Bibliography," *Great Lakes Review* 2 (1976): 75–85.

From Kentucky to Illinois to Iowa to the Ozarks, these collections testify to the essential similarity of the body of folk belief. There were of course localized customs, and when appropriate I indicate the location of the particular custom being discussed. Despite variations, however, I believe the general points made here to be valid for the precommercial Midwest as a whole. I agree with Vance Randolph that the Ozarks represented an extension into the twentieth century of the rural midwestern culture of the last. See Randolph, *The Ozarks: An American Survival of Primitive Society* (New York: Vanguard Press, 1931), pp. 83 ff.

55. Hyatt, *Folk-Lore from Adams County,* pp. 219–20; Thomas and Thomas, *Kentucky Superstitions,* p. 108.

56. Hyatt, *Folk-Lore from Adams County,* pp. 130–31.

57. Carl Degler, *Is There a History of Women?* (Oxford: Clarendon Press, 1975), p. 28, points out that nineteenth-century gynecology criticized American women for their belief that the fetus was not alive until after "quickening"—when fetal movements were first felt by the mother. For a path-breaking general history of birth control in the United States, see Linda Gordon, *Woman's Body, Woman's Right: A Social History of Birth Control in America* (New York: Grossman, 1976).

58. Randolph and Wilson, *Down in the Holler,* p. 114.

59. Onstot, *Pioneers,* p. 136.

60. Randolph, *Ozark Superstitions,* p. 192.

61. Carl Hamilton, *In No Tme at All* (Ames: Iowa State University Press, 1975), p. 39.

62. Hyatt, *Folk-Lore from Adams County,* pp. 133–36.

63. Ibid., pp. 154–57.

64. For a brief discussion of the professionalization of health care and a guide to the historical literature, see Barbara Ehrenrich and Dierdre English, *Witches, Midwives and Nurses: A History of Women Healers* (Old Westbury, N. Y.: Feminist Press, 1973), and *Complaints and Disorders: The Sexual Politics of Sickness* (Old Westbury, N. Y.: Feminist Press, 1973).

65. Spencer Ellsworth, *Records of the Olden Times* (Lacon, Ill.: Home Journal Steam Printing Establishment, 1880), p. 221.

66. Onstot, *Pioneers,* p. 136.

67. Henry C. Taylor, *Tarpleywick: A Century of Iowa Farming* (Ames: Iowa State University Press, 1970), pp. 12–13; Buley, *Old Northwest,* 1: 256.

68. Hyatt, *Folk-Lore from Adams County,* p. 193.

69. Frank, "Log-rolling," p. 81. At harvest, however, each farm wife seems to have been solely responsible for fixing the dinner for the hungry harvesters.

70. Oliver, *Eight Months,* p. 76.

71. Elizabeth Wells Robertson, *American Quilts* (New York: Studio Publications, 1948), p. 57.

72. Ibid., pp. 40–46. See also plates 61–150 for beautiful examples, many from the antebellum Midwest.

For an introduction to American quilting, see Patsy and Myron Orlofsky, *Quilts in America* (New York: McGraw-Hill, 1974); Patricia Cooper and Norman Bradley Bufferd, *The Quilters: Women and Domestic Art* (New York: Doubleday, 1977); and Beth Gutcheon, *The Perfect Patchwork Primer* (New York: Penguin Books, 1973). Also see Gutcheon's "Sewing the Blues," *New York Times Magazine,* July 20, 1975, pp. 36–37.

73. Hyatt, *Folk-Lore from Adams County,* pp. 472–74, 478.

74. Ibid., p. 47.

75. Ibid., p. 470.

76. Ibid., pp. 469–70. Joseph Doddridge, *Notes on the Settlement and Indian Wars of the Western Parts of Virginia and Pennsylvania,* reprinted in Samuel Kercheval, *A History of the Valley of Virginia* (Strasburg, Va: Shenandoah, 1925), pp. 260–63, describes a frontier wedding scene in which the couple retires to the loft and the party continues below. Doddridge's account was picked up and reprinted in nearly every nineteenth-century book of western description, and many a county history ("the ways of early settlers"). Other than these reprintings I can find no evidence that the practice of the guests' bedding the couple down was widespread in the Midwest. Cf. Lybarger, "Every Day Life," pp. 109 ff.

77. Ketcham, "From Ithaca," pp. 255–56.

78. Maria Parsons Belshaw, "Diary," p. 324.

79. Sixty-three percent of the women diarists consistently used the "I," but only 46 percent of the men. Like the other measures employed in this section, the basis of this evaluation is essentially subjective. But by making explicit the indicators I have used and by carefully noting in the case of each diary the reasons for my evaluation, I hoped to lend more precision to my notion that men and women composed their diaries in very different modes. This is not intended, however, to pass for a true sociolinguistic analysis, but merely a suggestion of the range of linguistic differences.

80. P. V. Crawford, "Journal of a Trip across the Plains, 1851," p. 139.

81. John L. Johnson, "Diary of an Overland Journey," p. 87. For another example of the male use of "we," see p. 90.

82. Agnes Stewart, "Journey to Oregon," p. 81.

83. Ninety-four percent of the women diarists and 44 percent of the men

explicitly placed themselves in relation to time and space at least once in their accounts.

84. James Frazier Reed, "Diary," p. 259.

85. Seventy-five percent of women and 39 percent of men used exact names, dates, and places in their accounts.

86. Mrs. Elizabeth Dixon Smith Geer, "Diary," p. 161.

87. Seventy-nine percent of women and 22 percent of men used one or more of these forms of extended description at least once.

88. Twenty-nine percent of men diarists wrote primarily about people, versus 64 percent of women diarists.

89. William T. Newby, "Diary of the Emigration," p. 235.

90. Ward, *Prairie Schooner Lady*, pp. 70–71.

91. Basil Bernstein, "Elaborated and Restricted Codes: Their Social Origins and Consequences," in Alfred G. Smith, ed., *Communication and Culture* (New York: Holt, Rinehart, and Winston, 1966), p. 429.

92. Basil Bernstein, "A Socio-Linguistic Approach to Socialization: With Some Reference to Educability," in *Class, Codes and Control* (London: Routledge and Kegan Paul, 1971), p. 144.

93. Arthur Ponsonby, *English Diaries*, 2d ed. (London: Methuen, 1923), p. 5. See also Dennis Lawton, "Social Class Language Differences in Language Development: A Study of Some Samples of Written Work," *Language and Speech* 6 (1963); 120–43, for an example of a study that quite successfully applies the insights of speech analysis to writing. Dell Hymes, "Models of the Interaction of Languages and Social Setting," *Journal of Social Issues* 23 (1967): 18, also would include writing in the analysis of codes. For a criticism of the approach employed here, however, see I. J. Gelb, *A Study of Writing* (Chicago: University of Chicago Press, 1952), pp. 10–11 f.

94. For those who would belittle male culture because of its apparent inarticulateness, Dell Hymes's reminder is pertinent: "The more the genre has become a shared meaningful expression within a group, the more likely that the crucial cues will be efficient, that is, slight in scale. If one balks at such detail, perhaps because it requires technical skills in linguistics, musicology or the like, one should face the fact that one is simply refusing to take seriously the human meaning of one's object of study and the scientific claims of one's field of inquiry." Hymes, "Models," p. 23.

95. For both codes, see Bernstein, "Elaborated and Restricted Codes," pp. 428–29, and "A Socio-Linguistic Approach to Socialization," pp. 145–61. See also the path-breaking article by Leonard Schatzman and Anselm Strauss, "Social Class and Modes of Communication," in Alfred G. Smith, ed., *Communication and Culture* (New York: Holt, Rinehart, and Winston, 1966), pp. 442–55, for a suggestive analysis of syntactical categories. For other perspectives on linguistic differences by sex, see Mary Ritchie Kay, *Male/Female Language: With a Comprehensive Bibliography* (Metuchen, N. J.: Scarecrow Press, 1975), and Barne Thorne and Nancy Henley, eds., *Language and Sex: Difference and Dominance* (Rowley, Mass.: Newberry House, 1975).

96. Oliver, *Eight Months*, p. 185.

97. Ibid., p. 195.

98. Avery Craven, "The Advancement of Civilization into the Middle West in the Period of Settlement," in Dixon Ryan Fox, ed., *Sources of Culture in the Middle West* (New York: Appleton-Century, 1934), p. 45.

99. Written June 1, 1843; published in the *New Orleans Daily Picayune*, November 21, 1843; reprinted in Matthew C. Field, *Prairie and Mountain Sketches*, ed. Kate L. Gregg (Norman: University of Oklahoma Press, 1957), p. 26.

100. For a good description of this masculine social life, see William A. Maxwell, *Crossing the Plains*.

101. William Thompson, *Reminiscences of a Pioneer*, pp. 3–4.

102. Moritz Busch, *Travels between the Hudson and the Mississippi, 1851–1852*, ed. and trans. Norman Binger (Lexington: University Press of Kentucky, 1971), pp. 151–52.

103. Oliver, *Eight Months*, pp. 202–03.

104. Written May 21, 1843; published in the *New Orleans Daily Picayune*, November 11, 1843; reprinted in Field, *Prairie and Mountain Sketches*, p. 25.

105. "Shoot the Buffalo," an old midwestern play-party song, quoted in Paul Van Riper, "Reminiscences of a Hill-Billy," ed. Victor M. Bogle, *Indiana Magazine of History* 62 (1966): 24.

106. Celinda E. Hines, "Diary of Celinda E. Hines," pp. 104–05.

107. Ketcham, "From Ithaca," p. 282.

108. Mrs. Margaret A. Frink, *Journal of the Adventures of a Party of California Gold-Seekers*, p. 67.

109. Mrs. Benjamin G. Ferris, *The Mormons at Home*, p. 18.

110. Catherine M. Haun, "A Woman's Trip across the Plains," p. 30.

111. Mrs. Velina A. Williams, "Diary of a Trip across the Plains in 1853," p. 192.

112. Louise M. Rahm, "Diary," n.p.

113. Mrs. Francis H. Sawyer, "Overland to California," p. 10.

114. Esther and Joseph Lyman, *Letters*, p. 3.

115. J. Orin Oliphant, ed., "Mrs. Lucy A. Ide's Diary 'In a Prairie Schooner, 1878,' " pp. 279–80.

116. Sixteen births for 122 women during the roughly seven months away from home converts to a gross birth rate of 254/1,000 (254 annual live births per 1,000 women aged 15–44). The comparable rates for the U.S. as a whole were: 1840, 222; 1850, 194; 1860, 184. U.S., Bureau of the Census, *Historical Statistics of the United States . . . to 1970* (Washington, D. C.: Government Printing Office, 1975), p. 49.

117. Merritt G. Kellogg, *Notes concerning the Kelloggs*, pp. 102–03.

118. Unless otherwise indicated, all quoted material in the following pages is from Charlotte Emily Pengra, *Diary of Mrs. Bynon J. Pengra*.

119. Williams, "Diary," p. 189.

120. For a similar story of a broken party, see Agnes Stewart, "Journey to Oregon," pp. 80–84; Helen Marnie Stewart, *Diary*, pp. 3–23.

121. Mariett Foster Cummings, "Second Trip across the Continent," p. 138.

122. Eleanor Allen, *Canvas Caravans: Based on the Journal of Esther Belle McMillan Hanna*, p. 24.

123. Agnes Stewart, "Journey to Oregon," p. 85.

CHAPTER 6

1. Arthur Calhoun, *A Social History of the American Family*, 2 vols. (New York: Barnes & Noble, 1945; original ed. 1917), 2: 11.

2. John Minto, "Reminiscences," p. 129.

3. William Oliver, *Eight Months in Illinois* (Chicago: W. M. Hill, 1924), p. 122.

4. Ibid., p. 77.

5. Mrs. P. T. Chapman, *A History of Johnson County Illinois* (n.p., 1925), p. 80.

6. Loren B. Hastings, "Diary of Loren B. Hastings," p. 17.

7. Quoted in Benjamin P. Thomas, *Lincoln's New Salem*, rev. ed. (New York: Knopf, 1954), p. 41.

8. Chapman, *Johnson County*, p. 81; Mary Alicia Owen, "Social Customs and Usages in Missouri during the Last Century," *Missouri Historical Review* 15 (1920): 184–86; *History of St. Joseph County, Indiana* (Chicago: C. C. Chapman, 1880), p. 373.

9. Mary Burrell, "Mary Burrell's Book," p. 31; Wesley Tonner in ibid., pp. 42–43.

10. Jacob Wright Harlan, *California '46 to '88*, p. 126; Susan Thompson Lewis Parrish, "Westward in 1850," p. 2.

11. Calculated from family reconstitution forms.

12. Earl J. Stout, *Folklore from Iowa*, American Folk-Lore Society Memoirs, vol. 29 (New York, 1936), p. 148; Daniel L. Thomas and Lucy P. Thomas, *Kentucky Superstitions* (Princeton: Princeton University Press, 1920), p. 50.

13. Henry M. Hyatt, *Folk-Lore from Adams County, Illinois*, 2d rev. ed. (New York: Alma Egan Hyatt Foundation, 1965), p. 395.

14. For courtship and wedding lore, see Hyatt, *Folk-Lore from Adams County*, pp. 390–451; Stout, *Folklore from Iowa*, pp. 144–50; and Thomas and Thomas, *Kentucky Superstitions*, pp. 25–63. Cf. Vance Randolph, *Ozark Superstitions* (New York: Columbia University Press, 1947), pp. 174 ff., for a body of essentially similar lore.

15. Peter Burnett, "Letters," p. 406.

16. Edward Shorter, *The Making of the Modern Family* (New York: Basic Books, 1975), pp. 15, 65.

17. Eleanor Allen, *Canvas Caravans: Based on the Journal of Esther Belle McMillan Hanna*; Katherine Dunlap, "Journal"; Mrs. Margaret A. Frink, *Journal of the Adventures of a Party of California Gold-Seekers*; Mrs. Francis H. Sawyer, "Overland to California."

18. Oliver, *Eight Months*, p. 76. See also Ocie Lybarger, "Every Day Life on

the Southern Illinois Frontier" (Master's thesis, Southern Illinois University, 1951), pp. 31–32.

19. Ralph Leslie Rusk, *The Literature of the Middle Western Frontier*, 2 vols. (New York: Columbia University Press, 1925), 1: 311; Lybarger, "Every Day Life," p. 16.

20. See collections by Paul G. Brewster, ed., *Ballads and Songs of Indiana* (Bloomington: Indiana University Press, 1940); Charles Neely, ed., *Tales and Songs of Southern Illinois* (Menasha, Wisc.: Banta Publishing Company, 1938); Henry Belden, ed., *Ballads and Songs Collected by the Missouri Folklore Society*, 2d ed. (Columbia: University of Missouri Press, 1955); Vance Randolph, ed., *Ozark Folksongs*, 4 vols. (Columbia: State Historical Society of Missouri, 1946–50). The dominance of the British songs was determined by G. Malcolm Laws, Jr., *Native American Balladry: A Descriptive Study and a Bibliographical Syllabus* (Philadelphia: American Folklore Society, 1964), pp. 101–02, after he surveyed these collections.

For a sensitive critique of antiquarian folk-song collecting and a plea for the use of song as historical evidence, see John Greenway, "Folksongs as Socio-Historical Documents," *Western Folklore* 19 (1960): 1–9.

21. Laws, *Native American Balladry*, p. 103.

22. See Tristram P. Coffin, *The British Traditional Ballad in North America* (Philadelphia: American Folklore Society, 1963), for an introduction to the study of American textual variation.

23. A complete study of midwestern song was beyond the means of this study; I chose instead to look at some of the most popular of the antebellum songs. I used Alan Lomax, *The Folk Songs of North America in the English Language* (Garden City, N.Y.: Doubleday, 1960), as my standard of popularity. Of his 317 songs, I selected those which appeared in at least one of the midwestern state collections and which could be assigned an approximate antebellum date. Of these 44 songs, 27 were British, and nearly half concerned sexual relations, the largest single thematic category.

24. "Lily Munroe," Belden, *Ballads and Songs*, p. 171; Lomax, *Folk Songs*, p. 164.

25. Lomax, *Folk Songs*, p. xxix. Roger D. Abrahams and George Foss, *Anglo-American Folksong Style* (Englewood Cliffs, N. J.: Prentice-Hall, 1968), p. 94 f., comment on this.

26. "Fair and Tender Ladies," Brewster, *Ballads and Songs*, p. 328; Belden, *Ballads and Songs*, p. 477; Lomax, *Folk Songs*, p. 205.

27. "Omie Wise," Belden, *Ballads and Songs*, p. 322; Lomax, *Folk Songs*, p. 268.

28. "The House Carpenter," Brewster, *Ballads and Songs*, p. 136; Stout, *Folklore from Iowa*, p. 11; Belden, *Ballads and Songs*, p. 79; Lomax, *Folk Songs*, p. 182.

29. Bertrand H. Bronson, *The Ballad as Song* (Berkeley: University of California Press, 1969), p. 167.

30. "I Never Will Marry," Belden, *Ballads and Songs*, p. 167; Lomax, *Folk Songs*, p. 222.

31. "Grandma's Advice," Brewster, *Ballads and Songs*, pp. 243–44.

32. "Single Girl," Stout, *Folklore from Iowa*, p. 92; Belden, *Ballads and Songs*, p. 473; Lomax, *Folk Songs*, p. 166. For a variant from a masculine point of view, see Stout, *Folklore from Iowa*, p. 93.

33. "Our Goodman," Brewster, *Ballads and Songs*, p. 149; Stout, *Folklore from Iowa*, p. 13; Belden, *Ballads and Songs*, p. 89.

34. "The Wife Wrapt in Wether's Skin," Brewster, *Ballads and Songs*, p. 151; Belden, *Ballads and Songs*, p. 92. See the Lomax variation, "Gentle Fair Jenny," *Folk Songs*, p. 167.

35. Even here the husband covers his wife in a sheep's hide when he beats her, so when she threatens to tell her father he claims he was only tanning his hide. True patriarchal power included spousal discipline, but here the husband must disguise it.

36. "The Farmer's Curst Wife," Brewster, *Ballads and Songs*, p. 155; Belden, *Ballads and Songs*, p. 94; Lomax, *Folk Songs*, p. 187.

37. The lyric tradition, as a whole, of course, is informed by an awareness of male social dominance, but this seems more a reflection of reality than a projected cultural vision. There is a small repertoire of masculine songs of lament at marriage, but they seem to have been responses to and variants of the female traditions; see, for example, n. 32 and pp. 152–53.

38. Lomax, *Folk Songs*, p. 169; Rusk, *Literature*, 1: 311.

39. "Lady Isabell and the Elf Knight," Brewster, *Ballads and Songs*, p. 31; Belden, *Ballads and Songs*, p. 5; Lomax, *Folk Songs*, p. 18.

40. "Barbara Allen," Brewster, *Ballads and Songs*, p. 99; Neely, *Tales and Songs*, p. 137; Stout, *Folklore from Iowa*, p. 8; Belden, *Ballads and Songs*, p. 60; Lomax, *Folk Songs*, p. 183. Coffin, *British Traditional Ballad*, p. 84, assesses "Barbara Allen's" popularity on the basis of the great number of variants.

41. See Lybarger, "Every Day Life," pp. 36–37.

42. Hyatt, *Folk Lore from Adams County*, p. 472.

43. "The Cambric Shirt," Brewster, *Ballads and Songs*, p. 23; Belden, *Ballads and Songs*, p. 1. See the Lomax variant, "Strawberry Lane," *Folk Songs*, p. 17.

44. "The Young Man Who Wouldn't Hoe His Corn," Brewster, *Ballads and Songs*, p. 307; Stout, *Folklore from Iowa*, pp. 91–92; Belden, *Ballads and Songs*, p. 440.

45. John Lewis Peyton, *Over the Alleghanies and across the Prairies* (London: Sunkin, Marshall, 1870), pp. 319–20.

46. "Hog and Hominy," Neely, *Tales and Songs*, p. 203.

47. Stout, *Folklore from Iowa*, p. 147; Thomas and Thomas, *Kentucky Superstitions*, p. 39.

48. See Henry Nash Smith, *Virgin Land: The American West as Symbol and Myth*, rev. ed. (Cambridge, Mass.: Harvard University Press, 1970), pp. 131, 135 f., and book 3, passim. Missouri, of course, was a haunt of slavery, but many of the Missouri emigrants were moving precisely because of what they considered the degrading competition of slave labor there (see, for example, Lindsey Applegate, "The Applegate Route," *Oregon Historical Quarterly* 22 [1921]: 12–45).

49. See the imaginative commentary of Frank R. Kramer, *Voices in the*

Valley: Mythmaking and Folk Belief in the Shaping of the Middle West (Madison: University of Wisconsin Press, 1964), pp. 64–65.

50. Calhoun, *Social History of the American Family*, 2: 11.

51. William Wadsworth, *The National Wagon Road and Guide* (San Francisco: Whitton, Towne, 1858), pp. 140–41.

52. Sarah Royce, *A Frontier Lady*, pp. 85–86.

53. Luzena Stanley Wilson, *Luzena Stanley Wilson, '49er*, p. 9. See also Virginia Wilcox Ivins, *Pen Pictures of Early Western Days*, p. 116; Frink, *Journal of the Adventures*, p. 22; and Royce, *Frontier Lady*, pp. 83–84.

54. Enoch W. Conyers, "Diary," p. 464. See also Randall H. Hewitt, *Across the Plains and over the Divide*, p. 464.

55. Wesley Tonner, in Burrell, "Mary Burrell's Book," p. 43.

56. Tallmadge B. Wood, "Letter from Willamette," p. 398.

57. William M. Case, "Reminiscences," p. 270.

58. I have found the following the most helpful on nineteenth-century legal marriage and common law: Elizabeth Warbasse, "The Changing Legal Rights of Married Women, 1800–1861" (Ph.D. diss., Radcliffe, 1960); Ruth A. Gallaher, *Legal and Political Status of Women in Iowa* (Iowa City: State Historical Society of Iowa, 1918); and Leo Kanowitz, *Women and the Law: The Unfinished Revolution* (Albuquerque: University of New Mexico Press, 1969).

59. Indiana, however, after the reforms of the early 1850s gained the reputation as an easy divorce state; see Calhoun, *Social History of the American Family*, 2: 46–49.

60. Ibid., vol. 2, chap. 2; Gallagher, *Legal and Political Status of Women*, p. 65. For elaboration and details on the restrictions catalogued in the last two paragraphs, consult Warbasse, "Legal Rights," chap. 1; Kanowitz, *Women and the Law*, pp. 35–38, 47, 77; and Gallagher, *Legal and Political Status of Women*, chap. 1.

61. By 1861 all the states under study here—Indiana, Illinois, Iowa, Missouri, California, and Oregon as well— had amended the common law in regard to married women's rights. In the case of Indiana there had been substantial improvement in several areas in addition to the easing of divorce regulations (see n. 59); in the case of Missouri, at the other extreme, only the most minimal reform was achieved. The other states fell in between, most allowing married women to hold real property in their married names but not touching their disabilities in contracts, wills, right to wages, and so on. In the Midwest, as elsewhere, reform was piecemeal and sometimes contradictory. See Warbasse, "Legal Rights," pp. 205, 375–87. See also the interesting Oregon debate on reform, which included some prominent emigrants, some of whose names appear in these pages, in Helen Krebs Smith, *The Presumptuous Dreamers: A Sociological History of the Life and Times of Abigail Scott Duniway (1834–1915)* (Lake Oswego, Ore.: Smith, Smith and Smith, 1974), pp. 49–50.

62. Kanowitz, *Women and the Law*, p. 40; Warbasse, "Legal Rights," chap. 4.

63. Mary A. Jones, "Story of My Life," p. 2.

64. Sarah J. Cummins, *Autobiography and Reminiscences*, p. 19.

65. Mrs. Matthew P. Deady, "Crossing the Plains to Oregon in 1846," p. 57.

66. Elias J. Draper, *Autobiography of . . . a Pioneer of California*, pp. 9–10.

67. "The Rolling Stone," Belden, *Ballads and Songs*, p. 351. Randolph, *Ozark Folksongs*, 1: 213, 216, copies essentially the same text from a Missouri broadside dated 1852. Theodore C. Blegen, *Grass Roots History* (Minneapolis: University of Minnesota Press, 1948), p. 33, reports widespread popularity in the East and Midwest during the 1850s and sixties with Wisconsin and other destinations substituted for California.

68. Garland, cited and song quoted in Blegen, *Grass Roots History*, p. 32.

69. Ibid., p. 34.

70. Basil G. Parker, *The Life and Adventures of Basil G. Parker*, p. 18.

71. Mary Jane Hayden, *Pioneer Days*, pp. 7–8.

72. Wilson, *Luzena Stanley Wilson*, p. 1.

73. Enos Ellmaker, "Autobiography," p. 9 (emphasis added).

74. Minto, "Reminiscences," p. 127.

75. See chapters 2 and 3.

76. Royce, *Frontier Lady*, p. 8.

77. Remembrance Hughes Campbell, *A Brief History of Our Trip across the Plains with Ox Teams in 1853*, p. 4.

78. Royce, *Frontier Lady*, pp. 8–9.

79. Edwin Bryant, *What I Saw in California*, p. 71.

80. Ward, *Prairie Schooner Lady*, pp. 61, 95.

81. Charles Frederick True, *Covered Wagon Pioneers*, p. 42.

82. Lavinia Honeyman Porter, *By Ox Team to California*, p. 82.

83. Charlotte Emily Pengra, *The Diary of Mrs. Bynon J. Pengra*, p. 52.

84. Porter, *By Ox Team*, p. 91.

85. True, *Covered Wagon Pioneers*, p. 90.

86. Albert Jerome Dickson, *Covered Wagon Days*, p. 91.

87. Eleanor Allen, *Canvas Caravans*, p. 28.

88. Mrs. Lodisa Frizzell, *Across the Plains to California in 1852*, p. 29.

89. Mrs. Velina A. Williams, "Diary," p. 182.

90. Lucy Rutledge Cooke, *Crossing the Plains in 1852*, pp. 5, 7, 9.

91. Margaret A. Hecox, *California Caravan*, p. 31.

92. J. Orin Oliphant, ed., "Mrs. Lucy A. Ide's Diary 'In a Prairie Schooner, 1878,' " p. 129.

93. Mrs. Elizabeth Dixon Smith Geer, "Diary," pp. 165–66.

94. Adrietta Applegate Hixon, *On to Oregon!*, p. 18. For more discussion of the turnarounds, see John D. Unruh, "The Plains Across: The Overland Emigrants and the Trans-Mississippi West, 1840–1860" (Ph.D. diss., University of Kansas, 1975), pp. 178 ff.

95. "Crossing the Plains," in Richard A. Dwyer and Richard E. Lingenfelter, *The Songs of the Gold Rush* (Berkeley: University of California Press, 1964), p. 42, copying an 1855 midwestern songster.

96. Royce, *Frontier Lady*, p. 11.

97. Porter, *By Ox Team*, pp. 6–8, 41. See also Arrazine Angeline Cooper, "Pioneer across the Plains," p. 139.

98. Allen, *Canvas Caravans*, pp. 24, 27, 32, 88, 111.

99. Sawyer, "Overland to California," p. 15.

100. Mary L. Rockwood Powers, "The Overland Route: Leaves from the Journal of a California Emigrant," *Amateur Book Collector* 1 (January 1951): 11.

101. Agnes Stewart, "Journey to Oregon," p. 81.

102. Maria Parsons Belshaw, "Diary," p. 330.

103. Gordon W. Allport, *The Nature of Prejudice* (Reading, Mass.: Addison-Wesley, 1954), p. 147.

104. Catherine M. Haun, "A Woman's Trip across the Plains," p. 7.

105. Ketcham, "From Ithaca to Clatsop Plains," p. 263.

106. Maria Parsons Belshaw, "Diary," p. 328.

107. Royce, *Frontier Lady*, p. 5.

CHAPTER 7

1. "The Wagoneer's Lad," Charles Neely, *Tales and Songs of Southern Illinois* (Menasha, Wisc.: George Banta, 1938), p. 236; Earl J. Stout, *Folklore from Iowa*, American Folk-Lore Society Memoirs, vol. 29 (New York, 1936), p. 49; Henry Belden, *Ballads and Songs Collected by the Missouri Folklore Society* (Columbia: University of Missouri Press, 1955), p. 474; Alan Lomax, *The Folk Songs of North America in the English Language* (New York: Doubleday, 1960), p. 220.

2. M. Kay Martin and Barbara Voorhies, *Female of the Species* (New York: Columbia University Press, 1975), p. 295.

3. See Heidi Hartmann, "Capitalism, Patriarchy, and Job Segregation By Sex," *Signs* 1, no. 3, pt. 2 (1976): 137–69, for a firm statement of this position. Cf. the rather inadequate formulation of the patriarchy question in the otherwise excellent article by Ann D. Gordon, Mary Jo Buhle, and Nancy E. Schrom, *Women in American Society* Radical America pamphlet (Boston: New England Free Press, 1971). Taken together these two articles are fundamental reading for the history of American women.

4. Abigail Scott Duniway, *Path Breaking: An Autobiographical History of the Equal Suffrage Movement in the Pacific Coast States*, 2nd ed. (Portland, Ore.: James Kerns & Abbot, 1914), p. 8.

5. Mary P. Ryan, *Womanhood in America: From Colonial Times to the Present* (New York: New Viewpoints, 1975), pp. 139–42, suggests that nineteenth-century women's roles were formed in the East and exported as an ideology to the West. This she attributes to the creation of a national culture, principally through print media, in the years 1830–60. This interesting idea deserves investigation. But on the other side, the changed conditions of social life for eastern and urban women (the end of productive work in the home, the beginnings of female employment in the public world) which produced those new role prescriptions were not present on the frontier, not present in Oregon, for instance, until well into the century. Thus feminine ideology, while a factor, was not as important as the social facts of pioneer wifery. Gordon, Buhle, and Schrom, *Women in American Society*, p. 27, suggest that eastern role prescriptions, because of their inapplicability to western (as well as working) women, were intensely oppressive.

6. Jack D. Eblen, "An Analysis of Nineteenth Century Frontier Populations," *Demography* 2 (1965): 399.

7. Caroline Bird, *Born Female: The High Cost of Keeping Women Down* (New York: David McKay, 1968), p. 22.

8. Page Smith, *Daughters of the Promised Land: Women in American History* (Boston: Little, Brown, 1970), p. 221.

9. Arthur Calhoun, *A Social History of the American Family*, 3 vols. (Barnes & Noble, 1945), 2: 106–07, 109.

10. David M. Potter, "American Woman and the American Character," in Don E. Fehrenbacher, ed., *History and American Society: Essays of David M. Potter* (New York: Oxford University Press, 1973), p. 283, calls this a "frontier aphorism," and it turns up frequently in contemporary writing. Everett N. Dick, *The Sod House Frontier* (New York: Appleton-Century, 1937), p. 232, quotes a "traveler of the fifties" as saying, "There is profound truth in the remark that 'plains travel and frontier life are peculiarly severe upon women and oxen.' " Patrick Sheriff, *A Tour through North America* (Edinburgh: Oliver and Boyd, 1835), p. 242, wrote that his two female traveling companions "agreed in thinking Illinois a hard country for women and cattle."

11. John Ludlum McConnel, *Western Characters* (New York: Redfield, 1853), pp. 131–32.

12. Abigail Scott Duniway, *Captain Gray's Company* (Portland, Ore.: S. J. McCormick, 1859), p. iii.

13. Duniway, *Path Breaking*, p. 14.

14. For a notable exception, see Potter, "American Women." See also the brief but sensitive comments of Edeen Martin, "Frontier Marriage and the Status Quo," *Westport Historical Quarterly* 10 (1975): 99–108, especially pp. 100 and 107.

15. The American West was not only rural, of course; it was also the scene of "instant cities," where women's status may have been positively improved. For some reflections on this, see Duniway, *Path Breaking*. My comments are reserved for the rural West.

APPENDIX II

1. I was unable to examine about 150 relevant documents at western libraries.

2. For a full discussion of family reconstitution as a historical tool, see E. A. Wrigley, *An Introduction to English Historical Demography* (New York: Basic Books, 1966).

3. See John Mack Faragher, "Midwestern Families in Motion: Women and Men on the Overland Trail to Oregon and California, 1843–1870," (Ph.D diss., Yale University, 1977), figure A.1., p. 303.

4. P. G. Herbst, "The Measurement of Family Relationships," *Human Relations* 5 (1952): 10.

5. See Faragher, "Midwestern Families," figure A.2., pp. 304–05.

6. Robert F. Berkhofer, Jr., *A Behavioral Approach to Historical Analysis* (New York: Free Press, 1969), chap. 5 and 6.

7. Ralph K. White, "Value Analysis: A Quantitative Method for Describing

Qualitative Data," *Journal of Social Psychology* 19 (1944): 351–58, and *Value Analysis: The Nature and Use of the Method* (Glen Gardiner, N. J.: Society for the Psychological Study of Social Issues, 1951). For a demonstration of the application of White's method, see his *"Black Boy: A Value-Analysis," Journal of Abnormal and Social Psychology* 42 (1947): 440–61.

8. Despite John A. Garraty's appeal for its attractiveness. See "The Applications of Content Analysis to Biography and History," in Ithiel de Sola Pool, ed., *Trends in Content Analysis* (Urbana: University of Illinois Press, 1959), pp. 171–88.

9. Milton Rokeach, *The Nature of Human Values* (New York: Free Press, 1973); Bernard Farber, "An Index of Marital Integration," *Sociometry* 20 (1957): 117–39.

Selected Bibliography

I. The Overland Trail

This study relies principally on the great volume of contemporary overland trail materials: diaries and recollections of emigrants and books, articles, and letters of trail observation. The following listing of overland trail materials is divided into four sections. The first includes (1) the diaries and recollections of men and women who traveled as members of families and (2) several diaries and recollections of single men (and in one case a single woman) who traveled in the company of families. These diaries and recollections are arranged alphabetically without regard to sex or family status, for ease of consultation. The second section includes contemporary books and articles intended to inform and advise the emigrants. The third section lists contemporary observations of life along the trail, and the fourth includes secondary books and articles of overland trail history.

In order to draw together the diaries and recollections used in this study, it was necessary to examine a much larger body of diaries and recollections than are listed here, primarily because the majority of male accounts were written by single men. Although I have utilized single men's accounts, for insights about their traveling arrangements, for instance, except for a few accounts from which I have quoted extensively (and which are included in the first section of this bibliography), I have not listed single men's materials here. For a fuller bibliography of overland accounts, consult Merrill Mattes, *The Great Platte River Road* (Lincoln: Nebraska State Historical Society, 1969), pp. 523–71.

A. DIARIES AND RECOLLECTIONS

Ackley, Mary E. *Crossing the Plains and Early Days in California*. San Francisco: privately printed, 1928.

Adair, Sarah D. "Pioneer of 1843." *Transactions of the Oregon Pioneer Association* (1900): 65–82.

Adams, Mrs. Cecelia Emily McMillen. "Crossing the Plains in 1852." *Transactions of the Oregon Pioneer Association* (1904): 288–329.

Agatz, Cora Wilson. "A Journey Across the Plains in 1866." *Pacific Northwest Quarterly* 27 (1936): 170–74.

Akin, Jr., James. *Journal.* . . . Edited by Edward Everett Dale. *University of Oklahoma Bulletin*, no. 9 (Norman, 1919).

Allen, A. J. *Ten Years in Oregon.* Ithaca: Main, Andrus, 1848.

Allen, Edward Jay. "Oregon Trail." *Pittsburg Daily Dispatch*, 1852. Clippings in Beinecke Library, Yale University.

Allen, Eleanor. *Canvas Caravans: Based on the Journal of Esther Belle McMillan Hanna.* . . . Portland, Ore.: Binfords & Mort, 1946.

Allyn, Henry. "Journal of 1853." *Transactions of the Oregon Pioneer Association* (1928): 372–435.

Angell, Susan P. "Sketch of Mrs. Susan P. Angell, A Pioneer of 1852." *Transactions of the Oregon Pioneer Association* (1928): 55–56.

Applegate, Jesse. "A Day with the Cow Column in 1843." *Oregon Historical Quarterly* 1 (1900): 371–83.

Aram, Capt. Joseph. "Reminiscences. . . ." *Journal of American History* 1 (1907): 617–32.

Arthur, John. "Pioneer of 1843." *Transactions of the Oregon Pioneer Association* (1887): 96–104.

Bailey, Mary S. "Journal, Ohio to California." MS. Huntington Library, San Marino, Calif.

Barlow, William. "Reminiscences of Seventy Years." *Oregon Historical Quarterly* 12 (1912).

Barnett, Joel. *A Long Trip in a Prairie Schooner.* Whittier, Calif.: Western Stationery Company, 1928.

Belshaw, George. "Journey from Indiana to Oregon." MS. Beinecke Library, Yale University.

———. "Letters." In Gwen Castle, "Belshaw Journey, Oregon Trail, 1853." *Oregon Historical Quarterly* 32 (1931): 217–39.

Belshaw, Maria Parsons. "Diary." Edited by J. W. Ellison. *Oregon Historical Society Quarterly* 33 (1932): 318–33.

Bogart, Nancy M. (Hembree) Snow. "Reminiscences of a Journey Across the Plains in 1843 with Dr. Marcus Whitman's Caravan and Early Life in Oregon." MS. Huntington Library, San Marino, Calif.

Bonney, Benjamin F. *Across the Plain by Prairie Schooner.* Eugene, Ore.: Kohe-Tiffany, 1923.

Bradley, Nancy J., and Bradley, Henry. "Journal." MS. Beinecke Library, Yale University.

Bray, T. Emery. "The Great American Trail [includes Eliza Bray Vincent's Oral History]." In *Bray Family Genealogy and History.* Edited by Emery T. Bray. N.p., n.d., pp. 9–12.

Bryant, Edwin. *What I Saw in California.* New York, 1849.

Breen, Patrick. "Diary." In *Overland in 1846: Diaries and Letters of the*

California-Oregon Trail, 1:306. Edited by Dale Morgan. Georgetown, Calif.: Talisman Press, 1963.

Brooks, Elisha. *Pioneer Mother of California*. San Francisco: Herr Wagner, 1922.

Brooks, Noah. "The Plains Across." *Century Magazine* 63 (1902): 803–20.

Brown, Mrs. Tabitha. "Letter to Brother and Sister: August, 1854." *Oregon Historical Quarterly* 5 (1904): 199–205.

Burnett, Peter H. "Letters." *Oregon Historical Quarterly* 3 (1902): 398–426.

————. *Recollections and Opinions of an Old Pioneer*. New York: D. Appleton, 1880.

Burlingame, Mr. and Mrs. "Journals." In Mrs. C. V. Waite, *Adventures in the Far West*. Chicago: C. V. Waite, 1882.

Burrell, Mary. "Mary Burrell's Book." MS. Beinecke Library, Yale University.

Campbell, Remembrance Hughes. *A Brief History of Our Trip across The Plains with Ox Teams in 1853*. N.p., n.d.

Carpenter, Helen. "A Trip Across the Plains." MS. Huntington Library, San Marino, Calif.

Carriger, Nicholas. "Diary." In *Overland in 1846: Diaries and Letters of the California-Oregon Trail*, 1:143–58. Edited by Dale Morgan. Georgetown, Calif.: Talisman Press, 1963.

Case, William M. "Reminiscences." *Oregon Historical Quarterly* 1 (1900): 269–77.

Chambers, Andrew J. "Pioneer History. A Brief Account of a Trip across the Plains." *Washington Standard* (Olympia, Wash.), May 15, 1908. Clipping in Beinecke Library, Yale University.

Chambers, Margaret White. *Reminiscences*. N.p., 1903.

Clinkinbeard, Philura V. *Across the Plains in '64: By Prairie Schooner to Oregon*. Edited by Anna Dell Clinkinbeard. New York: Exposition Press, 1953.

Collins, Martha Elizabeth Gilliam. "Reminiscences. . . ." *Oregon Historical Quarterly* 17 (1916): 358–72.

Conyers, Enoch W. "Diary." *Transactions of the Oregon Pioneer Association* (1905): 423–512.

Cooke, Lucy Rutledge. *Crossing the Plains in 1852: Narrative of a Trip from Iowa to "The Land of Gold," As Told in Letters Written during the Journey*. Modesto, Calif.: privately printed, 1923.

Cooper, Arrazine Angeline. "Pioneer across the Plains." In *Growing Up Female in America: Ten Lives*. Edited by Eve Merriam. New York: Dell, 1971.

Cosgrove, Hugh. "Reminiscences." *Oregon Historical Quarterly* 1 (1900): 253–69.

Cramer, Thomas. "Diary of a Journey from Kansas to California." MS. Beinecke Library, Yale University.

Crawford, C. F. *Scenes of Earlier Days, Etc.* Chicago: Quadrangle, 1962.

Crawford, P. V. "Journal of a Trip across the Plains, 1851." *Oregon Historical Quarterly* 25 (1924): 136–69.

Cummings, Mariett Foster. "Second Trip across Continent." In *The Foster Family: California Pioneers*, pp.115–43. Edited by Lucy Foster Sexton. Santa Barbara, Calif.: Schauer Printing Studio Press, 1925.

Cummins, Sarah J. *Autobiography and Reminiscences*. Walla Walla, Ore.: Walla Walla Bulletin, 1920.

Curry, George L. "Letter of May 11, 1846." In *Overland in 1846: Diaries and Letters of the California-Oregon Trail*, 1:520–23. Edited by Dale Morgan. Georgetown, Calif.: Talisman Press, 1963.

Deady, Mrs. Matthew P. "Crossing the Plains To Oregon in 1846." *Transactions of the Oregon Pioneer Association* (1928): 57–64.

Dickenson, Luella. *Reminiscences of a Trip across the Plains in 1846*. San Francisco: Whitaker & Ray, 1904.

Dickson, Albert Jerome. *Covered Wagon Days*. Edited by Arthur Jerome Dickson. Cleveland: Arthur H. Clark, 1929.

Dinwiddie. "The Dinwiddie Journal." Edited by Margaret Booth. In *Frontier Omnibus*, edited by John W. Hakola. Helena: Montana State University Press, 1962.

Donnell, Camilla Thomson. "The Oregon Pilgrimage." In Origen Thomson, *Crossing the Plains*. Greenburg, Ind.: O. Thomson, 1896.

Draper, Elias J. *Autobiography of . . . a Pioneer of California*. Fresno: Evening Democrat Print, 1904.

Dunham, E. Allene. *Across the Plains in a Covered Wagon*. N.p., n.d.

Dunlap, Katherine. "Journal." Photocopy of typescript. MS. Bancroft Library, University of California, Berkeley.

Eccles, Mrs. David. Interview. In *Frontier Omnibus*, edited by John W. Hakola. Helena: Montana State University Press, 1962.

Ellmaker, Enos. "Autobiography." In *Ellmaker Narrative, Oregon, 1853: Genealogy and Letters*. Eugene, Ore.: Lane County Pioneer-Historical Society, 1962.

Ferris, Benjamin G. *Utah and the Mormons*. New York: Harper & Brothers, 1854.

Ferris, Mrs. Benjamin G. *The Mormons at Home, with Some Incidents of Travel*. New York: Dix & Edwards, 1856.

Forsdick, Stephen. "On the Oregon Trail to Zion." *Denver Westerners Brand Book* 9 (1953): 33–55.

Foster, Isaac. "Journal of the Route to Alta, California [including letters written home]." In *The Foster Family: California Pioneers*, edited by Lucy Foster Sexton, pp. 14–85. Santa Barbara; Schauer Printing Studio Press, 1925.

Foster, Roxanna C. "The Third Trip across the Continent." In *The Foster Family: California Pioneers*, edited by Lucy Foster Sexton, pp. 187–98. Santa Barbara, Calif.: Schauer Printing Studio Press, 1925.

Francis, Samuel Dexter. "Journal." MS. Beinecke Library, Yale University.

Frink, Mrs. Margaret A. *Journal of the Adventures of a Party of California Gold-Seekers.* . . . Oakland, Calif., 1897.

Frizzell, Mrs. Lodisa. *Across the Plains to California in 1852*. Edited by Victor Hugo Paltsits. New York: New York Public Library, 1915.

Frost, Mary Perry. "Experience of a Pioneer." *Washington Historical Quarterly* 7 (1916): 123–25.

Garrison, Rev. A. E. *Life and Labours of Rev. A. E. Garrison*. N.p., 1943.

Geer, Mrs. Elizabeth Dixon Smith. "Diary." *Transactions of the Oregon Pioneer Association* (1907): 153–85.

Gilfry, Henry H. "Annual Address." *Transactions of the Oregon Pioneer Association* (1905): 411–23.

Gillette, Martha Louise Hill. *Overland to Oregon*. Ashland, Ore.: Lewis Osborne, 1971.

Glassock, C. B. *Lucky Baldwin*. Indianapolis, 1933.

Gowdy, Mrs. John T. *Crossing the Plains: Personal Recollections of the Journey to Oregon in 1852*. N.p., 1906.

Gray, George W. "Incidents of the Trip of the Gray Party." In Origen Thomson, *Crossing the Plains*. Greenburg, Ind.: O. Thomson, 1896.

Hadley, Mrs. E. A. "Diary." Typescript from MS. Privately owned.

Hancock, Samuel. *Narrative of Samuel Hancock*. New York: R. M. McBride, 1927.

Handsacker, Sarah Johnson. "Coming to Oregon." In Samuel Handsacker, *Pioneer Life*. Eugene, Ore.: privately printed, 1908.

Handsacker, Samuel. *Pioneer Life*. Eugene, Ore.: privately printed, 1908.

Hanna, Joseph A. "Letter, March 18, 1904." In Robert H. Blossom, "First Things Pertaining to Presbyterianism on the Pacific Coast," *Oregon Historical Quarterly* 15 (1914): 95–97.

Harlan, Jacob Wright. *California '46 to '88*. San Francisco: Bancroft, 1888.

Harter, George. *Crossing the Plains: An Account of the George Harter Family's Trip.* . . . Edited by Doris Harter Chase. Sacramento: privately printed, 1957.

Hastings, Loren B. "Diary of Loren B. Hastings. . . . " *Transactions of the Oregon Pioneer Association* (1923): 12–26.

Haun, Catherine M. "A Woman's Trip across the Plains." MS. Huntington Library, San Marino, Calif.

Hayden, Mary Jane. *Pioneer Days*. San Jose, Calif.: Murgotten's Press, 1915.

Hecox, Margaret M. *California Caravan: The 1846 Overland Trail Memoir of Margaret M. Hecox*. Edited by Richard Dillon. San Jose, Calif.: Harlan-Young Press, 1966.

Herndon, Sarah. *Days on the Road*. New York: Burr Printing House, 1902.

Hester, Sallie. "The Diary of a Pioneer Girl." *The Argonaut* 97 (September–October, 1925).

Hewitt, Randall H. *Across the Plains and over the Divide*. New York: Argosy Antiquarian, 1964.

———. *Notes by the Way*. Olympia: Washington Standard, 1863.

Hines, Celinda E. "Diary of Celinda E. Hines." *Transactions of the Oregon Pioneer Association* (1918): 69–125.

Hixon, Adrietta Applegate. *On to Oregon! A True Story of a Young Girl's Journey into the West*. Wesler, Idaho: Signal-American Printers, 1947.

Holtgrieve, Elizabeth R. "Recollections of Pioneer Days." *Washington Historical Quarterly* 19 (1928).

Hunt, Nancy A. "By Ox-Team to California." *Overland Monthly* 67 (April 1916).

Ivins, Virginia Wilcox. *Pen Pictures of Early Western Days*. N.p., 1905.

Johnson, John A. "Letters to His Wife, 1849." In *Pioneering on the Plains*. Kaukauna, Wisconsin, 1924.

Johnson, John L. "Diary of an Overland Journey." MS. Beinecke Library, Yale University.

Jones, Mary A. "Story of My Life." Typescript. California Pioneer Collection, Bancroft Library, University of California, Berkeley.

Judson, Phoebe Goodell. *A Pioneer's Search for an Ideal Home*. Bellingham, Wash.: United Printing, Binding and Stationery Company, 1925.

Kahler, William. "Diary, 1852." MS. Beinecke Library, Yale University.

Keil, William. "Letters from . . . Missouri to Oregon." *Missouri Historical Review* 48 (1953): 23–41.

Kellogg, Jane D. "Memories of Jane D. Kellogg." *Transactions of the Oregon Pioneer Association* (1913): 86–94.

Kellogg, Merritt G. *Notes Concerning the Kellogg's.* . . . Battle Creek, Mich., 1927.

Ketcham, Rebecca. "From Ithaca to Clatsop Plains." *Oregon Historical Quarterly* 62 (1961): 237–87, 337–402.

Keyes, Elizabeth. "Across the Plains. . . ." *Colorado Magazine* 10 (1933): 71–78.

Kingerly, Solomon. "Three Letters to Parents and Friends." MS. Beinecke Library, Yale University.

Knight, Mrs. Amelia Stewart. "Diary of an Oregon Pioneer of 1853." *Transactions of the Oregon Pioneer Association* (1928): 38–53.

Larkin, William. "Letter of June 27, 1864." *Pacific Historian* 2 (1958): 2–4.

Leach, A. J. *Early Day Stories.* Norfolk, Neb.: Huse, 1916.

Lenox, Edward Henry. *Overland to Oregon in the Track of Lewis and Clarke.* Edited by Robert Whitaker. Oakland, Calif.: Dowdle Press, 1904.

Long, Mrs. Mary Jane. *A True Story: Crossing the Plains in the Year of 1852 with Ox Teams.* McMinnville, Ore., 1915.

Longmire, James. "Narrative of a Pioneer." *Washington Historical Quarterly* 23 (1932): 47–60.

Looney, Mrs. M. A. *A Trip across the Plains in 1853.* Albany, Ore.: Albany Printing Company, 1912.

Lord, Mrs. Elizabeth. *Reminiscences of Eastern Oregon.* Portland, Ore.: Irwin-Hodson, 1903.

Lyman, Esther, and Lyman, Joseph. *Letters.* Eugene, Ore.: Lane County Pioneer-Historical Society, 1960.

Lyon, Bessie L. "Jasons of 1860." *The Palimpsest* 17 (1936): 217–34.

McClure, Andrew S. *The Diary.* Eugene, Ore.: Lane County Pioneer-Historical Society, 1959.

McIntosh, Walter H. *Allen and Rachel: An Overland Honeymoon in 1853.* Caldwell, Idaho: Caxton Printers, 1938.

Mathers, James. "Diary." In *Overland in 1846: Diaries and Letters of the California-Oregon Trail,* 1:219. Edited by Dale Morgan. Georgetown, Calif.: Talisman Press, 1963.

Maxwell, William A. *Crossing the Plains.* . . . San Francisco: Sunset, 1915.

Meeker, Ezra. *Covered Wagon Centennial and Ox Team Days.* Yonkers-on-Hudson, N.Y.: World Book Company, 1922.

Miller, J. D. "Early Oregon Scenes." *Oregon Historical Quarterly* 31 (1930): 55–68.

Miller, Joaquin. *Overland in a Covered Wagon.* New York: D. Appleton, 1830.

Minto, John. "Biography of Robert W. Morrison." *Transactions of the Oregon Pioneer Association* (1894): 53–57.

———. "Reminiscences. . . ." *Oregon Historical Quarterly* 2 (1901): 119–67.

Morgan, Mrs. Martha M. *A Trip across the Plains in the Year 1849*. San Francisco: Pioneer Press, 1864.

Murphy, Virginia Reed. "Across the Plains in the Donner Party (1846)." *Century Magazine* 42 (July 1891): 409–26.

Nash, Marie. "Diary." Typescript. California State Library, Sacramento.

Nesmith, James W. "Diary of the Emigration." *Oregon Historical Quarterly* 7 (December 1906): 329–59.

Newby, William T. "Diary of the Emigration." *Oregon Historical Quarterly* 40 (1939): 219–42.

Nobles, William. "Memoirs of Pioneer Life." Typescript. California Pioneer Collection, Bancroft Library, University of California, Berkeley.

Oliphant, J. Orin, ed. "Mrs. Lucy A. Ide's Diary 'In a Prairie Schooner, 1878.'" *Washington Historical Quarterly* 18 (1927): 125–31, 191–98, 277–88.

Olmsted, Juliet F. "Random Sketches." In *The Foster Family: California Pioneers*, edited by Lucy Foster Sexton, pp. 243–61. Santa Barbara, Calif.: Schauer Printing Studio Press, 1925.

Palmer, Harriet Scott. *Crossing over the Plains by Ox-Wagons*. N.p., 1931.

Parker, Basil G. *The Life and Adventures of Basil G. Parker: An Autobiography*. Plano, Calif.: F. W. Reed, 1902.

Parker, Mrs. Inez Eugenia Adams. "Early Recollections of Oregon Pioneer Life." *Transactions of the Oregon Pioneer Association* (1928): 17–35.

Parrish, Edward E. "Crossing the Plains." *Transactions of the Oregon Pioneer Association* (1888): 82–121.

Parrish, Susan Thomson Lewis. "Westward in 1850." MS. Huntington Library, San Marino, Calif.

Peabody, Frances C. "Across the Plains DeLuxe in 1865." *Colorado Magazine* 18 (1941): 71–76.

Pengra, Charlotte Emily. *Diary of Mrs. Bynon J. Pengra*. Eugene, Ore.: Lane County Pioneer-Historical Society, n.d.

Penter, Samuel. "Recollections of an Oregon Pioneer." *Oregon Historical Quarterly* 7 (1906): 56–61.

Perry, Elizabeth Higginbotham. "Mrs Perry, at Age of 88, Recalls Her Pioneer Days." In *Frontier Omnibus*, edited by John W. Hakola. Helena: Montana State University Press, 1962.

Porter, Lavinia Honeyman. *By Ox Team to California: A Narrative of Crossing the Plains in 1860.* Oakland, Calif.: Oakland Enquirer Publishing Company, 1910.

Potter, Theodore Edgar. *Autobiography.* Concord, N.H.: Rumford Press, 1913.

Powers, Mary L. Rockwood. Letters to Her Mother. In W. P. Powers, *Some Annals of the Powers Family.* Los Angeles: privately printed, 1924.

————. "The Overland Route: Leaves from the Journal of a California Emigrant." *Amateur Book Collector* 1, nos. 1–5 (September 1950–January 1951).

Pringle, Virgil K. "Diary. . . . " *Transactions of the Oregon Pioneer Association* (1920): 281–300.

Prosch, Thomas W. *David S. Maynard and Catherine T. Maynard: Biographies of Two of the Overland Immigrants of 1850.* Seattle: Lowman & Hanford Stationery & Printing Company, n.d.

Rahm, Louise M. "Diary." Photocopy. Bancroft Library, University of California, Berkeley.

Reed, James Frazier. "Letter of June 16, 1846" and "Diary." In *Overland in 1846: Diaries and Letters of the California-Oregon Trail*, 1:245. Edited by Dale Morgan. Georgetown, Calif.: Talisman Press, 1963.

Richey, Stuart, and Richey, Caleb. "Letters." *Transactions of the Oregon Pioneer Association* (1912): 586–662.

Royce, Sarah. *A Frontier Lady: Recollections of the Gold Rush and Early California.* Edited by Ralph Henry Gabriel. New Haven: Yale University Press, 1932.

Rudd, Lydia Allen. "Diary of Overland Journey from St. Joseph, Mo., to Burlington, Ore., by way of the Oregon Trail, the Dalles, Oregon City & Salem." MS. Huntington Library, San Marino, Calif.

Sawyer, Mrs. Francis H. "Overland to California." Typescript. Newberry Library, Chicago.

Schallenberger, Moses. *The Opening of the California Trail.* Edited by George R. Stewart. Berkeley: University of California Press, 1953.

Sexton, Lucy Foster, ed. *The Foster Family, California Pioneers.* Santa Barbara, Calif.: Schauer Printing Studio Press, 1925.

Sharp, Cornelia A. "Diary: Crossing the Plains from Missouri to Oregon in 1852." *Transactions of the Oregon Pioneer Association* (1903): 171–88.

Sharp, James M. *Brief Account of the Experiences of James Meikle Sharp.* Satiroy, Calif., 1931.

Sharp, Joseph A. "Crossing the Plains. . . . " *Transactions of the Oregon Pioneer Association* (1885): 91–95.

Shively, J. M. *Route and Distances to Oregon and California*. Washington, D.C.: W. Greer, 1846.

Shrode, Mrs. Maria Hargrave. "Overland by Ox-Train in 1870." *Historical Society of Southern California Quarterly* 26 (1944): 9–37.

Stearns, Orson A. "Appendix [to Mrs. Williams Diary: Recollections]." *Transactions of the Oregon Pioneer Association* (1919): 227–40.

Stewart, Agnes. "The Journey to Oregon. . . . " *Oregon Historical Quarterly* 29 (1928): 77–98. Also, *The Diary of Agnes Stewart, 1853*. Eugene, Ore.: Lane County Pioneer-Historical Society, 1959.

Stewart, Helen Marnie. *The Diary of Helen Marnie Stewart*. Eugene, Ore.: Lane County Pioneer-Historical Society, 1961.

Stevens, Charles. "Letters. . . . " Edited by E. Ruth Lockwood. *Oregon Historical Quarterly* 37 (1936): 137–59.

Stoughton, John A. "Passing of an Emigrant of 1843." *Washington Historical Quarterly* 15 (1924): 205–10.

Tetherow, Samuel. *Captain Sol Tetherow, Wagon Master*. Edited by Fred Lockley. Portland, Ore., 1923.

Thompson, William. *Reminiscences of a Pioneer*. San Francisco, 1912.

Thomson, Origen. *Crossing the Plains*. Greenburg, Ind.: O. Thomson, 1896.

Thornton, Jessy Quinn. *Oregon and California in 1848*. New York: Harper & Brothers, 1849.

True, Charles Fredrick. *Covered Wagon Pioneers*. Madison: College Printing Company, 1966.

Tuller, Mrs. Miriam A. "Crossing the Plains in 1845." *Transactions of the Oregon Pioneer Association* (1895): 87–90.

Udell, John. *John Udell Journal*. Los Angeles: N. A. Kovach, 1946.

Waite, Mrs. Catherine V. *Adventures in the Far West*. Chicago: C. V. Waite, 1882.

Walker, Margaret Hall. "Crossing the Plains." In *The Hall Family Crossing the Plains*, pp. 9–21. San Francisco: Wallace Kibbee, 1952.

Ward, Dilles Burgess. *Across the Plains in 1853*. Seattle, Wash.: Ball Brothers, 1911.

Ward, Harriet Sherrill. *Prairie Schooner Lady: The Journal of Harriet Sherrill Ward, 1853*. Edited by Ward D. Dewitt and Florence Stark Dewitt. Los Angeles: Westernlore Press, 1959.

Warner, Mary Elizabeth. "Wagon Train to California." MS. Huntington Library, San Marino, Calif.

Warren, Daniel K. "Narrative of a Pioneer." *Oregon Historical Quarterly* 3 (1902): 296–309.

Waters, Lydia Milner. "A Trip across the Plains in 1855." *Quarterly of the Society of California Pioneers* 6 (1929): 59–79.

Waugh, Lorenzo. *Autobiography*. Oakland, Calif.: Pacific Press Printer, 1883.

Whipple-Haslam, Mrs. Lee. *Early Days in California: Scenes and Events of the '50s As I Remember Them*. Jamestown, Calif., 1923.

White, Thomas. *To Oregon in 1852: Letter of Dr. Thomas White, La Grange County, Indiana, Emigrant*. Indianapolis: Indiana Historical Society, 1964.

Williams, Mrs. Velina A. "Diary of a Trip across the Plains in 1853." *Transactions of the Oregon Pioneer Association* (1919): 178–226.

Wilson, Luzena Stanley. *Luzena Stanley Wilson, '49er*. Mills College, Calif.: Eucalyptus Press, 1937.

Winne, Peter. "Across the Plains. . . ." Edited by Robert G. Athearn. *Iowa Journal of History* 41 (1951): 221–40.

Wisner, Sarah A. "A Trip across the Plains." Typescript. Newberry Library, Chicago.

Wood, Elizabeth. "Journal of a Trip to Oregon, 1851." *Oregon Historical Quarterly* 26 (1926): 192–203.

Wood, Tallmadge B. "Letter from Willamette." *Oregon Historical Quarterly* 3 (1902): 395–98.

Word, Samuel. "Diary . . . Trip across the Plains. . . ." *Contributions, Historical Society of Montana* 8 (1917): 37–92.

Zieber, John S. "Diary. . . ." *Transactions of the Oregon Pioneer Association* (1920): 301–35.

B.   GUIDEBOOKS AND ARTICLES

"Advice to Prospective Emigrants to Oregon." *Iowa Capitol Reporter*, March 25, 1843. Reprinted in *Oregon Historical Quarterly* 15 (1914): 295–99.

Buchanan, George W. "Oregon and California." *Western Expositor*, n.d. Reprinted in *Oregon Historical Quarterly* 11 (1910): 307–12.

Child, Andrew. *Overland Route to California*. Los Angeles: N. A. Kovach, 1946; original edition, 1852.

Edwards, P. L. *Sketch of Oregon Territory; or, Emigrant's Guide*. N.p., 1952.

Gilmore, S. M. "Letter from Oregon, from *Western Journal*, March 15, 1845." *Oregon Historical Quarterly* 4 (1903): 203–04.

Hastings, Lansford W. *Emigrant's Guide to Oregon and California*. Princeton: Princeton University Press, 1932; original edition, 1845.

Johnson, Overton, and Winter, William H. *Route across the Rocky Mountains*. Princeton: Princeton University Press, 1932; original edition, 1846.

Marcy, Randolph B. *The Prairie Traveler: A Hand-Book for Overland Expeditions*. London: Trübner, 1863.

Martin, William J. "Letter to *St. Joseph Gazette*, Jan. 5, 1846." Reprinted in *Overland in 1846: Diaries and Letters of the California-Oregon Trail*, 2:476–77. Edited by Dale Morgan. Georgetown, Calif.: Talisman Press, 1963.

"Oregon Meeting." *Ohio Statesman*, April 26, 1843. Reprinted in *Oregon Historical Quarterly* 2 (1902): 390–93.

Palmer, Joel. *Journal of Travels*. In *Early Western Travels, 1748–1846*, edited by R. G. Thwaites, vol. 30. Cleveland: Arthur H. Clark, 1906.

Platt, P. L., and Slater, N. *Traveler's Guide across the Plains upon the Overland Route to California*. San Francisco: J. Howell, 1963; original edition, 1848.

Ware, Joseph E. *The Emigrants' Guide to California*. Princeton: Princeton University Press, 1932; original edition, 1845.

C.   CONTEMPORARY OBSERVATION

Carleton, J. Henry. *The Prairie Logbooks*. Edited by Louis Pelzer. Chicago: Caxton Club, 1943.

Clyman, James. *James Clyman, Frontiersman; The Adventures of a Trapper and Covered-Wagon Emigrant As Told in His Own Reminiscences and Diaries*. Edited by Charles L. Camp. Portland, Ore.: Champoeg Press, 1960.

Field, Matthew C. *Prairie and Mountain Sketches*. Edited by Kate L. Gregg. Norman: University of Oklahoma Press, 1957.

Fremont, John Charles. *Report of the Exploring Expedition to the Rocky Mountains in the Year 1842, and to Oregon and North California in the Years 1843–44*. Vol. 1 of *The Expeditions of John Charles Fremont*, edited by Donald Jackson and Mary Lee Spence. Urbana: University of Illinois Press, 1970.

Holt, Thomas. "Journal." In *Overland in 1846: Diaries and Letters of the California-Oregon Trail*. Georgetown, Calif.: Talisman Press, 1963.

Linforth, James, ed. *Route from Liverpool to Great Salt Lake Valley*. Liverpool: F. D. Richards, 1855.

McConnel, John Ludlum. *Western Characters; or, Types of Border Life in the Western States*. New York: Redfield, 1853.

Parkman, Francis. *The Oregon Trail*. New York, New American Library, Signet Classics, 1950.

———. *The Oregon Trail Journal*. Vol. 2 of *The Journals of Francis Parkman*, edited by Mason Wade. New York: Harper, 1947.

Wadsworth, William. *The National Wagon Road Guide*. San Francisco: Whitton, Towne, 1858.

Watkins, Albert, ed. *Publications of the Nebraska State Historical Society* 20 (Lincoln, 1922).

D.   SECONDARY WORKS ON THE OVERLAND TRAIL

Altrocchi, Julia Cooley. *The Old California Trail*. Caldwell, Idaho: Caxton Printers, 1945.

Applegate, Lindsey. "The Applegate Route." *Oregon Historical Quarterly* 22 (1921): 12–45.

Bancroft, Huburt Howe. *History of California*. 5 vols. San Francisco: History Publishing Company, 1886.

———. *History of Oregon*. 2 vols. San Francisco: History Publishing Company, 1886.

Barlow, Mary S. "History of the Barlow Road." *Oregon Historical Quarterly* 3 (1902): 71–81.

Bell, James C. *Opening a Highway to the Pacific: 1838–1846*. New York: Columbia University Press, 1921.

Billington, Ray Allen. "Books That Won the West: The Guide Books of the Forty-Niners and Fifty-Niners." *American West* 4 (1967): 25–32, 72–75.

———. *Westward Expansion: A History of the American Frontier*, 4th ed. New York: Macmillan, 1974.

Clark, Roland Keith, and Tiller, Lowell. *Terrible Trail: The Meek Cutoff, 1845*. Caldwell, Idaho: Caxton Printers, 1966.

Coons, Frederica B. *The Trail to Oregon*. Portland, Ore.: Binfords & Mort, 1954.

Dale, Harrison C. "The Organization of the Oregon Emigrating Companies." *Oregon Historical Quarterly* 16 (1915): 205–27.

DeVoto, Bernard. *Across the Wide Missouri*. Boston: Little, Brown, 1947.

———. *The Year of Decision, 1846*. Boston: Little, Brown, 1943.

Dick, Everett. *Vanguards of the Frontier*. New York: D. Appleton-Century, 1941.

Eide, Ingvard Henry. *Oregon Trail*. Chicago: Rand McNally, 1973.

Ghent, W. J. *The Road to Oregon: A Chronicle of the Great Emigrant Trail*. New York: Tudor Publishing Company, 1934.

Gregg, J. R. *A History of the Oregon Trail, Santa Fe Trail, and Other Trails*. Portland, Ore.: Binfords & Mort, 1955.

Guthrie, A. B., Jr. *The Way West*. New York: William Sloane Associates, 1949.

Hafen, Leroy, and Young, Francis Marion. *Fort Laramie and the*

Pageant of the West, 1834–1890. Glendale, Calif.: Arthur H. Clark, 1938.

Hunt, Thomas H. *Ghost Trails to California*. Palo Alto: American West Publishing Company, 1974.

Jacobs, Melvin Clay. *Winning Oregon: A Study of an Expansionist Movement*. Caldwell, Idaho: Caxton Printers, 1938.

Kroll, Helen B. "The Books That Enlightened the Emigrants." *Oregon Historical Quarterly* 45 (1944): 102–23.

Langrin, David J. "Pioneer Justice on the Overland Trails." *Wyoming Historical Quarterly* 5 (1974): 421–39.

Laut, Agnes C. *The Overland Trail: The Epic Path of the Pioneers to Oregon*. New York: McGraw-Hill, 1963.

McGlashan, C. F. *History of the Donner Party. A Tragedy of the Sierras*. Truckee, Calif.: Chonsky & McGlashan, 1879.

Mattes, Merrill J. *The Great Platte River Road: The Covered Wagon Mainline via Fort Kearny to Fort Laramie*. Lincoln: Nebraska State Historical Society, 1969.

Morgan, Dale, ed. *Overland in 1846: Diaries and Letters of the California-Oregon Trail*. 2 vols. Georgetown, Calif.: Talisman Press, 1963.

Moynihan, Ruth Barnes. "Children and Young People on the Overland Trail." *Western Historical Quarterly* 6 (1975): 279–94.

Munkres, Robert L. "The Plains Indian Threat on the Overland Trail before 1860." *Annals of Wyoming* 40 (1968): 193–221.

———. "Wives, Mothers, Daughters: Women's Life in the Roads West." *Annals of Wyoming* 42 (1970): 191–224.

Paden, Irene. *The Wake of the Prairie Schooner*. New York: Macmillan, 1943.

Potter, David M. Introduction to *The Trail to California: The Overland Journal of Vincent Geiger and Wakeman Bryarly*. New Haven: Yale University Press, 1962.

Read, Georgia Willis. "Women and Children on the Oregon-California Trail in the Gold-Rush Years." *Missouri Historical Review* (1944–45).

Robertson, Frank C. *Fort Hall: Gateway to Oregon Country*. New York: Hastings House, 1963.

Rucker, Maude A. *The Oregon Trail and Some of Its Blazers*. New York: Walter Neale, 1930.

Stewart, George R. *The California Trail: An Epic with Many Heroes*. New York: McGraw-Hill, 1962.

———. *Ordeal by Hunger: The Story of the Donner Party*. New York: Henry Holt, 1936.

Taylor, P. A. M. "Emigrants' Problems in Crossing the West, 1830–1870." *University of Birmingham Historical Journal* 5 (1955): 83–102.

Troxel, Katherine. "Food of the Overland Emigrants." *Oregon Historical Quarterly* 56 (1955): 12–26.

Unruh, John D. "The Plains Across: The Overland Emigrants and the Trans-Mississippi West, 1840–1860." Ph.D. dissertation, University of Kansas, 1975.

Vestal, Stanley. *The Old Sante Fe Trail.* Boston: Houghton Mifflin, 1939.

Webster, Jean. "The Myth of Pioneer Hardship on the Oregon Trail." *Reed College Bulletin* 24 (January 1946): 27–46.

Young, F. G. "The Oregon Trail." *Oregon Historical Quarterly* 1 (1900).

II.   Midwestern Farm Life

A.   DEMOGRAPHIC STUDIES

Coale, Ansley J., and Zelnik, Melvin. *New Estimates of Fertility and Population in the United States.* Princeton: University Press, 1963.

DeBow, J. D. B. *Statistical View of the United States . . . Compendium of the Seventh Census.* Washington, D.C.: U.S. Census Office, 1854.

Eblen, Jack D. "An Analysis of Nineteenth Century Frontier Populations." *Demography* 2 (1965): 399–411.

Forster, Colin, and Tucker, G. S. L. *Economic Opportunity and White American Fertility Ratios, 1800–1860.* New Haven: Yale University Press, 1972.

Grabill, W. H., Kiser, C. V., and Whelpton, P. K. *The Fertility of American Women.* New York: John Wiley & Sons, 1958.

Kennedy, Joseph C. G. *Preliminary Report on the Eighth Census, 1860.* Washington, D.C.: Government Printing Office, 1862.

Oregon State Archives. *Pioneer Families of the Oregon Territory, 1850.* Bulletin no. 3, Publication no. 17. Eugene, 1951.

Whelpton, Pascal K. *Cohort Fertility: Native White Women in the United States.* Princeton: Princeton University Press, 1954.

Wrigley, E. A. *An Introduction to English Historical Demography.* New York: Basic Books, 1966.

Yasuba, Yasukirchi. *Birth Rates of the White Population in the United States, 1800–1860.* Baltimore: Johns Hopkins Press, 1962.

B.   MIDWESTERN POLITICAL ECONOMY

Bardolph, Richard. "Illinois Agriculture in Transition, 1820–1870." *Journal of the Illinois State Historical Society* 41 (1948): 244–64.

Bidwell, Percy W., and Falconer, John L. *History of Agriculture in the Northern United States, 1820–1860*. Washington, D.C.: Carnegie Institute, 1925.

Bogue, Allan G. *From Prairie to Corn Belt: Farming on the Illinois and Iowa Prairies in the Nineteenth Century*. Chicago: University of Chicago Press, 1963.

Carter, Harvey L. "Indiana in Transition, 1850–1860." *Agricultural History* 20 (1946): 107–21.

Chayanov, A. V. *The Theory of Peasant Economy*. Homewood, Ill.: American Economic Association, 1966.

Curti, Merle. *The Making of an American Community*. Stanford: Stanford University Press, 1959.

Danhof, Clarence H. "Agriculture." In *The Growth of the American Economy*, edited by Harold Williamson, pp. 133–53. New York: Prentice-Hall, 1951.

———. *Change in Agriculture: The Northern United States, 1820-1870*. Cambridge, Mass.: Harvard University Press, 1969.

———. "Farm Making Costs and the Safety Valve." *Journal of Political Economy* 44 (1941): 317–59.

David, Paul. "The Mechanization of Reaping in the Ante-Bellum Midwest." In *Industrialization in the Two Systems*, edited by Henry Rosovsky, pp. 3–39. New York: John Wiley & Sons, 1966.

Easterlin, Richard. "Interregional Differences in Per Capita Income, Population and Total Income, 1840–1950." In National Bureau of Economic Research, *Trends in the American Economy in the Nineteenth Century*, pp. 73–140. Studies in Income and Wealth, vol. 24. Princeton: Princeton University Press, 1960.

Galeski, Boguslaw. *Basic Concepts of Rural Sociology*. Manchester: University of Manchester Press, 1972.

Gates, Paul W. *Agriculture and the Civil War*. New York: Knopf, 1965.

———. *The Farmer's Age: Agriculture, 1815–1860*. New York: Holt, Rinehart, and Winston, 1960.

Herretta, James. *The Evolution of American Society, 1700–1815: An Interdisciplinary Analysis*. Lexington, Mass.: D. C. Heath, 1973.

Hillard, Sam Bowers, *Hog Meat and Hoecake: Food Supply in the Old South, 1840–1860*. Carbondale: Southern Illinois University Press, 1972.

Hooper, Luther. "The Loom and Spindle: Past, Present and Future." In Smithsonian Institute, *Annual Report* (Washington, D.C., 1914), pp. 629–78.

Hunter, Louis L. *Steamboats on the Western Rivers*. Cambridge, Mass.: Harvard University Press, 1949.

Jarchow, Merrill E. *The Earth Brought Forth: A History of Minnesota Agriculture to 1865*. St. Paul: Minnesota Historical Society, 1949.

Lemmon, George F. "Farm Machinery in Ante-Bellum Missouri." *Missouri Historical Review* 40 (1946): 467–80.

Loehr, Rodney C. "Self Sufficiency on the Farm." *Agricultural History* 26 (1952): 37–41.

Nelson, Lowry. *Rural Sociology*. New York: American Book Company, 1948.

North, Douglas C. "Agriculture in Regional Economic Growth." In *American Economic History: Essays in Interpretation*, edited by Stanley Cohen and Forest G. Hill, pp. 258–66. Philadelphia: J. B. Lippincott, 1966.

Odum, Howard W., and Moore, Harry Estill. *American Regionalism: A Cultural-Historical Approach to National Integration*. New York: Henry Holt, 1938.

Pease, Theodore C. *The Frontier State, 1818–1848*. Springfield: Illinois Centennial Commission, 1918.

Pressly, Thomas J., and Scofield, William H. *Farm Real Estate Values in the United States by Counties, 1850–1959*. Seattle: University of Washington Press, 1965.

Riegel, Robert E. "Trans-Mississippi Railroads during the Fifties." *Mississippi Valley Historical Review* 10 (1923): 153–72.

Rogin, Leo. *Introduction of Farm Machinery in Its Relation to the Productivity of Labor in the Agriculture of the United States during the Nineteenth Century*. Berkeley: University of California Press, 1931.

Ross, Earle D. *Iowa Agriculture: An Historical Survey*. Iowa City: State Historical Society of Iowa, 1951.

Rusk, Ralph Leslie. *The Literature of the Middle Western Frontier*. 2 vols. New York: Columbia University Press, 1925.

Sawerson, Durgert. *Rural Sociology and Rural Social Organization*. New York: John Wiley & Sons, 1942.

Schlebecker, John T. *Bibliography of Books and Pamphlets on the History of Agriculture*. Santa Barbara: Clio, 1969.

———. *Whereby We Thrive: A History of American Farming, 1607–1972*. Ames: Iowa State University Press, 1975.

Schmidt, Huburt. "Farming in Illinois a Century Ago As Illustrated in Bond County." *Journal of the Illinois State Historical Society* 31 (1938): 138–59.

Schrob, David E. *Hired Hands and Plowboys: Farm Labor in the Midwest, 1815–1860*. Urbana: University of Illinois Press, 1975.

Throne, Mildred. "Southern Iowa Agriculture, 1833–1890: The

Progress from Subsistence to Commercial Corn-Belt Farming." *Agricultural History* 24 (1950): 124–30.

Towne, Marvin W., and Rasmussen, Wayne D. "Farm Gross Product and Gross Investment." In National Bureau of Economic Research, *Trends in the American Economy in the Nineteenth Century.* Studies in Income and Wealth, vol. 24. Princeton: Princeton University Press, 1960.

Tryon, Rolla Milton. *Household Manufactures in the United States, 1840–1860.* Chicago: University of Chicago Press, 1917.

Winther, Oscar Osburn. *The Old Oregon Country: A History of Frontier Trade, Transportation, and Travel.* Indiana University Social Science Series no. 7. Bloomington: Indiana University Press, 1950.

C. SOCIAL LIFE: TRAVELERS' ACCOUNTS

Berger, Max. *The British Traveler in America: 1836–1850.* New York: Columbia University Press, 1943.

Brown, William. *America: A Four Years' Residence.* Leeds: privately printed, 1849.

Buckingham, J. H. *Illinois As Lincoln Knew It.* Springfield, Ill., 1938.

Busch, Mority. *Travels between the Hudson and the Mississippi, 1851–1852.* Edited and translated by Norman Binger. Lexington: University Press of Kentucky, 1971.

Flagg, Edmund. *The Far West, 1836–1837.* In Early Western Travels, 1748–1846, edited by R. G. Thwartes, vol. 26. Cleveland: Arthur H. Clark, 1906.

Hubach, Robert R. *Early Midwestern Travel Narratives: An Annotated Bibliography, 1634–1850.* Detroit: Wayne State University Press, 1961.

Latrobe, Charles J. *The Rambler in North America.* London: R. B. Seeley & N. Burnside, 1835.

Martineau, Harriet. *Retrospect of Western Travel.* 3 vols. London: Saunders and Otley, 1838.

Murray, Charles A. *Travels in North America.* London: Richard Bentley, 1854.

Oliver, William. *Eight Months in Illinois.* Chicago: W. M. Hill, 1924; original edition, 1843.

Peyton, John Lewis. *Over the Alleghanies and across the Prairies.* London: Sunkin, Marshall, 1870.

Sherreff, Patrick. *A Tour through North America.* Edinburgh: Oliver and Boyd, 1835.

D.   SOCIAL LIFE: RECOLLECTIONS AND AUTOBIOGRAPHIES

Brush, Daniel Harmon. *Growing Up with Southern Illinois, 1820 to 1861*.
Chicago: Lakeside Press, 1944.
Byers, S. H. M. "Out West in the Forties." *Iowa Historical Record* 5
(1889): 365–74.
Duniway, Abigail Scott. *Captain Gray's Company; or, Crossing the Plains
and Living in Oregon*. Portland, Ore.: S. J. McCormick, 1859.
———. *Path Breaking: An Autobiographical History of the Equal Suffrage
Movement in the Pacific Coast States*. 2nd ed. Portland, Ore.: James
Kerm & Abbott, 1914.
Frank, Cliff. "The Indiana Log-Rolling." *Folk-Say: A Regional Miscel-
lany* 1 (1929): 79–85.
Haines, James. "Social Life and Scenes in the Early Settlement of
Southern Illinois." *Transactions of the Illinois State Historical Society*
10 (1906).
Hamilton, Carl. *In No Time at All*. Ames: Iowa State University Press,
1975.
Hoppin, Ruth. "Personal Recollections of Pioneer Days." *Michigan
Pioneer and Historical Collections* 38 (1912).
Howells, William Cooper. *Recollections of Life in Ohio from 1813 to 1840*.
Cincinnati: Robert Clarke, 1895.
Kirkland, Caroline Matilda. *A New Home; or, Life in the Clearings*.
Edited by John Nerver. New York: G. P. Putnam's Sons, 1953.
Major, Noah J. "Pioneers of Morgan County." *Indiana Historical Society
Publication* 5 (1915).
Onstot, T. G. *Pioneers of Menard and Mason Counties*. Forest City, Ill.:
privately printed, 1962.
Parker, B. S. "Pioneer Life." *Indiana Magazine of History* 3 (1907):
1–11, 51–57, 125–37, 182–88.
Willard, Samuel. "Personal Reminiscences of Life in Illinois, 1830–
1880." *Transactions of the Illinois State Historical Society* 11 (1906):
73–87.

E.   SOCIAL LIFE: FOLKLORE MATERIALS

Abrahams, Roger D., and Foss, George. *Anglo-American Folksong Style*.
Englewood Cliffs, N. J.: Prentice-Hall, 1968.
Belden, Henry M. *Ballads and Songs Collected by the Missouri Folklore
Society*. Columbia: University of Missouri Press, 1955.
Brewster, Paul G. "Folktales from Indiana and Missouri." *Folklore*
50 (1939): 294–310.

———. "Some Folk Songs from Indiana." *Journal of American Folk Lore* 57 (1944): 282–87.

———. *Ballads and Songs of Indiana*. Bloomington: Indiana University Press, 1940.

Brown, Rollo Walter. "A Word List from Western Indiana." *Dialect Notes* 3 (1912): 570–93.

Coffin, Tristram P. *The British Traditional Ballad in North America*. Philadelphia: American Folklore Society, 1963.

Dale, Edward Everett. "The Speech of the Pioneers." *Arkansas Historical Quarterly* 6 (1947): 117–31.

Dwyer, Richard A., and Lingenfelter, Richard E. *The Songs of the Gold Rush*. Berkeley: University of California Press, 1964.

Eddy, Mary O. *Ballads and Songs from Ohio*. New York: J. J. Augustin, 1939.

Hanley, O. W. "Dialect Words from Southern Indiana." *Dialect Notes* 2 (1906): 113–23.

Harris, Jesse W. "The Dialect of Appalachia in Southern Illinois." *American Speech* 21 (1946): 96–99.

Hyatt, Henry M. *Folk-Lore from Adams County, Illinois*. 2d rev. ed. New York: Alma Egan Hyatt Foundation, 1965.

Laws, G. Malcolm, Jr. *Native American Balladry: A Descriptive Study and a Bibliographical Syllabus*. Philadelphia: American Folklore Society, 1964.

Leach, MacEdward. "Folklore in American Regional Literature." *Journal of the Folklore Institute* 3 (1966): 376–97.

Lomax, Alan. *The Folk Songs of North America in the English Language*. Garden City, N.Y.: Doubleday, 1960.

Kramer, Frank R. *Voices in the Valley: Mythmaking and Folk Belief in the Shaping of the Middle West*. Madison: University of Wisconsin Press, 1964.

McDavid, Ruben I. "Folk Speech." *Journal of American Folklore* 67 (1954): 327–30.

Machwardt, A. H. "Folkspeech in Indiana and Adjacent States." *Indiana Historical Bulletin* 17 (1940): 120–40.

Neely, Charles. *Tales and Songs of Southern Illinois*. Menasha, Wisc.: George Banta, 1938.

Randolph, Vance. *Ozark Folksongs*. 4 vols. Columbia: State Historical Society of Missouri, 1946–50.

———. *Ozark Mountain Folks*. New York: Vanguard Press, 1932.

———. *Ozark Superstitions*. New York: Columbia University Press, 1947.

————. *The Ozarks: An American Survival of Primitive Society*. New York: Vanguard Press, 1931.

————, and Wilson, George P. *Down in the Holler*. Norman: University of Oklahoma Press, 1953.

Read, Allen Walker. "Attitudes toward Missouri Speech." *Missouri Historical Review* 29 (1935): 259–71.

Rice, W. O. "The Pioneer Dialect of Southern Illinois." *Dialect Notes* 2 (1902): 225–49.

Stout, Earl J. *Folklore from Iowa*. American Folk-Lore Society Memoirs, vol. 29. New York, 1936.

Thomas, Daniel L., and Thomas, Lucy B. *Kentucky Superstitions*. Princeton: Princeton University Press, 1920.

F.   SOCIAL LIFE: SECONDARY STUDIES

Allen, John Willis. *It Happened in Southern Illinois*. Carbondale: Southern Illinois University Press, 1968.

Atkeson, Mary Meek. *The Woman on the Farm*. New York: Century, 1924.

Blegen, Theodore C. *Grass Roots History*. Minneapolis: University of Minnesota Press, 1948.

Bracke, William B. *Wheat Country*. New York: Duell, Sloane & Pearce, 1950.

Britton, Wiley. *Pioneer Life in Southwestern Missouri*. Kansas City: Smith-Greves, 1929.

Buley, R. C. *The Old Northwest Pioneer Period, 1815–1840*. 2 vols. Indianapolis: Indiana Historical Society, 1950.

Burris, Evadene A. "Building the Frontier Home." *Minnesota History* 15 (1934): 43–49.

————. "Frontier Food." *Minnesota History* 14 (1933): 378–92.

————. "Furnishing the Frontier Home." *Minnesota History* 15 (1934): 181–93.

————. "Keeping House on the Minnesota Frontier." *Minnesota History* 14 (1933): 265–75.

Chapman, Mrs. T. T. *A History of Johnson County Illinois*. N.p., 1925.

Clark, Thomas D. *Frontier America*. New York: Charles Scribner's Sons, 1958.

————. "Manners and Humors of the American Frontier." *Missouri Historical Review* 35 (1940): 3–24.

————. *The Rampaging Frontier: Manners and Humors of Pioneer Days in the South and Middle West*. Indianapolis: Bobbs Merrill, 1939.

Craven, Avery. "The Advance of Civilization into the Middle West in the Period of Settlement." In *Sources of Culture in the Middle West*, edited by Dixon Ryan Rex, pp. 39–71. New York: Appleton-Century, 1934.

Dale, Edward Everett. "The Food of the Frontier." *Journal of the Illinois State Historical Society* 40 (1947): 38–61.

Dick, Everett N. *The Dixie Frontier.* New York: Knopf, 1948.

———. *The Sod House Frontier, 1854–1859: A Social History of the Northern Plains.* . . . New York: Appleton-Century, 1937.

Esarey, Logan. *A History of Indiana from Its Exploration to 1850.* Indianapolis: B. F. Bowen, 1915.

———. *The Indiana Home.* Crawfordsville, Ind.: R. E. Banta, 1943.

Gronert, Ted. *Sugar Creek Saga: A History and Development of Montgomery County [Indiana].* Crawfordsville, Ind.: Wabash College, 1958.

Hall, Dr. W. W. "Health of Farmers' Families." In *Report of the Commissioner of Agriculture for the Year 1862*, pp. 453–70. Washington, D.C.: Government Printing Office, 1863.

Johnson, Charles Albert. *The Frontier Camp Meeting: Religion's Harvest Time.* Dallas: Southern Methodist University Press, 1955.

Johnson, Charles Beneulyn. "Everyday Life in Illinois near the Middle of the Nineteenth Century." *Transactions of the Illinois State Historical Society* 13 (1914): 44–53.

———. *Illinois in the Fifties.* Champaign, Ill.: Flanigan-Pearson, 1918.

Krueger, Lillian. "Motherhood on the Wisconson Frontier." *Wisconsin Historical Magazine* 29 (1945): 157–83.

———. "Social Life in Wisconsin: Pre-Territorial through the Mid Sixties." *Wisconsin Magazine of History* 22 (1938).

Loehr, Rodney. "Minnesota Farmers' Diaries." *Minnesota History* 18 (1937): 284–97.

Lybarger, Ocie. "Every Day Life on the Southern Illinois Frontier." Master's thesis, Southern Illinois University, 1951.

McGinnis, R. J., ed. *The Good Old Days: An Invitation to Memory.* New York: Harper & Brothers, 1960.

Mackey, Margaret Gilbert, and Sooy, Louise Pickney. *Early California Costumes, 1769–1847.* Stanford: Stanford University Press, 1932.

Manahan, Leuty. *Early American Life: Historical Paintings and Text.* Columbus, Ohio: Franklin County Historical Society, 1961.

Mainardi, Patricia. "Quilts: The Great American Art." *Radical America* 7 (1973): 36–38.

Mitchell, Edward B. "The American Farm Woman As She Sees Herself." U.S., Department of Agriculture, *Yearbook of Agriculture, 1914.* Washington, D.C.: Government Printing Office, 1915.

Owen, Mary Alicia. "Social Customs and Usages in Missouri during the Last Century." *Missouri Historical Review* 15 (1920): 176–90.

Power, Richard Lyle. *Planting Corn Belt Culture.* Indianapolis: Indiana Historical Society, 1953.

Robertson, Elizabeth Wells. *American Quilts.* New York: Studio Publications, 1948.

Sandburg, Carl. *Abraham Lincoln: The Prairie Years.* New York: Harcourt, Brace, 1927.

Schmiedeler, Edgar. *The Industrial Revolution and the Home: A Comparative Study of Family Life in County, Town and City.* Washington, D.C., 1927.

Sloane, Eric. *The Seasons of America Past.* New York: Wilfred Funk, 1958.

Smith, Helen Krebs. *The Presumptuous Dreamers: A Sociological History of the Life and Times of Abigail Scott Duniway (1834–1915).* Lake Oswego, Ore.: Smith, Smith and Smith, 1974.

Taylor, Henry C. *Tarpleywick: A Century of Iowa Farming.* Ames: Iowa State University Press, 1970.

Taylor, Marjorie Caroline. "Domestic Arts and Crafts in Illinois (1800–1860)." *Journal of the Illinois State Historical Society* 33 (1940): 278–303.

Thomas, Benjamin P. *Lincoln's New Salem.* Rev. ed. New York: Knopf, 1954.

Van Wagenen, Jared, Jr. *The Golden Age of Homespun.* Ithaca: Cornell University Press, 1953.

Vogel, William. "Home Life in Early Indiana." *Indiana Magazine of History* 10 (1914).

Wannah, Edward, and Pitz, Henry. *Early American Costume.* New York: Century, 1929.

Wilson, Charles Morrow. *Backwoods America.* Chapel Hill: University of North Carolina Press, 1934.

Wilson, George R. *History of DuBois County [Indiana].* Jasper, Ind., privately printed, 1910.

III. Theoretical and Methodological Studies

A. DIARY WRITING

Allport, Gordon W. *The Use of Personal Documents in Psychological Science.* New York: Social Science Research Council, 1942.

Gottschalk, Louis, Kluckhohn, Clyde, and Angell, Robert. *The Use of Personal Documents in History, Anthropology and Sociology.* Washington, D.C.: Social Science Research Council, 1945.

Ponsonby, Arthur. *English Diaries*. 2d ed. London: Methuen, 1923.
————. *More English Diaries*. London: Methuen, 1927.

B.   CONTENT ANALYSIS

Berelson, Bernard. "Content Analysis." In *Handbook of Social Psychology*, edited by G. Lindzey, pp. 488–513. Reading, Mass.: Addison-Wesley, 1964.

Carney, T. F. "Content Analysis: A Review Essay." *Historical Methods Newsletter* 4 (March 1971): 52–61.

Farber, Bernard. "An Index of Marital Integration." *Sociometry* 20 (1957): 117–39.

Garraty, John A. "The Application of Content Analysis to Biography and History." In *Trends in Content Analysis*, edited by Ithiel de Sola Pool. Urbana: University of Illinois Press, 1959.

Holsti, Ole. *Content Analysis for the Social Sciences and Humanities*. Reading, Mass.: Addison-Wesley, 1969.

Rokeach, Milton. *Beliefs, Attitudes, and Values: A Theory of Organization and Change*. San Francisco: Jossey-Bass, 1968.

Schutz, William C. "On Categorizing Qualitative Data in Content Analysis." *Public Opinion Quarterly* 22 (1958): 503–15.

White, Ralph K. "*Black Boy:* A Value Analysis." *Journal of Abnormal and Social Psychology* 42 (1947): 440–61.

————. "Value-Analysis: A Quantitative Method for Describing Qualitative Data." *Journal of Social Psychology* 19 (1944): 351–58.

————. *Value-Analysis: The Nature and Use of the Method*. Glen Gardiner, N.J.: Society for the Psychological Study of Social Issues, 1951.

C.   SOCIO-LINGUISTICS

Bernstein, Basil. "Elaborated and Restricted Codes: Their Social Origins and Consequences." In *Communication and Culture*, edited by Alfred G. Smith, pp. 427–41. New York: Holt, Rinehart, and Winston, 1966.

————. "A Socio-Linguistic Approach to Socialization: With Some Reference to Educability." In *Class, Codes and Control*, pp. 143–69. London: Routledge & Kegan Paul, 1971.

Bradley, Henry. "On the Relations between Spoken and Written Language." *Proceedings of the British Academy* 6 (1913–14): 212–32.

Brown, Roger, and Gillman, Albert. "The Pronouns of Power and Solidarity." In *Readings in the Sociology of Language*, edited by Joshua A. Fishman. Paris: Mouton, 1968.

Gelb, I. J. *A Study of Writing*. Chicago: University of Chicago Press, 1952.

Hymes, Dell. "Models of the Interaction of Languages and Social Setting." *Journal of Social Issues* 23 (1967).

Kay, Mary Ritchie. *Male/Female Language: With a Comprehensive Bibliography*. Metuchen, N.J.: Scarecrow Press, 1975.

Lawton, Dennis. "Social Class Language Differences in Language Development: A Study of Some Samples of Written Work." *Language and Speech* 6 (1963): 120–43.

Schatzman, Leonan, and Straus, Anselm. "Social Class and Modes of Communication." In *Communication and Culture*, edited by Alfred G. Smith, pp. 442–55. New York: Holt, Rinehart, and Winston, 1966.

Thorne, Barre, and Henley, Nancy, eds. *Language and Sex: Difference and Dominance*. Rowley, Mass.: Newberry House, 1975.

Uldall, H. J. "Speech and Writing." In *Readings in Linguistics II*, edited by Eric P. Harp et al., pp. 147–51. Chicago: University of Chicago Press, 1966.

D.   WOMEN

Albert, Ethel M. "The Roles of Women: A Question of Values." In *The Potential of Women*, edited by Seymour M. Farrer and Roger H. L. Wilson. New York: McGraw-Hill, 1963.

Bosenrup, Esther. *Women's Role in Economic Development*. London: Allen & Unwin, 1970.

Brown, Judith K. "A Note on the Division of Labor by Sex." *American Anthropologist* 70 (1970): 1073–78.

Degler, Carl N. *Is There a History of Women?* Cambridge: Clarendon Press, 1975.

Dick, Everett N. "Sunbonnet and Calico: The Homesteader's Consort." *Nebraska History* 47 (1966): 3–13.

Ehrenreich, Barbara, and English, Dierdre. *Witches, Midwives and Nurses: A History of Women Healers*. Old Westbury, N.Y.: Feminist Press, 1973.

Friedl, E. *Women and Men: An Anthropologist's View*. New York: Holt, Rinehart, and Winston, 1975.

Gallaher, Ruth A. *Legal and Political Status of Women in Iowa*. Iowa City: State Historical Society of Iowa, 1918.

Gattey, Charles Nelson. *The Bloomer Girls*. New York: Coward-McMann, 1968.

Gonzales, Nanice L. S. "Lactation and Pregnancy: A Hypothesis." *American Anthropologist* 66 (1964): 873–78.

Gordon, Ann D., Buhle, Mari Jo, and Schrom, Nancy E. *Women in American Society*. A Radical America pamphlet. Boston: New England Free Press, 1971.

Gordon, Linda. *Woman's Body, Woman's Right: A Social History of Birth Control in America*. New York: Grossman, 1976.

Hartmann, Heidi. "Capitalism, Patriarchy and Job Segregation By Sex." *Signs* 1, no. 3, pt. 2 (1976): 137–69.

Henry, L. "Some Data on Natural Fertility." *Eugenics Quarterly* 8 (1961): 87, 200–11.

Jacobs, Sue Ellen. *Women in Perspective: A Guide for Cross Cultural Studies*. Chicago: University of Illinois Press, 1974.

Kanowitz, Leo. *Women and the Law: The Unfinished Revolution*. Albuquerque: University of New Mexico Press, 1969.

Kelly-Gadol, Joan. "The Social Relations of the Sexes: Methodological Implications of Women's History." *Signs* 1 (1976): 809–823.

Maccoby, Eleanor Emmons, ed. *The Development of Sex Differences*. Stanford: Stanford University Press, 1965.

————, and Jacklin, Carol Nagy. *The Psychology of Sex Differences*. Stanford: Stanford University Press, 1974.

Martin, M. Kay, and Voorhies, Barbara. *Female of the Species*. New York: Columbia University Press, 1975.

Mead, Margaret. *Male and Female: A Study of the Sexes in a Changing World*. New York: William Morrow, 1949.

————. *Sex and Temperament in Three Primitive Societies*. New York: William Morrow, 1935.

Mitchell, Juliet. *Woman's Estate*. New York: Pantheon, 1970.

Nerlove, S. B. "Women's Workload and Infant Feeding Practices: A Relationship with Demographic Implications." *Ethnology* 13 (1974): 207–14.

Oakley, Ann. *Housewife*. London: Allen Lake, 1974.

————. *Sex, Gender, and Society*. London: Temple Smith, 1974.

————. *The Sociology of Housework*. Bath: Martin Robertson, 1974.

Percy, A. P., et al. "Timing and Sequence of Resuming Ovulation and Menstruation after Childbirth." *Population Studies* 25 (1971): 491–503.

Potter, David M. "American Woman and the American Character." In *History and American Society: Essays of David M. Potter*, edited by Don E. Fehrenbacher, pp. 277–303. New York: Oxford University Press, 1973.

Potter, R. G. "Birth Intervals: Structure and Change." *Population Studies* 17 (1963): 155–66.

Reiter, Reyna, ed. *Toward an Anthropology of Women*. New York: Monthly Review Press, 1974.

Rosaldo, Michelle Z. "Women, Culture and Society: A Theoretical Overview." In *Women, Culture and Society*, edited by Michelle Z. Rosaldo and L. Lamphere, pp. 17–42. Stanford: Stanford University Press, 1974.

Ryan, Mary P. *Womanhood in America: From Colonial Times to the Present*. New York: New Viewpoints, 1975.

Sanday, P. R. "Toward a Theory of the Status of Women." *American Anthropologist* 75 (1973): 1682–1700.

Scott, Joan W., and Tilly, Louise A. "Women's Work and the Family in Nineteenth Century Europe." In *The Family in History*, edited by Charles E. Rosenberg. University of Pennsylvania Press, 1975.

Smith-Rosenberg, Carroll. "The Female World of Love and Ritual: Relations between Women in Nineteenth Century America." *Signs* 1 (1975): 1–29.

Sprague, William Forrest. *Women and the West: A Short Social History*. Boston: Christopher Publishing House, 1940.

Vogel, Lise. "The Earthly Family." *Radical America* 7 (1973): 9–50.

Warbasse, Elizabeth. "The Changing Legal Rights of Married Women, 1800–1861." Ph.D. dissertation, Radcliffe College, 1960.

Welter, Barbara. "The Cult of True Womanhood: 1820–1860." *American Quarterly* 18 (1966): 151–74.

E.   FAMILY STUDIES

Calhoun, Arthur W. *A Social History of the American Family from Colonial Times to the Present*. 3 vols. Cleveland: Arthur H. Clark, 1917–19.

Glick, Paul. "The Family Cycle." *American Sociological Review* 12 (1947): 164–74.

Glick, Paul, and Parke, Robert, Jr. "New Approaches in Studying the Life Cycle of the Family." *Demography* 2 (1965): 187–202.

Shorter, Edward. *The Making of the Modern Family*. New York: Basic Books, 1975.

F.   STUDIES OF FAMILY POWER

Giele, Janet Zollinger. "Cenutries of Womanhood: An Evolutionary Perspective on the Feminine Role." *Women's Studies* 1 (1972): 97–110.

Heer, Donald M. "The Measurement and Bases of Family Power: An Overview." *Marriage and Family Living* 25 (1963): 133–39, 477–78.

Herbst, P. G. "The Measurement of Family Relationships." *Human Relations* 5 (1952): 3–30.

Murdoch, G. P. "Comparative Data on the Division of Labor by Sex." *Social Forces* 15 (1935): 551–53.

———. "Ethnographic Roles: A Summary." *Ethnology* 6 (1967): 108–236.

———, and Provost, C. "Factors in the Division of Labor by Sex: A Cross-Cultural Analysis." *Ethnology* 12 (1973): 203–25.

Paxton, L. M., and Barry, H. III. "Infancy and Early Childhood: Cross Cultural Codes 2." *Ethnology* 10 (1971): 466–508.

Wolfe, D. M. "Power and Authority in the Family." In *Studies in Social Power*, edited by Darwin Cartwright, pp. 99–117. Ann Arbor: Institute for Social Research, 1959.

Yamaura, D. S. "A Note on the Usefulness and Validity of the Herbst Family Questionnaire." *Human Relations* 9 (1956): 213–21.

G.   GENDER ROLES

Allport, Gordon W. *The Nature of Prejudice.* Reading, Mass.: Addison-Wesley, 1954.

Angrist, Shirley S. "The Study of Sex Roles." *Journal of Social Issues* 25 (1969): 215–32.

Banton, Michael P. *Roles: An Introduction to the Study of Social Relations.* London: Tavistock Publications, 1965.

Cochran, Thomas C. "The Historical Use of Social Role." In *Generalization in the Writing of History*, edited by Louis Gottschalk. Chicago: University of Chicago Press, 1963.

Hochschild, A. R. "A Review of Sex-Role Research." *American Journal of Sociology* 78 (1973): 1011–29.

Hiller, E. T. *Social Relations and Structures: A Study in Principles of Sociology.* New York: Harper & Brothers, 1947.

May, Mark A., and Doob, L. W. *Competition and Cooperation.* New York: Social Science Research Council, 1937.

———, Allport, Gordon, and Murphy, Gardner. *Memorandum on Research in Competition and Cooperation.* New York: Social Science Research Council, 1937.

H.   MISCELLANEOUS

Bauman, Zygmunt. "Marxism and the Contemporary Theory of Culture." *Co-Existence* 5 (1968): 161–71.

Berkhofer, Robert. *A Behavioral Approach to Historical Analysis.* New York: Free Press, 1969.

Frankfurt Institute of Social Research. *Aspects of Sociology*. Boston: Beacon Press, 1972.

Floud, Roderick. *An Introduction to Quantitative Methods for Historians*. Princeton: Princeton University Press, 1975.

Genoveşe, Eugene D. "American Slaves and Their History." In *In Red and Black: Marxian Explorations in Southern and Afro-American History*, pp. 102–28. New York: Pantheon, 1971.

White, Leslie A. "The Concept of Culture." In *Culture and the Evolution of Man*, edited by A. F. Ashley-Montagu, pp. 38–64. New York: Oxford University Press, 1962.

Index